A HEART TURNED
EAST

A HEART TURNED
EAST

Among the Muslims
of Europe and America

ADAM LEBOR

ST. MARTIN'S PRESS ⚉ NEW YORK

A THOMAS DUNNE BOOK.
An imprint of St. Martin's Press.

A HEART TURNED EAST. Copyright © 1997 by Adam LeBor. All
rights reserved. Printed in the United States of America. No part
of this book may be used or reproduced in any manner whatsoever
without written permission except in the case of brief quotations
embodied in critical articles or reviews. For information, address
St. Martin's Press, 175 Fifth Avenue, New York, N.Y. 10010.

ISBN: 0-312-18109-4

First published in Great Britain by Little, Brown and Company

First U.S. Edition: January 1998

10 9 8 7 6 5 4 3 2 1

For my parents, for everything

'God has made you brethren one to another, so be not divided. An Arab has no preference over a non-Arab, nor a non-Arab over an Arab; nor is a white one to be preferred to a dark one, nor a dark one to a white.'

Muhammad speaking at Arafat, shortly before his death

'The western countries have the material goods and we have spirituality. But you cannot live only with material things and you cannot live only with spirituality. So we are like a couple, a man and a woman, and to have normal happiness we have to share them together.'

Mustapha Tougui, lecturer in Islamic theology,
the Paris Mosque

CONTENTS

ACKNOWLEDGEMENTS

Without the help of dozens of people – Muslim, Christian and Jew – family, friends and colleagues, spread across a dozen countries, this book would never have been written. They all deserve a mention, but my thanks must go first to my agent Jennifer Kavanagh, in whose office the idea for *A Heart Turned East* was conceived. She had the faith to take on an untried first-time author, encourage me – and cajole when necessary – to carry out this project, from initial idea to publication. All that holds too for my editor Alan Samson, whose unflagging enthusiasm was always a source of inspiration, and whose advice has kept me motivated and focused. I am also indebted to Professor Akbar Ahmed, of Selwyn College, Cambridge, for his support and help, especially for his valuable guidance on points of Islamic theology.

Then, the others: their numbers are legion. Some took to the road with me, others I met on the way, but they all helped by being there, especially in the war-zones. In Bosnia and the former Yugoslavia: Peter Maass (best slalom driver in the Lasva Valley), Patrick Bishop, Cathy Jenkins, Michael Montgomery, Tim Judah, Yigal Chazan, Adrian Brown, Charles Lane, Isabelle Laserre, Laura Pitter, Joel Brand, Matt Frei, Paul Lowe, Amra Abadžić, Miloš Vasić, Dessa Trevisan, Philip Sherwell, Richard Carruthers, Tony Gallagher, Martin Nangle, Julian Borger, Mirijana Miličević, Ian Traynor, Tamara Levak, the reception staff at the Hotel Esplanade in Zagreb, everyone at the BBC Kiseljak office in the winter of 1992/1993, and Kurt Schork, who once drove me down Sniper's Alley to Sarajevo airport in a soft-skinned VW Golf. Thanks, Kurt.

In Hungary and the Balkans: Chris Condon and Simon

Evans at the Budapest International Press Centre. Chris for his rigorous reading of this manuscript and thoughtful editorial advice; Simon, together with Tom Popper, heroic transcribers of many interview tapes. My much-loved friends: Nora Milótay, Vesna Kojić, Vlada Vlaškalić, John Nadler, Julius Strauss, Steve Boggan, Meriel Beattie, Dóra Czuk, Miles Graham, Desmond McGrath, Colin Woodard, Rick Bruner and my brother Jason. Thanks also to Anna Szőke, my muse and more while I wrote most of this book. Also, everyone at *Budapest Week*, my workplace in the summer of 1995, particularly Krisztina Krizsán, Carl Kovac and Stephen Loy.

In Turkey: Andrew Finkel, for good-humoured expert advice. In Albania: Justin Leighton, best friend and road-trip companion for almost a decade and hopefully many more. In Germany: Frederick Schulenberg, Heidi Modro and Henning Angerer. In France: Emmanuelle Richard, Elizabeth Johnston, Amy Oberdorfer, Sacha Smith, John Randall, Fred Guilledoux, Frederick Tristram, Muriel Bouquet and Peter Sinclair. In the USA: Sam Loewenberg, for his unfailing lengthy hospitality, Daniel Felber and Joshua Freeman. In Britain: Dr Ahmad Khalidi, Rabbi David J. Goldberg, and Tony Earnshaw at the *Yorkshire Post*.

Among my colleagues at *The Times*: former foreign editors Richard Owen and Martin Ivens, for first sending me to Bosnia and printing my despatches as I wrote them, which is as much as any journalist can ask for. Also at *The Times*: Anne McElvoy, Michael Binyon, Tom Rhodes, Michael Evans and especially Julia Llewellyn-Smith, a reassuring voice at the end of the telephone during some dangerous days. But my biggest thanks there go to Roger Boyes, a fine friend and mentor, ever-ready with advice and novel ideas.

I am indebted also to Steve Crawshaw and Godfrey Hodgson, who first sent me abroad to Budapest as a correspondent for the *Independent*. Thanks also to my other editors who have shown consistent faith in me over the years: Susan Ward Davies at *Elle*, David Meilton at the *European*, Andrew McLeod at the *Scotsman*, Joe Millis at the *Jewish Chronicle*, Sandra Harris at *Business Life* magazine, Maggie Pringle and the late Les Daly.

There are several others too, in various countries, who agreed to be interviewed, and pointed me in the right directions. They have asked that their names not be published. Doubtless there are some individuals whom I have forgotten to include. To all, I say thank you.

I would also like to acknowledge here the many works of Professor Bernard Lewis, historian of Islam, which have inspired and instructed me during the writing of this book, and in addition, H.T. Norris' treasure-trove of a work: *Islam in the Balkans*. Any errors are mine.

Finally I must thank the several organisations that provided me with goods and services. Dr János Muth at Compuserve Hungary, who provided me with a complimentary account and invaluable access to Compuserve's databases, while I researched the lives of Muslims in the West. British Rail International, for providing me with several complimentary Interrail 26+ tickets with which I travelled across Europe and the staff at Phipps PR for helping arrange them. Finally, thanks to Mr Bashir of Regent's Park Mosque, who gave me a beautiful copy of the Quran. *Shukran*!

INTRODUCTION

'He who leaveth home in search of knowledge, walketh in the path of God,' said Muhammad. He also instructed his followers to 'seek knowledge even unto China'. I didn't go to China, but I did visit a dozen countries across Europe as well as the United States while researching this book. My aim was simple: to travel to where Muslims live in the West, speak to them, report on their lives and aspirations, and give them a voice. And from that, analyse the implications of this fresh stage in history, when for the first time, both Europe and the United States are home to a sizeable part of the *ummah*, the brotherhood of the world's Muslims.

Like every traveller before me I carried my own baggage: of stereotypes and preconceptions about Islam and Muslims, which gradually shrank and withered as I roamed the continent and entered, however briefly, their lives, and they, mine. I found an extraordinary national and cultural diversity that enriches life in Europe and the United States. Western Muslims are Bosnian soldiers in Sarajevo, Turkish musicians in Berlin, Algerian artists in Marseilles, Pakistani lawyers in Bradford, exiled Arab dissidents, modernising Muslim scholars in London and Islamic political activists in Washington DC. Each of their lives was shaped by Islam, but each was also moulded by their new homes. From these something new and unique is emerging: a modern, western Islam.

Just as Islam evolves in the environment in which it exists, for life in medieval Muslim Spain was radically different to present-day Saudi society, each of the West's Muslim minorities is grappling with issues specific to the new lands among which they now live.

This book opens in Sarajevo, where for over three years Muslims struggled just to stay alive as the world's first ethnocide to be broadcast live on prime-time television unfolded, literally, on their bloodied doorsteps. In France, Muslims must grapple with Islamophobia, a problem certainly not helped by the spate of bombs on the Paris metro last summer that were attributed to Algerian Muslim terrorists. Even so French Muslims have never suffered the murderous attacks of German neo-Nazis on Muslim immigrants. Most French Muslims are in fact French citizens. Only a tiny minority of Turkish immigrants in Germany have German citizenship, a result of that nation's obsession with nineteenth-century ideas of pure bloodlines, and a citizenship law dating back to 1913, the Imperial Naturalisation Act, specifically designed to keep the *Volk* pure from foreign blood, then Jewish.

For French Muslims the issue is dignity and respect. For German ones, it is the security that citizenship would provide. For British Muslims, the overwhelming majority of whom hail from the Indian sub-continent, it is a combination of both, combating an imperialist legacy that imported them from former bits of empire such as India and Pakistan to do the dirty work in Bradford factories that had been rejected by native Britons, but at the same time denying Muslims the legal protection of the Race Relations Act. In Britain, though, just as in the United States, Muslims are slowly building their own political lobbying organisations to try to make their voices heard in the West's corridors of power. Many, such as the American Muslim Council, or the Bradford Council of Mosques, draw directly on the lessons of the Jewish immigrant experience, and it is heartening that the Jewish Board of Deputies is actively advising Muslim groups on issues such as securing the provision of halal meat in British schools.

Modern Muslim life also demands compromises from Muslims, or at least an understanding of how politics work in the West. When, for example, Bradford Muslims incinerate a copy of *The Satanic Verses*, nailed to a stick like a literary crucifixion, tongues of fire charring the pages as it burns in front of a crowd of angry Muslim demonstrators, that image rebounds around the world, confirming the atavistic fears of many in the West that Islam is set on an inevitable collision course with life in a liberal western democracy.

As Ayad Abu Chakra, a senior editor at the London-based Saudi-funded newspaper *Ash-Sharq Al-Awsat* (Middle East) told me, there must also be a two-way process and Muslims must give as well as take, if they wish to be accepted. 'What is required is understanding by both sides. The Muslims might not like this, but I think I have to be realistic, you don't expect people to accept you in their culture if you are not ready to concede something. I for one have no right to impose my values on the British. I am gaining from them, I can give to them if they want to get something from me, but I don't impose myself on them. But if they want to know more about my culture I am ready to give them, to give them the best I can. We need concessions from both sides. A civilised society has to be open-minded.'

Which also means being open to the contribution that Muslims want to give to the West. An Islamic perspective can bring much to life in a modern industrial society, says Dr Dalil Boubakeur, rector of the Paris Mosque. The alternative, of continued prejudice and marginalisation, will only help spawn an angry Islamic underclass that will turn increasingly to a radical, confrontational Islam and polarise further the divisions between the West's Muslims and their host countries. Better by far, then, to let Muslims in the West introduce a new approach – or rather a much older one – founded in spiritual values, rather than material ones, says Dr Boubakeur.

'Muslims who are living in another country than their original one have a new way to discuss life, religion, nationality, philosophy, which are not only about the problems of life in their own countries. Islamic life can be a part of communal life in France, and Muslim values can help provide answers to problems of modern life, to make an *Ijtihad* [intellectual renewal]. For instance on artificial insemination, that brings a lot of theological problems in Islam, on abortion, on genetic engineering, problems of malformed fetuses.'

The right to eat *halal* meat in Bradford, or to wear a headscarf to school in Bordeaux, this is the stuff of Muslims' daily struggle to live an Islamic life. But from these debates spring other, more fundamental long-term questions that also demand answers. Modern Muslim life in Islam's new lands – where events in Algeria rebound almost instantly in Amiens – means a reconsideration of the nature of Europe, its ideal and reality, as the slowly-uniting continent struggles to forge its structure for the twenty-first century. It demands a new look at the very nature of nationalism and the cultural diversity of the modern nation-state; about citizenship laws and ethnic identity; and how Muslims can combine their loyalty to a single nation-state with a supra-national religious ideal.

About living a life in the West, with a heart turned East.

Running to avoid sniper fire, Sarajevo

Chapter 1

SARAJEVO: THE
SHOOTING GALLERY

---

*'From the ruins of a whole people, imperial ambitions
were already springing, which might one day threaten
all southern Europe.'*
John Reed, Serbia, 1915

'We must fight. The Muslims have the Islamic virus.'
Vojislav Savić, Bosnian Serb soldier, Zvornik, 1995

It was the smelliest and worst-fitting garment I had ever worn.
Designed apparently for someone five feet tall and four feet
wide, the flak-jacket hung stiffly on my shoulders, its rigid con-
tours wide and unyielding as I tried to bend down. Its armpits
stank of stale sweat and it lacked both a chest-plate to stop a
sniper's bullet and a slide-down groin flap, the latter especially
coveted by male journalists in Bosnia after a photographer with
Associated Press lost a testicle to mortar shrapnel.

But its large pockets were roomy enough to stash the foreign
correspondent's essential war-zone kit of notebooks, torch, Swiss
Army knife, cigarettes and hip-flask. And even this unlikely life-
saver was much more protection than most Sarajevans ever had.
Later that day, gratefully encased in the shrapnel-proof Kevlar,
I would nervously ask the foreign press, sitting at the bar in the
wrecked Sarajevo Holiday Inn, if I should sleep in it as well,
triggering guffaws of laughter. The black monster later disappeared, handed down the chain of reporters from *The Times*
who covered Bosnia. By the autumn I was kitted out in over
£1200-worth of body armour and helmet, an outfit that weighed
so much that one day in Mostar an old Muslim man even

offered me his seat, so hot and breathless was I in my armadillo-style gear. But that was several months away and my priority in July 1992 was getting into Sarajevo.

At five in the morning the Zagreb sky was slowly lightening as I picked up the flak-jacket, together with my luggage, and tramped downstairs to the lobby of the $158-a-night Hotel Esplanade. Its haute cuisine, chilled white Croatian wine and urbane staff made it a favourite haunt of the foreign press corps covering the wars in former Yugoslavia. Like the Commodore in Beirut and the Holiday Inn in Sarajevo, the Esplanade, wartime headquarters of the Gestapo, haunt of arms dealers, mercenaries and prostitutes in the Yugoslav wars, has entered journalistic folklore. Its ornate lobby and ballroom drip history and Balkan intrigue but I had more mundane concerns. The night manager summoned the bill as I checked out, again, and began another day trying to get into Sarajevo. There, under the gaze of the world's television crews, the unique culture of Bosnian Muslims, with its triple Turkish, Slavic and Muslim heritages, was being targeted for annihilation.

For a city under siege, blasted for months, and to be blasted for years to come by Bosnian Serb artillery, the guns a gift from Serbian president Slobodan Milošević's military henchmen, getting into Sarajevo was generally straightforward. The United Nations Protection Force, UNPROFOR, precursor of NATO's I-FOR, ran regular flights in and out of the city, open to aid agency staff, relief workers, journalists, UN personnel, foreign diplomats, almost anyone with an interest in the Bosnian war, except of course the people trapped inside the city. But the airlift often stopped and I had already spent three futile days sitting on the runway watching stationary C130s. Even the hotel staff raised an eyebrow, remarking dryly as I checked in again for the fourth time in as many days, 'Back again, Mr LeBor?' In fact I wasn't even sure that I wanted to get to the Bosnian capital, then one of the most dangerous places in the world, but this was my trial for a new job with *The Times*. If I filed enough stories, and came home in one piece – instead of the wooden boxes or air ambulances that too many of my colleagues left Sarajevo in – I would get the post.

No wonder the airlift was named 'Maybe Airlines' by the UN. The soldiers at the airport claimed that the name meant

8

'Maybe you will get shot down and maybe you won't,' but it seemed to me it meant 'Maybe you will get on a flight and maybe you won't.' The wasted days triggered a curious new emotion: the feeling of being desperate to get to a place I was secretly terrified of arriving at.

But just three hours later that morning we were roaring down the runway at Zagreb airport, strapped into a German C160 transporter plane. The plane's nose lifted and we sailed up into the clear Croatian sky, heading into Europe's latest battlefield, where Bosnian Serbs saw themselves as the new Crusaders against a wholly imagined Islamic threat. On board UN flight 267 were just over ten tons of food, several journalists cracking jokes and trying to look nonchalant about the possibility of being killed or injured over the next few days, and the aircrew, for whom this was just another day's work. It wasn't even nine o'clock yet, but we passed the brandy round and the plane banked, vibrating with the noise of the propeller engines, as we turned out to sea, out of range of the anti-aircraft guns of the Serbian army in occupied Croatia and flew over the Adriatic.

Standing up next to the piles of cooking oil and corned beef, the bland diet of Sarajevo's besieged citizens, I looked out of the window to see the Croatian coastline stretched out seventeen thousand feet beneath us, a beautiful panorama of jagged rocks with distant archipelagos dotting the azure sea. In the distance the mountains of central Bosnia that would, a few months later, see the start of the war between Bosnian Croats and Muslims, shimmered in the morning heat. The sea and the hills looked like a shot from a tourist-board video, from the C160's window, but Bosnia's welcome that summer was always violent and sometimes fatal. We flew down the coast over Zadar, the ancient Roman port of Split, and then descended to land at Sarajevo airport. It took just forty minutes to leave tranquil early-morning Zagreb and land in hell on earth.

I had seen the wreckage of war before, in the Croatian war, and heard the boom of shells fired in anger. The vista of destruction in the debris of former Yugoslavia was almost universal: a house outside Osijek hit by an air-to-ground missile, collapsed into rubble with its red roof tiles scattered outside; the almost delicate symmetry of shrapnel spray marks that a mortar left when it exploded across the ancient paving stones of

Dubrovnik; the eerie ghost town that was Vukovar, with its empty shells of houses, where an immaculate multi-volume biography of Tito lay among the glass, symbolism almost too obvious to be notable. In Slavonski Brod I had sat silently in a hospital basement with a doctor while we listened to a whistle. It was clear and sharp, subtly altering its tone until it ended in a not very distant explosion. It was the tune a shell played as it soared overhead and all conversation in the room stopped when it cut through the autumn afternoon air. Life itself seemed to be suspended, hanging on a thread of a Serb gunner's trajectory, while we waited to hear where the shell landed. It missed the hospital and landed in an apartment block. A few minutes later the first casualties were brought in on trolleys, rushed into a makeshift operating theatre in the hospital's gymnasium. The floor was awash with blood, crimson rivulets flowing back and forth, and pools of red sticky under the bright lights.

But nothing, not even the reports of the Sarajevo press corps that I had read and watched, prepared me for the horrible reality of the Bosnian capital that would be made bloody manifest later that morning, although the airport was a good introduction. Its wrecked buildings were carpeted with shards of glass, glinting in the hot morning sun, the remaining windows shot through. Spent cartridges littered the inside of the terminal, a reminder of the battle between government troops and the Bosnian Serbs at the start of the war. The tense UN soldiers stood guard behind sandbagged positions made it clear that we must leave the area immediately, for standing on the Tarmac we were in easy range of both sides.

It was the noise, a racket that sounded in the city for years, that was the most unnerving. It resounded all day and most of the night, echoing around the mosques and churches, the narrow Ottoman streets, the maze of the smashed shops and stalls of Baščaršija, the old market section, and across the former stadium for the 1984 Winter Olympics, where Torvill and Dean had won their gold medal, now a giant graveyard. The Bosnian Serbian artillery provided the back beat, with a regular boom and rumble of the 155mm shells that the soldiers, safely hidden in their bunkers in the surrounding hillside, liked to lob into streets and markets crowded with civilians and children. The mortars added a lighter note, and made a sharper bang when they exploded downtown or in the suburbs. When things got too slow, there was the rattle of machine-gun fire and the whoosh of rocket-propelled grenades to up the tempo of death, punctuated by the sharp snap of sniper fire, like a dry branch cracking underfoot. Surrounded by hills, spread out down the banks of the river Miljacka, Sarajevo was a giant shooting gallery.

How could this happen in 1990s Europe, asked the world, as it watched the destruction of this once-beautiful, cosmopolitan Ottoman town with its medieval mosques and craftsmen's shops and narrow Turkish streets? When Iraq invaded Kuwait the world's armies amassed to expel Saddam Hussein's forces. But the west would never launch 'Operation Balkan Storm', said Sarajevans. For there was no oil in Bosnia, and anyway, for western politicians and diplomats, Muslim life is cheap.

From the airport I scrounged a lift from a television crew and we raced down Sniper Alley as fast as possible, the driver swerving and weaving like a racing professional as we bumped down side streets and back alleys to avoid any sniper fire. I looked around the almost empty streets and scribbled random words into my notebook, barely legible scrawls about destruction, artillery and incoming fire. We hurtled past the UN Checkpoint that controlled access into the airport, past the shell holes punched into the apartment buildings, the road signs riddled with bullet holes, the sand-bags and tank-traps, the mangled cars, the anti-sniping barricades and, bizarrely, several pedestrians, including a middle-aged woman wearing a green top picking a careful path to somewhere. But mostly the streets were empty, for the Bosnian Serb gunners had weaved a web of dread and terror through the city, one so thick it was almost tangible. It was a feeling of dread I had never experienced before. The very air itself seemed tensed and ready for violence, swollen with anticipation for the next impact that would surely tear it open with high-explosive and shrapnel, hurling bricks and mortar, limbs and blood across the pavements and along the road. Something coiled tightly, twisting in my stomach, as I shrank into my flak jacket, a fear raw and visceral such as I had never known before. It was the fear for my life.

My destination was the Holiday Inn, a hotel whose amazing powers of endurance have now ensured it a place in history. The

Holiday Inn was located in one of the most dangerous areas of the city, a couple of hundred yards away from the front-line. Its glass entrance had been shot to pieces and its rooms were in easy reach of Serb sniper, rocket and shellfire. Guests were requested to keep their curtains drawn, so as not to draw incoming fire, and a notice proclaimed that they would be asked to leave if they failed to do so. Many of the rooms had been wrecked and there were gory urban-myth stories about a supposed corpse that still lay somewhere on the tenth floor. I had tried to book a room before leaving home in Budapest for Sarajevo and had eventually got through to reception. The staff were not encouraging to would-be guests. 'Don't come. It's very dangerous,' I was told.

It was. The front entrance was covered by a Serb sniper and so guests and staff used the back door. The building shook regularly as it took yet more hits from the Serbs' high-calibre machine guns. When a staff member had to repair something in front of the building the manager stood at the door with a sub-machine gun, ready to give him covering fire. The receptionist kept an AK47 under the counter. With a curfew in force there was little to do in the evening, except drink and watch the battles erupting outside. The view from the hotel's upper floors of the sudden flash of the explosions and arcs of tracer fire back and forth through the darkness had a terrible beauty, if that is the word. Newcomers were barraged with survival tips, and that was just for staying alive inside the building. Use this staircase, don't use that entrance. Stay away from that side of the hotel, get a room on this side.

It seemed worse at night, when the silence of a city under curfew was broken in the early hours of the morning by the whoosh of rocket-propelled grenades past my bedroom window. One evening we were drinking in the foyer bar when the alcohol reached saturation point and I needed to visit the toilet. I couldn't find the way and was scared to blunder about in the darkness in a semi-drunken haze. A Bosnian soldier escorted me to the gents', his Kalashnikov at the ready in case of incoming fire. It was the first time I had been accompanied to the toilet for many years. The rules of survival inside the Holiday Inn were complicated, but you learnt fast. And even though the hotel was directly in the line of fire it survived, just, thanks to a complicated arrangement of black market deals that kept the Bosnian Serbs supplied with a good proportion of the dollars and Deutschmarks that poured in from the foreign press corps, and which were passed across the nearby front-lines to former friends and neighbours.

Somehow, even among the carnage, the niceties of luxury hotel etiquette continued. The toilets were cleaned daily, and a fresh paper wrapper appeared each evening on the seat, proclaiming it hygienically disinfected. A pianist played each afternoon on the mezzanine floor, giving a spirited rendition of some Viennese waltzes, followed by Chopin's *Revolutionary Etude*. Waiters dressed in tuxedos and bow ties gliding back and forth with trays of iced drinks only added to the air of surreality. One evening as we sat around mulling over the day's events, discussing whose turn it was to buy the drinks, a shell exploded loudly somewhere nearby. 'Whose round is it anyway?' someone asked. 'Bosnian army, I believe,' came the reply. The staff too kept a morbid sense of humour. One morning the press came down for breakfast to find the receptionist carefully sorting through a pile of publicity leaflets, emblazoned 'Holiday Inn, Sarajevo, Yugoslavia'. Black marker in hand, he carefully inked out the word 'Yugoslavia' on each flyer before neatly piling them up again. 'What are you doing?' someone asked. 'Dead country,' he replied, shaking his head.

But standing in the foyer that first morning, hot, confused, and scared, I watched in dismay as a blood-stained and disorientated CNN reporter suddenly wandered in, repeating over and over how frightened he was to anyone who would listen. Everyone rushed over to help him. Red splotches were spattered across his shoulder and he was bleeding from glass splinters as he walked across the foyer. He was, by Sarajevo standards, comparatively lucky, although his colleague travelling in the same vehicle was not.

The CNN van had taken a direct hit on Sniper Alley, just a short while after we had sped down the long straight road. The camerawoman travelling with him had been hit in the face by a Serb anti-aircraft bullet. It blew off her jaw and she was medivaced out by the UN. She lived, but she would never look the same again. For weeks afterwards the white CNN van stood alone in the corner of the Holiday Inn's underground car park, for when death can come in an instant and luck means all, the van gave off bad vibrations and nobody would park near it.

That was the morning's casualty toll, at least among the press. In the city outside the Bosnian Serb gunners and snipers continued their work, maiming and killing, and the government troops, outgunned and outnumbered, fought back. Later that evening as we chatted to some Canadian UN soldiers, a photographer slowly limped in. He had been shot through the leg that afternoon as he took pictures of soldiers in action on the front-line. He had even seen the soldier taking aim at him, he explained indignantly, but his cries not to shoot went unheeded.

As the graffitto on Sniper Alley said: 'Welcome to Hell.'

Hell had come to the heart of Europe, but Bosnia's neighbours did little to put out its fires. The grand notion of a common European home did not apply to Muslims, even European ones. Diplomats and envoys such as Lords Owen and Carrington, the best drones in suits the West could offer, flew in and out of former Yugoslavia, trying to stop the war. They apportioned equal blame to all parties and tut-tutted at the reluctance of the multi-national Bosnian government – nearly always reduced to the description of the 'Muslims' – to roll over and give up, all in the best tradition of Foreign Office appeasement. The international community soon excused itself from intervention to stop the Bosnian Serbs and save Bosnia's Muslims, by claiming the Bosnian conflict was a 'civil' war, yet as a conscience-salver simultaneously imposed sanctions on Yugoslavia for Belgrade's role in fomenting the conflict. One of the more illuminating examples of the role of hypocrisy in international relations.

In Bosnia words as well as people are casualties of war. Orwell's Ministry of Truth is alive and flourishing: not in its supposed natural home, the now-vanished Communist bloc, but in the luxurious corridors of the UN in New York and Geneva. There a 'safe haven' was one of the most dangerous places in the world and a 'peace plan' is code for surrendering to Bosnian Serb ethnocide. One of the more revolting sights of the Bosnian war was watching the sleek UN diplomats pretend to anguish over the carnage they could stop with one phone call to NATO, before they waddled self-satisfiedly off to the next Security Council session.

Lords Carrington and Owen failed to stop the war. All the UN's peace plans and proposals failed until they recognised the single salient fact of the war in Bosnia. The conflict was spawned and directed in Belgrade by Serbian president Slobodan Milošević, implemented on the ground by his hench-men, former psychiatrist and Bosnian Serb leader Radovan Karadžić – the clearest case yet of 'physician heal thyself' – and General Ratko Mladić, the Bosnian Serb military leader and the man with the bloodiest hands in Europe. It was planned years in advance, which is how the Bosnian Serbs, with their Yugoslav allies, were able to seize over half the country in just a few months. The arms were smuggled in, openly imported, or just handed over to the Bosnian Serbs by the Yugoslav National Army (JNA), the Bosnian Serb militias formed, the sites selected for the camps and the methodology of ethnic cleansing honed to maximum efficiency.

Europe was about to witness its first ethnocide since the end of the Second World War – the destruction of Muslim Bosnia, its buildings, its culture, its people and even its history. Many months later I encountered Radovan Karadžić in Geneva at one of the seemingly endless series of peace conferences organised under UN auspices to try and make the Bosnians roll over and give up. He stood in front of the microphone, flanked by his bodyguards, bullish and simultaneously aggrieved at the failure of the world to understand the terrible Islamic menace to Europe that only the Serbs could stop. 'You, who wades in blood, how can you sleep at night?' I wanted to yell at him. Instead I asked his view of some arcane point of the latest maps to slice up Bosnia.

Whitehall and Washington, Bonn and Brussels, all know this which is why Milošević, Karadžić and Mladić have been named as potential war criminals, but Milošević especially enjoyed the attentions of the world's statesmen and had a ready welcome in the international corridors of power when he chose to talk peace. One day he faces possible arrest, the next he is an hon-oured guest in the company of world statesmen, drinking slivovitz with American diplomat Richard Holbrooke in Dayton, Ohio as they carve up the corpse of Bosnia together on the diplomatic table. How they must have laughed at night for years in Belgrade and Pale, capital of the self-proclaimed quasi-fascist

Bosnian Serb Republic, as they danced rings around the hopeless emissaries from the self-serving international bureaucracies that are supposed to represent world security, and the barrage of futile acronyms in whose name they speak: the UN, NATO, EU, WEU, OSCE and NAA with their useless maps, and plans for new zones, republics, confederations, even minute details of flyovers and motorways.

Practitioners of violence such as Karadžić and Mladić understand one word: force. The summer 1995 massacres at Srebrenica when thousands of Bosnian Muslim men were slaughtered en masse, in a Nazi-style killing field, were too much even for the West to stomach, and waves of airstrikes followed that finally brought the Bosnian Serbs' puppet master, Slobodan Milošević, to the negotiating table. It was the worst atrocity in Europe since the Second World War. 'The Bosnian Serbs made a fatal error. They overplayed their hand when they went into Srebrenica,' said US Defense Secretary William Perry. Which begs the question as to what exactly, in the West's eyes, would have been a well-judged hand for General Mladić? But if the West could stop the war then, how much easier it would have been to hit Mladić's forces in 1992, how many more people would still be alive, how many homes still standing.

That said, the common view of the Bosnian war as the Serb, and Bosnian Serb, people, solidly united against all Muslims is both wrong and simplistic. For a start, it neglects the role of Croatian President Franjo Tuđjman in the death of multinational Bosnia. This is the ultra-nationalist leader who once felt it necessary to apologise to Jewish organisations for his antisemitism and the man in charge of the nearest thing to a quasi-fascist regime in Europe, where unwelcome local election results are annulled and troublesome Croat journalists are arrested. Croatia has the dubious honour of initially being refused entry to the Council of Europe, thanks to its human-rights record. Or lack of one. For Tuđjman's government organised, armed and financed the Bosnian Croat army, admittedly an occasional ally of Bosnian government troops, but far better known for its siege of Muslim Mostar, a mini-war that far outclassed the siege of Sarajevo in its brutality and destruction. Tuđjman was as keen as Milošević to slice up Bosnia – the only difference was he tried to present his regime as an oasis of western-style democracy in a swamp of Balkan nationalism. He failed.

At the same time the old Yugoslav ideals of multi-nationalism still lived, and live on, among many Serbs. A largely unreported footnote to the Bosnian war was the continued presence within Serbia proper of a large Muslim community in the Sandjak region, some of whom left to fight for the Bosnian government army. Serbia's tragedy was that a whole section of society that could form a liberal opposition to the war – students, writers, artists and much of the intelligentsia – simply uprooted and left the country in their tens of thousands, leaving the field clear for the nationalists. Several came to Budapest, and became close friends of mine. They too have scars, psychological rather than physical, for their country, the old Yugoslavia, no longer exists. At the same time, it was a peculiarity of the Bosnian war that some Muslim refugees fled to Belgrade, of all places. At first glance this appears a strange choice, but the city, while home to plenty of war profiteers and gangsters, kept enough of its cosmopolitan spirit alive to take them in.

Many Bosnians now admit they should have seen what was coming back in June 1991, when war erupted in Croatia and Slovenia. Then the JNA metamorphosed into the protector and armer of the rebel Serbs in Croatia, handing its extensive arsenal – for this was a force armed and trained to withstand possible attack from both NATO and the Warsaw Pact – to General Mladić's rebel Serb soldiers fighting newly independent Croatia. At the same time some Bosnian Muslim soldiers in the JNA fought under the Yugoslav flag, in effect aiding the Serbs during the Croatian war. They failed to realise that the lessons Serb fighters learnt in Vukovar and Pakrac, of shelling civilians, terrorising and killing anyone in their path, the ABC of ethnic cleansing, would be soon put to good use in Višegrad and Zvornik. That some Bosnian Muslims fought with the JNA would also be well remembered by the Bosnian Croats a couple of years later.

After Slovenia and Croatia declared their independence in June 1991, war in Bosnia was almost inevitable. The state in the making had several choices: to remain in rump Yugoslavia, in effect being absorbed into Greater Serbia; join Croatia in a federation; or go for independence. Bosnian Serb leaders repeatedly warned that the Serbs would not accept an independent Bosnia, which they claimed would be dominated by Muslims. Karadžić and his henchmen launched the most effective propaganda drive against the idea of a multi-national Bosnia since Goebbels' work for the Nazi cause. 'The Muslims are trying to dominate Bosnia. They want to create an Islamic state here, but we Serbs are not going to let them. You cannot force Christians to live in a Muslim state. It's just like Lebanon. We do not want to live under Oriental despotism,' said Karadžić.

The propaganda was directed at an international audience as well as those living inside Serb-controlled Bosnia. Bosnian Serb officials handed reporters covering the conflict a slickly produced 92-page booklet entitled *Bosnia-Herzegovina: Chronicle of an Announced Death*, which was an apt title as they had first pronounced the capital sentence on the nascent state. Its pages were filled with supposed captured documents, produced by Bosnian Muslims, claiming for example that: 'For one dead Muslim one hundred Serbs will be liquidated and for one wounded Muslim (depending on the severity of the wound) 10–15 Serbs.' A picture of a Muslim resting at the Zagreb mosque was captioned: 'A rest at the assembly centre in the Zagreb mosque before setting out to the holy war in Bosnia-Herzegovina.' The Serb cause also went online, and those interested could download more of the same from Serbnet, on the Internet. The various newsgroups soon filled up with furious arguments between rival supporters of each cause as the Bosnian war spread into cyberspace.

It was that fantastic vision of some reborn Ottoman empire run along Iranian lines that Karadžić used to rally the Bosnian Serbs to his bloody standard. It was a perfect example of the 'Big Lie' technique, for the more nonsensical the claims of the supposed Islamic dictatorship that was on its way, the more many Bosnian Serbs believed them. Reports that Bosnian Serb women would be forced to wear the veil and their men press-ganged into the mosque, in an independent Bosnia, were readily believed by the often unsophisticated rural Bosnian Serbs, even though they had lived among, and sometimes married, their Muslim neighbours for decades.

One of the grimmer ironies of the Bosnian war was that for

all the Serbs' supposed horror of the Bosnian Muslims' Turkish heritage, Milošević's Serbia far more resembled the declining Ottoman empire than the present day Europe it claimed to be protecting from the Islamic menace. From the country's rotten and corrupt bureaucracy and the paranoid fear of strangers in border areas, to Belgrade's use of assassination and murder as a tool of political control, modern day Serbia is a grandchild of Ottoman Turkey. Even the sawing oriental rhythms of Serbian nationalist 'turbo-folk' music draw on Turkey's musical heritage.

Ancient folk memories of the Turkish occupation, more recent ones of Croat and Muslim atrocities in the Second World War, the lack of any developed democratic culture or strong independent national media in Communist Yugoslavia, all meant that Bosnian Serb Television found a ready audience for the stream of lies it pumped out every night on its equipment, stolen from the BBC. In fact the roots of this maniacal nationalism extended back over a century. Here are the thoughts of Petar Petrović-Njegoš, poet, Montenegrin prince and monk, published in 1847, on the future of Islam and the 'Id Muslim festival in the southern Slav lands (Miloš Obilić, a Serbian knight, supposedly killed Sultan Murad I at the battle of Kosovo):

> So tear down the minarets and mosques,
> and kindle the Serbian yule logs,
> and let us paint our Easter eggs.
> Observe the two fasts honestly,
> and as for the remainder, do as you like.
> I swear to you by the creed of Miloš Obilić
> and by the trusty weapons that I carry,
> our faiths will be submerged in blood.
> The better of the two will rise redeemed.
> The 'Id can never live in peace
> with Christmas Day.

Almost 150 years later his instructions would be comprehensively carried out.

Under Karadžić's instructions many Bosnian Serbs boycotted the March 1992 nationwide referendum on independence, claiming that the plebiscite violated the principle of tri-national constitutional parity. There was here a legitimate political point.

Nobody could force the Bosnian Serbs to live in an independent Bosnia if they didn't want to. But, had there been the political will among the Bosnian Serb leadership, a solution could have been found to the conundrum of Bosnia's three nationalities. Joint Bosnian-Yugoslav citizenship; federation with Yugoslavia for a Serb-dominated region; confederation; cultural autonomy, political autonomy, territorial autonomy for a Bosnian Serb entity, open borders, any or all of these could have provided an answer. But the Bosnian Serb leaders were never interested in a peaceful solution. They had a more final version in mind.

In response they held their own referendum, which produced a result overwhelmingly against independence. Fighting erupted at the end of March and the eastern Bosnian city of Bijeljina was the first town to fall to the Bosnian Serbs. Its capture produced one of the most famous images of the war: a Bosnian Serb soldier, cigarette in hand, lazily kicking a pile of Muslim corpses. That shot handed the Bosnian government an early propaganda coup and has been used in pro-Bosnian posters across the world. The fighter was a member of the Tigers militia, commanded by Željko Ražnjatović, a.k.a. Arkan, and another on a list of alleged war criminals. Rumour had it that the soldier was subsequently severely, possibly fatally, disciplined, after the picture was published, but if so his only crime, by Bosnian Serb standards, was to be immortalised on film in the act of atrocity.

Whether they were religious or secular, Bosnian Muslims dismissed as ridiculous the Bosnian Serbs' barrages of propaganda, that claimed the government of President Alija Izetbegović aimed to set up an Iranian-style Islamic state. Drinkers of slivovitz, strong plum brandy, eaters of pork, for many Bosnian Muslims their only connections with Islam until the war were that they had names like Amra and Emir and left their shoes outside their houses. Bosnian Muslims were largely secular and those that were religious emphasised that they were 'European Muslims', something quite different to the Ayatollahs of Iran and the Islamic clergy of Saudi Arabia. All were proud of their multi-ethnic heritage and traditions of co-existence with both Orthodox and Catholic Christianity and Judaism.

As even one prominent Bosnian Serb leader explained to the

Belgrade magazine *NIN* in June 1990: 'In Serbia, the media are wrongly speaking of the dangers of [Islamic] fundamentalism in Bosnia . . . Our Bosnian Muslims are Slavs, of our same blood and language, who have chosen the European life along with their Muslim faith . . . We Serbs are closer to our Muslims than we are to that Europe.' But back then Radovan Karadžić was presenting a different face to the world. Even now though many Bosnian Serbs would agree with Karadžić's old analysis. Many have stayed loyal to the idea of a multi-ethnic Bosnia, and fight in the Bosnian army, such as General Jovan Divjac, or just try and survive in government-controlled towns such as Sarajevo and Tuzla. Loyal Bosnian Serbs who fight under the government's flag are usually singled for especially harsh treatment if they are captured by their religious kin on the other side of the front-lines, who regard them with loathing as traitors.

Until the outbreak of war many Bosnian Muslims were largely uninfected by the virus of nationalism that lurks just beneath the surface of so many southern Slavs, and were quite content in Yugoslavia. Bosnia's Muslims did not have their own independent state under Tito, but then neither did anyone shell their towns and cities. Unusually for the former Yugoslav republics, Bosnian public buildings often still had pictures of Tito hanging in offices. Even the barber in the dreary central Bosnian city of Zenica, where I once had my hair cut, still worked under Tito's benevolent gaze.

Right up to the outbreak of war, many identified themselves as Yugoslavs, rather than Serbs, Muslims or Croats, especially those of mixed marriages. This cosmopolitan tradition was highest in Sarajevo, where, according to the Bosnian government's Institute for Statistics, the capital reported the highest intermarriage rate for the whole country, with 34.1 per cent in 1991. But many cynics understandably wonder how, if the city was truly as tolerant and multi-cultural as everyone claimed, it degenerated so quickly into Europe's longest running urban-battleground since the Second World War. After the Dayton Peace accords were signed most Bosnian Serbs on the Serb side of the former front-lines left en masse for Serbia proper. The few who remained suffered repeated harassment by angry Muslims.

In Sarajevo, even as the JNA dug trenches around the city to prepare for the Bosnian Serbs' bombardment, few believed that a war was coming. When the war erupted in April 1992 the defence of the city was led by criminals who knew how to use guns and where to get them, such as the notorious 'Juka', who ran a black-market and extortion operation in the wartime city. Juka was repeatedly wounded and seemed to be held together by a collection of nuts and bolts but carried on fighting bravely and, it must be said, profitably. He later turned against the government and joined forces with the Bosnian Croats and was found shot to death near a motorway in Aachen, Germany.

A few prescient Sarajevans formed the 'Patriotic League' and secretly reconnoitered the JNA trenches being dug around the town, but their warnings went almost ignored. 'Nobody believed that war was coming. I didn't believe it,' said Arman, a former Sarajevo businessman turned fighter in the early days of the war. 'I remember that when someone asked me to join the Patriotic League early in 1992 I just laughed at him and said I was a pacifist. A few months later, after the war started, we met downtown. He was in a uniform, carrying a pistol. He shouted over to me: "Hey, Mr Pacifist! How are you now?"'

Rifles and pistols were passed from hand to hand, as during the Jewish Warsaw Ghetto revolt in 1943, and Bosnian soldiers ran up and down the trenches firing from different positions pretending to be more numerous than they were. By May 1992, one month into the war, there was still no war cabinet and no proper defence of the city, notes Misha Glenny in his book *The Fall of Yugoslavia*. 'When I ask Defence Minister Jerko Đoko what his strategy for the defence of the city is he replies: "Actually I come from Mostar and I've only been here a year so I don't know the city very well."' The Bosnian soldiers died in their hundreds, partly as a result of President Izetbegović's poor planning for war. 'Citizens of Sarajevo, sleep peacefully, there will be no war,' he famously proclaimed in a broadcast on 4 April 1992. Probably only he knows what kind of assurances he was given by Europe and America, that the West would ensure his nascent state's survival when he decided that Bosnia-Herzegovina should be an independent country without the consent of the Serb minority. Izetbegović's initial strategy, it seemed to many, was to let as many civilians be killed as necessary, until the West was galvanised into action to save Bosnia. It failed.

He also foolishly believed the repeated promises of the Yugoslav army that its soldiers were neutral and would stand between the two sides as a buffer. Muslim fighters were so nervous that Izetbegović would disarm their Green Beret militia that they met in secret. A day after the attack on Bijeljina the Green Berets stopped a JNA convoy on the road to Sarajevo. Hidden among the bananas were rockets and ammunition. President Izetbegović ordered that the convoy be allowed to continue on its way. The supposed great international Islamic plot to establish an Iranian-style Islamic state at the gates of Vienna did not seem very effective, at least militarily.

Many Serbs and Croats saw their Muslim compatriots as rather sleepy and disorganised. Just as British people tell 'Irish' jokes, Yugoslavs told Bosnian Muslim jokes, about a pair of peasants called 'Muljo and Suljo', mocking their supposed rural parochialism, although Sarajevo was at least as cosmopolitan as Belgrade or Zagreb. The latest joke about them is quite short: Muljo and Suljo are dead.

So were Senad Sačirović, Mirijana Milanović, Branko Pletikoša and Leo Sternberg. Just four of the Sarajevans laid to rest in one morning at the Lions cemetery overlooking the Olympic complex. The graveyard was divided into three sections: Muslim plots were marked with a star and crescent; Christian ones with a crucifix, and atheists with a star, symbol of the old Yugoslavia. Leo Sternberg was buried with the atheists, as Sarajevo's Jewish cemetery is now a front-line position.

Grief hung heavy in the air like a fog of human pain among the forest of cheap wooden grave markers. They stretched for rows up the hillside, each ending in the same year: 1992, the year of the start of the war. Bereaved relatives stood hunched over the fresh mounds, uniformed soldiers and policemen trying to keep their features composed while mothers, daughters and sisters sobbed out their pain. A woman's scream, sharp and agonised, pierced through the sounds of mourning as Branko Pletikoša's coffin was lowered into the ground. Space for corpses was so precious that old bones had been churned up in the ground. As I walked nearer to the funeral of Senad Sačirović, where his crying relatives kneeled down intoning the Muslim prayers for the dead, fragments of long-buried arms and legs poked through the earth. It was a truly dreadful place and I found myself biting my lip to keep my composure and stop myself from crying. A Muslim, a Serb, a mixed Serbo-Croat and a Jew. Bosnians could no longer live together in peace, but in death at least they were united, their funeral eulogy the rattle of machine-gun fire nearby.

But even in the midst of carnage, daily life, of a sort, sputtered on. Some cafés still functioned, where patrons nervously sipped black coffee among the wreckage, their faces tense as they puffed hard on cigarettes, their pistols and sub-machine guns lying ready on the table. An underground theatre was staging a play called *Die Like a Man*, in fact a comedy about two men and a girl. Death could, and did, come at any moment, but as Sarajevans said, nobody wants to stay indoors all day. Men and women still went to work in the morning, crunching through the broken glass, the women with make-up freshly applied as a personal gesture of defiance, the men clutching their briefcases. At each intersection downtown they stopped, checked for snipers and then ran across.

Even the traffic police carried on stopping cars for speeding and breaking the rules of the road. As one policeman said: 'Just because there's a war on, everyone thinks they can drive through red lights.' Police regularly pulled over our car, a beaten-up old Lada purchased in Split, driven by photographer Paul Lowe, because it lacked number plates. The plates, emblazoned with the Croatian red and white chequerboard, had sensibly been thrown away on the drive into the city before reaching the Bosnian Serb lines. But repeatedly sitting in the car in the middle of an often empty road, prone and exposed, while a Bosnian policeman demanded to see our documents and shellfire echoed around us was an unnerving experience. Eventually we tried to register the vehicle with Bosnian plates, and after a morning spent traipsing from office to office, we finally found the right one. Unfortunately though, the car could not be registered in Sarajevo for the moment, the clerk explained, laughing. Nobody had ever registered a foreign car in Bosnia before and so the procedure didn't exist.

But Sarajevo's veneer of normality was thin. One that could be instantly smashed by the curl of a Serb finger on the trigger a kilometre away in the hills, as we soon discovered one morning.

There was a set routine for getting out of the Holiday Inn, demanding a series of racing turns as fast as possible to avoid any sniper fire. As the passenger it was my job to check for other vehicles, for Paul had no time to look. 'Clear right?' he snapped, as we bumped out of the Holiday Inn's underground car park, racing up the concrete path onto ground level, whizzing past the danger spot where a Serb sniper often took pot-shots at passing cars. 'Clear left?' he demanded, and then we were off, heading downtown. The pavements were comparatively crowded at nine that morning as we weaved along the road and, the destruction aside, the city looked almost normal.

Until a bullet smacked into a building a few yards away and we leapt out of the car. Fear filled the air as the street erupted into pandemonium. Terrified pedestrians started screaming and running for cover. We ran too, rushing towards a doorway where, it seemed, twenty people were crammed into space for three or four, all scrabbling to get off the exposed pavement. An old lady sat in the middle of the road wailing out her terror, unable to move fast enough or get up alone. I watched scared and ashamed that I didn't go to help her, although someone braver did.

Somewhere in the hills a Bosnian Serb was smiling.

His commander General Mladić would have laughed as well, had he witnessed the parade one Saturday afternoon at the Bosnian Army headquarters downtown. If this was the crack force of fanatical Bosnian Mujahideen ready to bring Saudi Arabian-style Islam to Sarajevo, that so terrified the Serbs, they really had very little to worry about.

The soldiers, in name at least, lined up as the officer called them to attention. They looked as though they had just walked in off the street, which most of them had. Dressed in shirts and jeans, tracksuits and training shoes, the recruits, some with earrings and ponytails, looked around nervously. One gangly youth displayed all the awkwardness of adolescence, smiling eagerly with darting glances from side to side as he tried to keep in step. He was barely out of childhood and should have been out playing football or chasing girls, but instead he was going to war. Artists and accountants, musicians and mechanical engineers, anyone who could point and shoot a gun was being drafted.

The scene was a modern-day version of George Orwell's opening to his book *Homage to Catalonia*, when he first arrives at the barracks to join the rag-tag International Brigade. And just like the Republican forces of the Spanish Civil War, the Muslim-led army of independent Bosnia said it too was fighting against fascism.

The Old Town First Brigade was composed of grinning teenagers, tattooed bruisers and a sprinkling of middle-aged men with grimmer faces. They rose at seven for three hours of exercises, with breakfast at ten, followed by a course in shooting and destroying tanks. After two or three days' instruction they were despatched to the front-line. 'We teach them how to fight and how to go to war. We fight like partisans, because we have no weapons for any kind of fight. Their education is on the front-line. We have no choice,' said instructor Nijaz Sabgica. The Bosnian army was massively outgunned, but morale was high at the *ad hoc* military academy. Soldiers just back from the trenches, or about to be despatched, milled about, while in the corner a fighter in his twenties filled his pockets with hand-grenades. The strains of music from the Bosnian Army band drifted down the corridors. Couriers ran to and fro with messages and documents to be signed and orders to be ratified.

A few fighters had weapons, ancient bolt-action rifles and the occasional Kalashnikov. Adison Nezirović had a screwdriver. He pulled it out, exclaiming scornfully: 'What we have we use. I don't even have a knife.' Adison, son of a Muslim mother and Croat father, in former life an importer of china and cutlery, had seen action. An articulate young man in his twenties, he looked sadder and wearier than his new brothers-in-arms in the courtyard.

His was a familiar Sarajevo tale of betrayal, but one no less poignant for its telling. 'I've seen people I know fighting on the other side. Five of us were in school together, in the same class, and we saw our friend Cile fighting with the Serbs. We arrested him and told him to go home. We told our chief that we know him and we don't want him to fight. He went back to the hills. Don't ask me if I would kill him. I don't want to talk about it, because he was a very good friend of mine. Every Serb thinks the same now and I don't know how it can happen. I couldn't believe it when I saw him. He slept in my house a hundred times and now he is fighting against me and my friends.'

Adison had been wounded three months earlier, with shrapnel in his back, but he claimed that he was not scared before combat. 'If you don't go to the war, if they come here, they will kill you. I felt very bad the first time I killed someone with a hand-grenade. They were coming out of a car, I saw it and threw the grenade. I had never killed an ant before, but I had to do it because I was afraid for my people. At that time I wasn't sure what was happening but I thought now I have killed in my life. But in war you had to do it. Everyone said. I have to protect my mother and sister, but I don't know what I will do when the war is over, maybe go to Canada. I don't want to be here.'

Here was Sarajevo, capital of newly independent Bosnia-Herzegovina, but even many Bosnian Muslims were not quite sure what that meant. One day they were Yugoslavs, strolling by the Miljacka river, the next they were sheltering in their basements because their Bosnian Serb neighbours were shelling them on account of their Muslim religion.

So who, exactly, are the Bosnian Muslims? They are probably the only nation in the world to be defined by a religious criteria, in their case Islam, but at first glance that raises more questions than it answers. How can a people be described as Muslim, when most of them were secular unbelievers? And where does that leave Orthodox Bosnian Serbs and Catholic Bosnian Croats who want to be Bosnians first and Serbs and Croats second, not to mention Bosnian Jews and Gypsies?

For Serbian and Croatian nationalists the question is irrelevant. They believe Bosnian Muslims are really Orthodox Serbs or Catholic Croats who took a theological wrong turn and converted to Islam when Bosnia was part of the Ottoman empire and should now return to the fold. No Bosnians means no Bosnia. The logical conclusion of this argument were the secret accords reported to be signed by Presidents Tuđjman and Milošević carving up Bosnia between them, even as hostilities erupted between Serbs and Croats.

Certainly there is an argument that there is no such thing as a Bosnian *per se*, just as one can argue that there is no such thing as, for example, a Slovak. Like Serbs and Croats, Bosnian

Muslims are southern Slavs (Yugoslavs, in Serbo-Croat). They speak the same language, Serbo-Croat, and have no specific racial features to distinguish them from Serbs and Croats. Bosnian Muslims are dark-haired and brown-eyed or blond and blue-eyed, just like Serbs and Croats. All three peoples originated in the great migrations of Slavic tribes from the Volga basin over a thousand years ago that spilled across eastern Europe through Bulgaria and former Yugoslavia to the Czech Republic and Slovakia. But by these criteria Serbs are really Croats and vice-versa. Or even Poles, or Slovaks. What differentiates Bosnian Muslims from Serbs and Croats is their religion, Islam; their hybrid Turkic-Slavic culture and of course their history of continuous occupation on the same territory, adequate criteria in 1990s Europe for statehood.

The collapse of the Soviet Union and Communism has triggered an avalanche of new nation states which barely match Bosnia's claim to nationhood, yet which have been welcomed into the international community. Until 1 January 1993 there had never been an independent Slovakia, for example, although a Nazi puppet state had existed in the Second World War. There was not even a referendum on independence in Slovakia, but its claim to nationhood has gone largely unchallenged by most of the world. In Bosnia there was, and a majority voted for independence, even with the Serb boycott. So why should Bosnia be any different and its status as a independent state be continually marginalised and prevented from buying the arms to defend itself? The answer, many Bosnian and foreign Muslims believe, is because of the country's Islamic heritage. Fear of Islam has prompted the world to stand by while the country was destroyed by marauding Serbs.

But Bosnia-Herzegovina has at least as good a claim to statehood as Croatia and Serbia, no matter whether its citizens pray in a church, mosque or synagogue, if that claim is based on a desire of a majority of the population for self-determination and a history as a national entity. Bosnia was politically independent by 1100, but it was not until the late twelfth century that an independent country emerged, led by the 'Great Ban' Kulin. Medieval Bosnia had its own script and its royal family's symbol was the fleur-de-lys, now readopted by the current Bosnian government as the country's symbol, to the chagrin of many devout Muslims there who would have preferred an Islamic crescent.

Bosnia also had its own church, a key element of national identity in the Balkans. The Bosnian Church appears to have been a hybrid of Catholic and Orthodox, a fitting mix for a region that straddled the theological divide. The key event in Bosnian history was the disappearance of this Church and the replacement of Rome by Mecca as Bosnians steadily deserted Christianity for Islam after the arrival of the Turks in the fifteenth century. Many writers have sought to explain this switch by claiming that Bosnian Christians were in fact Bogomils. Bogomil(ism), meaning 'love of God' in Slavic, was a heresy modelled on Manichean dualism, a Babylonian doctrine based on the eternal conflict between light and dark. As Bogomils were perpetually at the mercy of either Rome or Byzantium, the argument goes, with no external protector of their own, they were more susceptible to the lure of Islam which gave them full citizenship in the Ottoman empire. Other historians, such as Noel Malcolm, completely reject the Bogomil hypothesis. He points out that Bosnian Christians used the sign of the cross, held masses, drank wine and ate meat, all forbidden for Bogomils.

Either way, probably by the late sixteenth or early seventeenth century Muslims were a majority in Bosnia. Just like the Bedouin, the Turks, the Gulf Arabs and North Africans, the Bosnians simply chose Islam. Many Bosnians' links to Christianity were tenuous, and converting to Islam brought immediate benefits under Ottoman rule. The first was the privileged status of Muslims: non-Muslims were discriminated against by the *Kanun-i-rayah*, which governed the status of subject peoples. Conversion also brought enhanced career prospects. Anyone hoping for a position as an Ottoman functionary had to be a Muslim.

Ottoman Islam also offered a civilised life-style for its subjects, at least by sixteenth- and seventeenth-century standards, as long as they observed the law and accepted Ottoman rule. Religious minorities, including the Serbian Orthodox Church, were allowed their own courts and given the powers to settle their own internal affairs. But wrongdoers, real or imagined, who threatened the stability of the Sublime Porte, were subjected to revolting punishments such as impaling. The prisoner would be held down and a stake fed into his rectum, passing through his body out of a cut in his shoulder, before he was raised up on the pole like a human kebab, to flop helplessly in agony. This was a calculated brutality, designed to control often restless subject peoples. The Ottoman executioners were specially trained in their job, easing the stake through so it bypassed vital organs. The wretched prisoner would often survive for several days, dangling helplessly as a grisly warning to passers-by of the price of law-breaking under the Turks.

That was the downside of Ottoman rule. So was the hated practice of *devshirme*, the state-organised kidnapping en masse of young males to Istanbul where they would be converted to Islam and trained in the army or Ottoman civil service. The benefits could be considerable for towns such as Travnik and Banja Luka, which quickly became important local centres. The Turks erected an urban infrastructure; not only mosques, but also markets, bath-houses, schools and bridges. Ghazi Husrev Beg, who lived in the sixteenth century, is immortalised in this Sarajevo folksong praising his endowments:

I built the medresa [school] *and imaret* [public kitchen]
I built the clock tower by it a mosque
I built Taslihan and the cloth market
I built three bridges in Sarajevo
I turned a village into the town of Sarajevo

Serbian towns too flowered under Ottoman rule. By the eighteenth century Užice, for example, had eighteen mosques, as well as the usual municipal buildings, and became a noted centre of Islamic learning. Under Ottoman rule Bosnians evolved their own Turkic-Slavic hybrid culture, just as the Bosnian Church adopted some but not all of the trappings of Catholicism. Bosnian Muslims wore Turkish dress but few learnt Turkish and married women were only half-veiled: 'Go to Bosnia if you want to see your wife,' said one Turkish saying.

Until the collapse of the great Austro-Hungarian and Ottoman empires in the First World War, the question of Bosnian independence was largely irrelevant. Bosnia was annexed by Austria in 1908 and later became part of the

Kingdom of Serbs, Slovenes and Croats, set up after the First World War. But during the Second World War, as victory drew nearer for Tito's Communist partisans, the question of Bosnian nationhood became a vitally important issue. At that time Bosnia had been absorbed into the Independent State of Croatia (NDH), a Nazi puppet-state led by Croatian fascist Anté Pavelić.

In 1942 the Muslim leadership sent a memo to Hitler, boasting of their supposed Gothic origins, complaining of killings of Muslims by Pavelić's Ustaša troops and asking for Bosnian autonomy. That was denied but the memo led to the formation of the first Bosnian SS division composed of Muslims, the 13th Handar, named after the Turkish knife, a move actively encouraged by Haj Amin El-Husseini, the Grand Mufti of Jerusalem, fervent anti-Semite and ally of Hitler. Spurred on by Bosnian Imams, at one stage 21,000 men joined up. Fifty years later the Bosnian Serbs would well remember the SS Handar division. But relations between the NDH and the Muslims soon drastically deteriorated after religious leaders across the country issued protests about the NDH's brutal treatment of Jews and Serbs, and by the end of 1944 the SS unit was disbanded as Muslims flocked to the partisans.

Post-war Yugoslavia though failed to deliver on its promises of religious freedom. Its first twenty years saw Islamic courts suppressed, veils outlawed together with teaching of children in mosques, and only one state-controlled Islamic association allowed. It was not until 1974 that nationhood for Muslims of both Bosnia and the Sandak, Muslim-inhabited parts of Serbia and Montenegro, was enshrined in the Yugoslav constitution, the first time in post-war Europe that a nation had been created on religious criteria. As Yugoslavia began to implode in the late 1980s and early 1990s Bosnia was pulled in two directions, between ethnic nationalists who saw themselves as Croats, Serbs or Muslims first, and Bosnian nationalists who supported the idea of a multi-ethnic state. The Muslims were not immune to the idea of ethnically based nationhood: the first nationalist party to be formed in Bosnia was their Party of Democratic Action, the SDA, in 1990.

The choice of Alija Izetbegović as leader of the SDA and subsequent president of Bosnia-Herzegovina gave Bosnian

Serbs their greatest propaganda coup. Born in Bosanski Samac in August 1925, he was sentenced to three years in prison in 1946 as Tito's secret police, beginning their crackdown against Muslim activists, charged him with 'pan-Islamic' activities. Tito's security services watched his development with interest over the next few decades and monitored his works such as *Islam Between East and West* and *Problems of the Islamic Renaissance*. In 1983, together with other Muslim nationalists, he was put on trial for 'counter-revolutionary acts derived from Muslim nationalism'. He received a fourteen-year sentence, of which he served six years. The prosecution's case rested on the *Islamic Declaration* that he had written in 1970, translated copies of which are easily obtained at the Serbian press centre in Belgrade, and are continuously quoted by Serb spokesmen.

The declaration appears to call for the establishment of some kind of Islamic order, based on the experience of Pakistan, another country where Islam defined a nation as well as a religious allegiance, although nowhere does it mention Bosnia by name. But the work, a rambling and contradictory treatise, is so hedged with qualifications that its alleged Islamic radicalism was best seen in the eye of the beholder. The declaration's repeated emphasis on the individual's conscience and moral behaviour places it firmly in the modern reformist tradition of Islam, and far from the Iranian or Saudi models, according to analysts such as Yahya Sadowski at the Brookings Institution.

Such important distinctions were lost on the Yugoslav prosecutors. At his trial Izetbegović defended the declaration as offering 'a vision of a democratic and humanistic social order', and said an Islamic order could only be established with a majority Muslim population. Izetbegović's defenders say the *Islamic Declaration* must be taken in context as a dissident document, written under a Communist regime, that used Islam as a tool to express opposition to a repressive Marxist dictatorship. If other Yugoslav leaders were judged on what they stood for twenty years ago, Serbian president Slobodan Milošević would remain a vote-rigging despot and Croatia's Franjo Tuđjman an authoritarian ultra-nationalist. Both of which are, in fact, still fairly accurate descriptions.

Defenders also point to the sentiments of Izetbegović's later book, *Islam Between East and West,* published in 1980. Writing in the *New Republic*, Professor Fouad Ajami of Johns Hopkins University described this confused tome, jammed with references to everyone from Albert Camus and Frederick Engels to Bertrand Russell, as an amateurish attempt to marry Bosnian Muslim traditions with those of Anglo-Saxon Europe. Hardly the views of an Islamic fundamentalist. This attempt to weld Islamic and modern European culture and norms was also evident in the interview Izetbegović gave to the first issue of the magazine *Ogledalo* [mirror], published in 1990, a few months before the first outbreak of war in the former Yugoslavia, where he refers to Jean-Paul Sartre. 'For the Bosnians, the fact that the people aren't the same, but different is totally natural. Hell is not otherness (remember Jean-Paul Sartre) but something you accept and understand. From the beginning we have been getting used to people that belong to other religions and nations. This situation is an extra experience and an extra wealth.'

But for Bosnia, that wealth, of four religions – Islam, Catholicism, Serbian Orthodoxy and Judaism – and as many cultures, now exacted a high price. A short walk through Sarajevo showed the true cost. Hurtling around town by car and living in the Holiday Inn, journalists were to some extent insulated from the lives of average Sarajevans. It was the trip on foot to Amra Abadžić's house in the old Turkish part of the city – a frightening combination of walking, sprinting and hiding in doorways – that brought home the grim reality of daily existence in the Bosnian capital.

Black-haired, slim and fine-boned, Amra was a law student and Communist party member before the war. She carried a Makarov pistol in her handbag and looked like a model, which may have been an added incentive to pay her family a call. I met Amra through Paul Lowe and they have since married, giving at least one happy ending to a story out of Bosnia. We walked out of the Bosnian army headquarters where her father Fuad was based, tramping downtown through the wreckage of war: shops with their fronts blown out, twisted remains of cars splayed across the road and everywhere, building façades pitted with shells and bullet holes. In the background the Sarajevo symphony played on, with its orchestra of rifles, mortars and artillery. For half a mile or so we ambled down the city's main street, named after Marshal Tito. Amra and her sister Elma walked along quite casually, but my stomach was clenched with tension. We were exposed; the only people on the street. At every intersection, favourite targets for snipers, we stopped, checked and ran across. Then we came to a small precinct, empty apart from smashed cars and twisted lamp-posts. 'Here we must run,' they said as we stopped in a doorway. 'Go across the square and over to that corner.' I ran as fast as I ever had, fear spurring me on. So fast in fact that I almost barged Amra and Elma out of the way as we reached the other side. From there, hearts pounding, we trekked up a steep hill into the warren of the old city. We tramped across gardens, up dusty alleys until finally we were home. As we went further into the relative safety of old Sarajevo, where children played in the streets, the tension began to drain away. But it never went.

Like many Bosnian Muslim families, the Abadžićs had always thought of themselves as Yugoslavs. Now though, they had discovered they had a new nationality as Bosnian Muslims – even Amra, the former communist. 'I loved Tito very much. When we were young they taught us about him. We sang for him and danced for him. I loved him for twenty years. I don't blame him for anything, he is part of my life. It was a good time under Tito. There was no war, we were together and we believed in something. Maybe it was stupid but at least we were together,' she said. As we spoke her mother Munira served us coffee, chocolate and biscuits. Lines of tension were etched onto her face and she looked tired and haggard.

Her husband Fuad had already been wounded three times, once as he stood outside the front door. In civilian life Fuad made belts, but now he was a Bosnian army officer. 'Before the war I could never have imagined this situation, that I would be a soldier or commander. I never thought about war. But if we all stay at home who will be in the front-line fighting? Once this war is over I will go back to my leather job. I want to do that,' he said.

Like most families in Sarajevo the Abadžićs survived with the help of UN food aid. Bread, beer and ice-cream were the only food readily available then, although if you were prepared to take the risky journey to the Bosnian Croat barracks, eggs, meat and vegetables were on sale, for Deutschmarks. A typical aid package might contain sardines, soap, pasta and a tin of goulash. The goulash, explained Munira, could be stretched to several meals by serving it with pasta. 'Oil and sugar would be more use. You can't live on a tin of goulash every two or three months. We do appreciate the UN aid of course, but if you wait for that you will die.' The war governed every aspect of daily existence, said Amra. 'In the beginning I felt awful, but now I'm used to it. I arrange my day around the war. I spend my day finding water, meeting my friends. We have good friends, our neighbours, we sit with them and play the guitar and listen to music or talk and play cards. You feel better when you have friends. You become really close when you spend all day and night together in the shelter.'

One evening, back home in Budapest, I turned on Sky television to see the belligerent *Daily Mail* columnist Richard Littlejohn hosting his chat show. Among his guests were the *Daily Mail*'s star feature writer Ann Leslie and Carol Sarler, a columnist with the *People* newspaper, two heavy hitters from Fleet Street's battalion of media worthies. Somehow the mention of Sarajevo came up. 'Sarah who?' quipped Littlejohn. His crowing guests guffawed with laughter. After years of war, the slow death of the Bosnian capital was, for these people, worth no more than a snigger.

But down on Marshal Tito boulevard, and high on the slopes of the Lions cemetery, nobody was laughing.

Refugees from Banja Luka, Travnik

Chapter 2

BOSNIA: ISLAM REBORN

'They are doing this to us because we are Muslims. We are all Muslims enough to be killed . . . this war can continue to the day of judgment if necessary.'
Dr Mustafa Cerić, Imam of Bosnia

'Allahu Egber [God is Great].'
Written in the dust on a BBC armoured vehicle,
Vitez, central Bosnia

When the morning sunlight glinted on the river Lašva, cutting through central Bosnia, and the mist rose through the bumpy mountain tracks snaking behind the front-lines, it was hard to believe that we were crossing a war-zone. Streams poured crystal water through the tree-covered hills, dogs barked in the distance, birds sang out their early morning call and school-children trudged along the road to Vitez on their way to classes, brightly coloured rucksacks on their backs. The soldiers at the checkpoints would lazily wave us through, as they lifted up the wooden pole blocking the road, their presence the only blight in this pastoral idyll. That, and the frequent funerals, as another cross or Muslim marker was added to the little forests of graves that spilled down the verdant hillsides.

But when tension rose between Bosnian government forces and their occasional allies in the Bosnian Croat army (HVO), usually a prelude to all-out fighting, the trip from the Bosnian Croat village of Kiseljak, just outside Sarajevo, to the old Turkish town of Travnik, was an unnerving journey. Then the checkpoints were transformed into combat positions and it was best to drive up very slowly. The fighters were alert and tensed, their Kalashnikovs cocked as they stopped each vehicle to check the occupants. Soldiers laid two lines of land-mines in a careful path that curved towards their position, often reinforced with a machine-gun. A British officer at the UN base in Vitez claimed that the mines were usually empty or not primed, but we weren't about to check when we gingerly drove between them. The sandbags would come out as well, together with lines of tank-traps, giant crosses of steel rails welded together that were slowly rusting, but no less menacing for it.

The journey after dark was the most unnerving. One night as we returned from the government-controlled town of Zenica, speeding away after an air-raid siren sounded, we reached the Bosnian Croat checkpoint at the Vitez turn-off. Heavily armed soldiers watched us warily in the darkness. A torch flashed in the night and an HVO fighter pulled us over. 'Go slowly, slowly,' he cautioned. 'The Muslims have put up barricades down the road.' Our interpreter Mirijana suddenly became very nervous, for she was a Bosnian Croat, and if Muslim soldiers had set up new checkpoints on the way home life could get complicated very quickly. Mirijana was a delightful young woman, twenty years old, pretty and brave, who had been a student in Sarajevo. 'Oh Sarajevo, how I would love to go back to Sarajevo,' she would sigh as she looked longingly down the road that led to the front-line Serb positions at Ilida. We would pick her up most mornings from her parents' house just outside Kiseljak before setting off in search of a story. Her father had run a small haulage business before the war, but now his trucks sat rusting in the garden. We thanked the HVO troops for the warning and slowly set off again down the badly lit road, past the Dutch UN troops at Busovača, until a torch beam again cut through the night. There were no barricades. A handful of ragged Bosnian army troops stood by the side of the road as we stopped. One peered inside the car and stared dolefully at us, saying only, 'Help us. Help Bosnia,' before letting us drive on.

In the government-controlled towns of Travnik and Zenica, Sarajevo and Tuzla, Bosnia's Muslims were at first puzzled, then bitter and incensed at the failure of the West to come to their aid. Food, medical supplies, even British toilets in prefabricated units, all these trundled up the dirt roads from the UN warehouses on the Croatian coast. Welcome as the relief aid was, it was not enough. Loyal Bosnians, of all faiths, wanted weapons, preferably artillery, tanks and fighter planes. Or as Nađija Ridić, a Bosnian army officer based in Travnik, put it: 'If someone kills your children with a hand-grenade, you don't want to be given a lunchbox.'

The Bosnian army, slowly evolving from a ragged band of fighters armed with pistols and ancient bolt-action rifles into a coherent fighting force, was a unique military phenomenon. For the first time since the collapse of the Ottoman empire soldiers in a Muslim-majority army – together with a minority of loyal Bosnian Serbs and Croats – were fighting in mainland Europe. But they were vastly outgunned by the Bosnian Serbs, who under the orders of Serbian President Slobodan Milošević had been handed the JNA's arsenal. Together with the HVO, government troops held barely a third of Bosnian territory. The Serb onslaught had been stopped, and a village here, a ridge there recaptured, but without arms deliveries it would take decades and thousands of lives to regain enough territory to make Bosnia a viable state.

But the West refused to supply weapons to Sarajevo, thanks to the UN arms embargo on all countries of the former Yugoslavia. Diplomats claimed the decision would slow down the fighting and help the cause of peace, but the reality on the front-lines of the arms embargo was to draw a moral equivalence between Muslim victims and Serb aggressors, further increasing Muslim anger. More importantly though, the arms embargo was providing an opportunity for less scrupulous, or perhaps more scrupulous, depending on your viewpoint, states to step into the military gap. If Washington would not help, then Tehran and Riyadh would. Bosnian Muslims had little sympathy for these Islamic countries' theocratic systems of government, but after months of pleading in vain with the West for guns they gladly accepted military and financial aid from Middle Eastern countries.

Fighters too came, hard-faced men from Saudi Arabia and Algeria, some veterans of the Afghan war, all ready to die in what they saw as a 'Jihad', a holy war to save their Muslim brethren. In fact there was little Islamic brotherhood in evidence between the Mujahideen and Bosnian soldiers. The foreign fighters were shocked at Bosnians' liberal ways and the presence of women fighters on the front-line, the Bosnians were alienated by the Mujahideen's Islamic orthodoxy. One UN officer gleefully related how, when a Mujahid ordered a Bosnian woman soldier off the front-line, she shot him. But ultimately a single armed Arab fighter was worth any number of European diplomats mouthing platitudes about the latest Serb atrocity. For Bosnian Serbs the presence of the Mujahideen was the proof they had been waiting for that Bosnian Muslims were Islamic fundamentalists. At the Bosnian Serb headquarters in Banja Luka, epicentre of ethnic cleansing, Serb officers showed visiting journalists a picture, supposedly found on a dead Saudi soldier, of a Mujahid holding up the severed head of a Serb. In Brussels and Washington too, diplomats feared that Bosnian Muslims would turn into Iranian-style Islamic radicals. But in front-line towns such as Travnik, where the Mujahideen prayed at the sixteenth-century multi-coloured mosque, a more subtle process, of awakening and realignment, was unfolding.

Travnik was for centuries a vital staging post on the trade routes from the Balkans to Vienna and Trieste. It had been home to Muslims, Croats, Serbs and a now-vanished Jewish community for centuries but the domes and the minarets of the mosques, the Turkish fountains and water towers, the urban heritage of the Ottoman empire dotted through its streets and alleys marked it as, culturally, a Muslim town. The city was immortalised in *Travnik Chronicle*, by Ivo Andrić, the only Yugoslav to win the Nobel Prize for Literature. 'No one in Travnik ever thought it was a town made for simple and everyday happenings,' he wrote. 'It is like a half-open book on whose pages on one side and the other are gardens, small streets, houses, fields, graveyards and mosques, like illustrations.'

Andrić was more prescient than he knew. Travnik, the disembarkation point for thousands of ethnically cleansed refugees, was regularly shelled by the besieging Serbs, although the presence of British UN troops in their Warrior armoured vehicles on patrol sometimes seemed to reduce the intensity. Still, plenty of shrapnel scars were splashed across houses in the ancient city centre. Some were large gashes from ground-burst shells, while others were a filigree of tiny holes, from rounds that exploded in mid-air, showering schools, markets and people with a deadly steel rain.

Sometimes the streets would rapidly empty as though the

inhabitants had been suddenly sucked away, alerted by some
communal sixth sense and doors would suddenly close. Or the
sirens would ring out across the narrow, winding lanes, warning
of impending attack and we would jump into our Lada Niva
four-wheel drives and tear off as fast as possible while the inhabitants fled to their basements. Important buildings such as the
headquarters of the Bosnian army and the HVO were boarded
up, to protect against shrapnel and blasts. So was the multi-
coloured mosque, with its minaret unusually positioned on its
eastern side and clutch of hairs said to come from the beard of
Muhammad. The mosque, in the centre of town, was always
crowded with soldiers returning to the front, or just back from
the fighting.

In Travnik at least, the mosques were still standing. In Serb-
controlled towns such as the northern Bosnian city of Banja
Luka, Bosnian Serbs not only forced Muslims from their homes,
killing and raping as they went, but also comprehensively
destroyed Muslims' history. Every one of Banja Luka's centuries-old mosques, part of a UNESCO heritage site, has now
been destroyed. Even the Muslim cemetery has been bulldozed
and the rubble of the mosques dispersed to prevent them ever
being rebuilt. Just as the Nazis attempted to eradicate Jewish
history in the Holocaust, by destroying cemeteries, synagogues
and schools, the Bosnian Serb army was dedicated to wiping out
Bosnia's Muslim heritage and history. One of the more shame-
ful footnotes to the Bosnian war has been the encouragement
that the Serbian Orthodox Church has given to its congregants
as they set about destroying every vestige of Islam in Bosnia.
The God of the Serbs, some believe, has no time for notions of
brotherhood or universal spirituality. As one Orthodox priest
reportedly said of the destruction of the Banja Luka mosques:
'They were in the wrong place.'

At the Blue Water hotel in Travnik, now a Bosnian army
headquarters, Emir Tica was bitter at the West's refusal to arm
Bosnia. Sophisticated and well-travelled, this U2 fan now had a
job organising transport for the Bosnian army. Each time we
met he looked increasingly fatigued, but he still carried an
increasingly dog-eared travel guide to the city, hidden away in
his combat fatigues, to show new foreign journalists that once
Travnik had been a popular tourist destination.

A clear stream gurgled down the side of the hotel in Travnik, and thick wooden boards had been placed at its sides to protect against shrapnel and flying glass. The dining room was crowded with soldiers, men and women in fatigues, as he spoke. 'If the Islamic countries break the arms embargo it is the shame of Europe. Europe made the embargo and cut off our chance to survive but the Islamic countries try to help. But if somebody wants to help me and I have to hide that, it's wrong. Somebody wants to save my life, so why should I have to hide it from the people who officially want to help.'

Like every Bosnian Muslim, Emir emphasised his European heritage. 'I want to be part of Europe. When I come to London I am more European than people from Paris or Berlin. Whether or not Europe wants me, I belong to it. I listen to U2 and Madonna. I have friends in Budapest and London. For me Europe does not mean living in Europe, it means the European dream. European governments don't listen to the people who want to help us. But where is Europe when somebody wants to shoot me? When we worked in Germany nobody was scared of Islamisation. Now when they try to kill us in Bosnia, they are. I only started to feel like a Muslim when they put a map on the table and separated Bosnia into Croat, Muslim and Serb.'

In towns such as Travnik, nearby Zenica, Vitez and Sarajevo, right across the sliver of government-controlled Bosnia, a new Bosnian Muslim identity was emerging, sired by both the West's inaction and the arms supplied by the Islamic world. None of the Bosnian Serbs seemed to realise, or more likely care, that the harder and more destructive their onslaught against their Muslim neighbours, the more they would turn to Islam to see the answers for the destruction and death that was spreading all around them in this peculiarly vicious and murderous conflict.

Every mosque reduced to rubble made Serb propaganda of a Bosnia allied to the Muslim world instead of the West more likely to be a self-fulfilling prophecy. Part of this was a strain of 'Ottoman-nostalgia', a longing for the days when it was Istanbul, not Belgrade, that dictated events in Bosnia. Then Muslims were the élite and it was Christians and Jews that were *rayahs* or subject peoples. Another was a slow shedding of western culture in favour of a Muslim one, based on the precepts of Islam. Young

Muslim women were exchanging jeans and skirts for the veil and baggy trousers, both sexes were greeting each other with the Arabic 'Marhaba' instead of 'hi' and starting to spend their free time in the mosque instead of bars and clubs.

Other Bosnian Muslims, especially victims of ethnic cleansing, began to compare themselves to the Palestinians, another dispossessed Muslim nation. 'We are similar. We will fight until we get our land back. Even if they give the Muslims a tiny bit of land we will have a liberation organisation and it's one hundred per cent certain I will join it. I will fight until the last,' said Samir Bidić. Bidić, 25, escaped from the Serb detention camp of Keraterm and made his way to Zenica. His home was a space on the floor of a fetid sports hall, shared with dozens of other malnourished, coughing refugees. 'As long as there are Muslims I will fight. Sometimes I get so tired and sick and I think I should leave everything. Then I get angry with Europe and I want to take a knife and kill Serbs.'

Even in the yellow-painted school building in Travnik, now home to hundreds of refugees huddling in dank, crowded rooms, the niceties of Muslim village life were carefully preserved. The soldiers, just back from the nearby front, left their shoes outside the room while they brewed coffee in a small brass pot over an open flame. Outside it was so cold that the refugees' washing had frozen solid into a jumble of ice-covered sweaters and trousers. Despair hung in the air, together with the fog of cigarette smoke. But in similar shabby and grimy refugee centres across Bosnia, and across Europe, Islam was taking root among a nation dispossessed, its homeland laid waste. The very methodology of the Bosnian war was helping this radicalisation. Fighting, at least at the outbreak of war, was organised to a different set of rules to conflicts such as the Second World War. Bosnian Serbs avoided military engagements against other soldiers as much as possible. Instead they shelled their target for a few days, sent in the paramilitaries to slaughter a few families and then the buses arrived to ship out the Muslims en masse, such as the Naderević family.

Amla Naderević told me her story one freezing winter morning in the Travnik schoolhouse that was now her home. She was seventeen, with short dark hair and remnants of puppy fat. But her voice was older than her years and she had a faraway look in her eyes as she spoke in the chill of the schoolroom. Hers was a common story, simply told.

'My family comes from Brezičani, a village near Prijedor, it was burnt down. We were brought here by bus in October 1992, but we didn't have to buy a ticket because our house was burnt down. We were given a lift by the Serb Red Cross to Mt Vlašić where we had to cross the front-lines and no-man's land. We were accompanied by Serb gunfire and they tried to take our money and jewellery. My father was in a camp at Prijedor for four and a half months. These were the worst days of my life. He was taken in June and held until October.

'I can say I hate Serbs but we are not capable of doing such things. It's hard to say what the real cause is, it's somewhere in the dark side of the brain. They represent a country which is capable of doing this for its own prosperity, to move people around and kill them. I can't explain why, perhaps it's because they want their own country to be bigger, stronger, greater. I had Serb friends but they were forbidden to contact us and forced to stay away.

'I work from 8.00 am to 2.00 pm as a civilian protection officer here. I have a job trying to help people who are suffering, dealing with problems delivering food, medicine and so on. The conditions here are very miserable, it is very cold, several degrees below freezing and the food supplies are very bad. Still I feel optimistic; after all the suffering we went through we are stronger and capable of enduring anything. All the people here, whatever faith they follow, have right on their side and they will win. My home has been burnt down but I will build another one. It's hard to think about the future. My best wish is for a normal life. Schools, parties, meeting people and to be at home. I won't stay here but someday I will return to Travnik, but next time as a tourist, just for fun.'

Bosnian Muslims accepted help from the Islamic world because they had been forgotten by Europe, said Effendi Nusret Abdibegović, the Imam of Travnik. 'To be a Muslim [now] is absolutely different. If you asked me before the war I would say it's nice to be European Muslim. But now I have to say that we don't feel like we used to feel in Europe. We are part of Europe and part of that is our religion. We still feel European because we felt that Europe will protect us. In Europe democracy is a symbol of a free life.'

Shrapnel scars pitted the walls of Imam's Abdibegović's house, a minute's walk from the multi-coloured mosque. As we spoke he served coffee and biscuits, the sweets still wrapped in their Arabic wrappers. 'But Europe forgets that we are also part of it. We have accepted help from our Muslim brothers because it's their duty to help us. We accept all kinds of help. If Milošević and Karadžić say they will defend Europe from Islam we say we will defend Europe from the Serb religion. Comparing us before the war and now, I wouldn't say Islam has grown stronger. In some places it's ruined, such as Bijeljina. But Muslims are awakening to their identity. Still the Muslims countries could do more. They must not allow what happened to Palestine happen to Bosnia. They should use their oil money.'

Foreign Muslims, particularly Iranians, were using their oil money to provide guns as well as biscuits. The many Islamic relief organisations based in Zagreb were running streams of relief convoys into central Bosnia packed with food and medical aid for the refugees. The Muslim hard men congregated in Zenica, home to the all-Muslim 7th Brigade. Members of the 7th Brigade, part of the Bosnian Army Third Corps, were either practising Bosnian or foreign Muslims. Unlike most Bosnian soldiers they were often hostile to the press. In fact it was best to avoid them completely, as BBC reporter Alan Little and his crew discovered in Zenica one day. Filming in the city the crew were arrested by soldiers from the 7th brigade and held for hours. The Muslim soldiers were so suspicious they even copied down the serial number on a Jubilee line ticket. The BBC crew had a lucky escape. A few months later a British aid driver was killed by Muslim soldiers in Zenica in a military-style execution. President Izetbegović triggered controversy across government-controlled Bosnia when he attended a commemoration of the brigade's founding in January 1995. Together with fellow presidency member Eyup Ganić he defended his attendance in a statement: 'The unit in question saved people from genocide. Their religion aided them in that and was a source of their strength.'

Life in Zenica became increasingly unpleasant for the remaining Serbs and Croats. They were harassed by Muslim fighters and many fled across the lines to their Serb brethren. There were reports of ethnic cleansing by government troops, arrests and imprisonment of non Muslims. Muslim fighters were also blamed for a massacre in a Bosnian village, when over thirty corpses were discovered. However, when it came to the slaughter of the innocents, government troops were always in the third division, trailing far behind the Bosnian Serbs and Croats.

Sometimes, hidden under the boxes of flour and cooking oil that trundled into Travnik and Zenica, lay freshly greased Kalashnikovs and boxes of ammunition. Much of the government forces' arms and ammunitions had been paid for by Islamic countries, working under the cover of relief organisations. One Iranian plane packed with weapons had been turned back at Zagreb airport, reportedly after the Croatian government had been tipped off by US intelligence.

Two years into the war a second attempt was more successful and any tip-offs from the CIA were ignored by the Croats. An Iranian air force transport plane, loaded with sixty tons of explosives and material for weapons production, landed at Zagreb in May 1994, its cargo destined for the Bosnian army. The Iranians maintained an unusually large embassy in Zagreb which was a central point for arms supplies to the Bosnian government forces. Tons of arms still sat at Maribor airport, in Slovenia, after a botched attempt to fly them to the Bosnian army via Hungary and the Arab world. But despite the UN arms embargo, a trickle of mostly small arms arrived in central Bosnia, depending on the current state of relations between Zagreb and Sarajevo. Plenty of western aid organisations and the United Nations were also bringing in aid convoys, but each Islamic relief convoy emblazoned with a green crescent logo, crammed with goods covered in Arabic writing, reinforced the growing impression that only Islamic countries cared about Bosnia.

But Christians too came to help, and increasingly, to fight, said Hamed Mesanović, Travnik's deputy commander. 'We have French, British, Italian, Hungarian and Slovenian volunteers. They are all fighting against evil. Their military significance is not great but they boost our forces. Their presence is morally significant. Some of the foreign Islamic fighters might be motivated by the possibility of fighting a holy war but I only wish there were more of them. They are welcome and their presence shames Europe.'

At one stage there seemed to be so many British volunteers (they said they weren't mercenaries because the pay was virtually non-existent) in the Bosnian army, that it became an almost daily occurrence to see a soldier wearing the blue and white Bosnian fleur-de-lys speaking in a broad Glasgow or Manchester accent.

There was John from Blackpool, a computer programmer who had previously fought with the Croatian army. He would often drop by the BBC office in Kiseljak, provoking fury from Kate Adie when he brought his weapon indoors with him. John was sick, suffering from a kidney infection, not helped by a diet for weeks on end of rice and beans. Like many British soldiers in the Bosnian army he had nothing but praise for the welcome he received from the people for whom he was fighting. 'In some ways they are more cultured than we are. They have manners that we have forgotten. They have a kindness and regard for each other. When a man sees you in the street he will walk up, shake your hand and say how are you? Even if he sees you every day. It is just a politeness. If you go into their homes they will give you everything they have. They are starving in some areas but they will give you the food from their mouths. It's very embarrassing sometimes to go into someone's house and be given a meal and then you realise it's their rations for a week or more,' he explained.

There were other, gorier stories as well, of throat-slitting and slaughter. 'I've killed Chetniks [Serbs] personally and in actions, I've been in countless actions. I've killed one as close as you are to me. He was a sentry and my patrol was attacking a village where the Chetniks had a front-line and they had two sentries patrolling in the woods. I killed one with a knife, my friend killed another with a knife. They had to be dealt with, quietly.' Another afternoon at the village of Pazaric just outside Sarajevo we met a middle-aged man with a bag emblazoned with a Red Cross. He claimed he was a field medic from Derbyshire. A couple of minutes later five young Britons appeared, all former soldiers in the British army, their faces covered in camouflage cream, full of bravado as they headed to the front nearby. They all claimed that the television pictures of Serbian detention camps had triggered their decision to fight for Bosnia. But there was always the suspicion that the better opportunities for killing

people in the Lašva valley than in Lancashire also helped influence their decision. At least two British volunteers would later
die a horrible death.

Ted Skinner and Derek Arnold, from Liverpool and Glasgow
respectively, were a common sight at the Blue Water hotel in
Travnik, eating their lunch of rice and bean soup with their
comrades in arms. They were well known to the Bosnian
Muslim fighters, having trained many of them. Skinner, in his
late thirties, had just spent Christmas staring down his Zastava
rifle's night-sight near Travnik before killing a Serb sniper, he
said. When he shot his enemy he felt nothing, he claimed, but
the killing sometimes haunted him in the early hours of the
morning. Both men worked as instructors teaching raw recruits
one end of an AK47 from the other. They described themselves
as 'soldiers of misfortune' and said they supplied their own uniforms and field dressings, although their guns were issued by the
Bosnian army.

Like most foreign fighters they were suspicious of outsiders
at first, and reluctant to talk. But after they had seen us a couple
of times in the army headquarters, they slowly opened up.
Skinner was an intelligent and articulate man who drew a parallel between the Bosnian and Spanish civil wars. 'That was a
practice run for Germany and a testing ground for the Condor
legion. It would be terrible if the same happened here. If they
get away with it in Bosnia who's to say they won't in Kosovo?'
But it was clear that the two men, both British army veterans,
had a cause in the Bosnian army that they could never get in the
civilian world. Arnold also taught field medicine to trainee
medics. 'They had four days to learn. A lot of them are kids, sixteen, seventeen or eighteen and many are girls. Some of them
are instinctively good fighters who would be welcome in
anyone's army.'

Like many in Travnik that winter they sensed the coming
battle between the HVO and the Bosnian army. They were
scathing about the shaven-headed Croat fighters who swaggered
around the old town's bars and cafés, shiny hand-grenades
clamped to their belts. Skinner and Arnold's bodies were found
a couple of months later, tied to trees near the front-line at
Turbe, just outside Travnik. They had been tortured and then
shot. Some blamed the HVO, others the Mujahideen. The two

were reportedly abducted from their flat in Travnik. They said they had ten years of military experience but it all proved useless. In the end, they were in too deep.

So, it appeared, were we, when we awoke one morning at 6.00 am to an early morning call of repeated rifle fire right outside our bedroom window in Vitez. We had arrived the night before at the Muslim-run guest house above a petrol station a couple of miles from the British UN base. The Bosnian soldiers downstairs assured us that everything was calm, and that the only recent trouble was an attempted armed robbery, which in Bosnian terms made the hotel reasonably safe. I noticed that one fighter had an AK47 clip in his trouser pocket, but it was late, we were tired, we had just been turned back from a checkpoint because of fighting nearby and we had to sleep somewhere. In the dark we didn't notice that a network of slit trenches had been dug around the forecourt. We had checked into a battlefield and we would be lucky to check out again alive.

It was the eve of the latest phase of the Bosnian war: the fight between government forces and their supposed allies against the Bosnian Serbs, the Bosnian Croats. The HVO had issued an ultimatum to government forces to submit to its authority in areas with a heavy Bosnian Croat presence by 15 April 1993. Under the leadership of the ultra-nationalist Mate Boban, the HVO attempted to carve out its own Croat minirepublic of Herceg-Bosna, with its capital in Mostar, which he and President Tuđjman planned to absorb into Croatia proper, even while the HVO was nominally allied to Sarajevo. Bosnian Croats claimed that Herceg-Bosna, a quasi-fascist statelet modelled on the Bosnian Serb Republic, was merely a temporary measure to ensure their protection while the war lasted. They were lying. One afternoon in Mostar Muslim leaders showed us a school registration form for the city, overprinted with the Bosnian Croat chequerboard. At the bottom, in tiny letters, was the printing imprint date, January 1992. The war in Bosnia started in April 1992.

Like the Bosnian Serbs, with whom they would soon be fighting against government forces, the Croats had long prepared for their annexation attempt. In Herceg-Bosna just as in Serbcontrolled Bosnia, Muslims were expelled en masse, murdered or incarcerated in concentration camps. Sporadic fighting between government and HVO troops had erupted since the previous autumn, and now an all-out war was about to explode. The Bosnian army refused to sign and the ultimatum expired at midnight. Six hours later the shooting started. Outside our front door. When the crump of mortar fire was added to the rattle of machine guns we decided to get out as fast as possible. The mortars were close enough for us to hear their baseplates rattle as the shells soared upwards. But it was hard to leave as there was a battle going on downstairs just a few feet away. As we stood in the corridor deciding what to do a bullet smashed through a window, flying right by us. The staccato cracking speeded up and the motel's windows and bathroom mirrors shattered all around us as the bullets smashed into the rooms.

We instantly dropped to the ground, noses virtually scraping the carpet as we crawled along the floor and gathered our luggage. Donning our flak jackets and helmets we sat on the stairs and waited while the battle unfolded a few feet beneath. There was nowhere to run, nowhere to hide. Shouts and screams filled the air as I listened, trying to dam the rush of nightmare scenarios pushing their way into my head and considering the possibility that we might not get out alive. Not only were we caught in a real live battle, even worse, we were trapped above a garage and its great tanks of petrol while bullets flew all around us. Peter Maass, a friend and colleague from the *Washington Post*, held the keys to our Lada Niva in his hand and pointed to the pocket in his flak jacket where he was placing the keys. The implication was clear: if something happens to me, this is your ticket out. Even my other friend and travelling companion, Cathy Jenkins of the BBC, a real veteran of the Yugoslav wars, was starting to look worried, for this was way beyond any adventure. It would make a great story around the dinner table of course, if we made it out alive.

The fighting lasted about a quarter of an hour, although at the time it seemed longer. Then a Bosnian Croat fighter ran up the stairs towards us, his face covered with a ski-mask and his AK47 cocked and ready for action. Here at last was my chance to shout the phrase I had carefully memorised in Serbo-Croat for just this sort of unhappy occasion: 'Foreign journalists! Don't shoot!' But all I could remember was 'novinar' (journalist). I shouted it anyway. Several times. It must have done the trick for the fighter, who thankfully was at least wearing proper fatigues with brigade badges and wasn't a freelance bandit, stopped. He demanded to see our press cards, which we all scrabbled to produce. 'Who are you?' we asked carefully. 'Don't ask. You don't want to know,' he replied.

He and his colleagues then put on a fine display of destruction for us, jumping in and out of rooms, waving their guns around and leaping through glass doors in their search for more Muslim soldiers, even though we said the other rooms were all empty, and emptying their magazines all over the place. Here at last was Rambovic in action, literally under our noses. It was a truly terrifying but also bizarre experience, for in a way I had moved beyond the Sarajevo-style fear of being shot and shelled when caught in a war-zone. Part of my brain just seemed to switch off and I watched the soldiers in a sort of interested, but dispassionate daze, like seeing a 3-D film. It is a curious feeling to contemplate the possibility of your own death in a war. Then the HVO soldiers beckoned us downstairs.

A stench of cordite filled the air and a hand-grenade lay on the floor. The young Muslim soldiers from the previous night stood against the wall, their hands in the air, their faces fearful. A Croat soldier ushered us out, gun in the air, ready to give us covering fire if there was a counterattack from government troops. Another waved us off with a Nazi style-salute. Thankfully our Lada was a hardy beast and Peter drove off down the road, weaving to avoid any sniper fire, until we reached the British base, where we were served a full English breakfast by the doughty and unflappable British UN troops. I couldn't eat anything. In fact I think I went into some sort of shock, for it was not until lunchtime that I was able to hold a reasonably coherent conversation. I tried to read a book, *A History of the World in 10½ Chapters* by Julian Barnes, to take my mind off the shooting and shelling all around us, but the words just danced across the page.

Incredibly, even in the midst of a battle unfolding around them, the daily necessities continued. Housewives hung their washing out and old men stood on their doorsteps wondering what the day held in store. This bizarre mix of the banal and the deadly that was Bosnia, was perhaps best summed up by a

British officer as a 'Bosnian mind-fuck'. Certainly my repeated trips to the war-zone began to fuck up my mind as my mental recovery period became longer and longer each time I left. I became irritable, short-tempered and twitchy. Unexpected noises made me jump. They still do, in fact. When I began to dream about Bosnia, even at home in Budapest or London, I knew it was time to think about getting out. I still remember one dream vividly. I was out on the front-line with a group of Bosnian army soldiers who were setting up a mortar position. But the mortar was pointing straight upwards, instead of being angled towards the enemy. 'If you fire that it will come straight back down and land on our heads,' I exclaimed to the fighters. I never found out what happened in that dream, for the telephone rang then, waking me.

We spent the rest of the day in a house where the British troops had set up a press base. Their presence was comforting but our immediate surroundings only made me more nervous. A Bosnian Croat, the local postman, sat at the bottom of the garden, every now and again lazily firing his high calibre mortar. The doors shook and the windows rattled every time the postman knocked and we all moved underground into the cellar. From the windows we watched the battle unfold as soldiers dodged between houses, some of them on fire. In the evening a British army doctor showed us how to apply an intravenous drip. I paid close attention thinking it might be a useful lesson but couldn't remember much. It was the longest day of my life.

I did not return to Bosnia after that. The next morning I hitched a lift back to Split in a UN vehicle with a British army soldier. We drove through the mountains on back roads, where fear and tension hung in the air like an almost tangible, brooding presence. Compared to Vitez, Split was a paradise, a gorgeous seaside town with atmospheric Roman ruins, where we dined every night on grilled seafood and watched leggy blondes zip around town on their boyfriends' scooters. It was hard to believe the war-zone was just a couple of hours' drive away, but the holiday cabins near the beach that were once filled with revellers were crowded with Bosnian women refugees, smoke from their cigarettes drifting across the lines of washing strung between the huts.

*

Fighting between the HVO and government forces lasted almost a year. In spring 1994 Bosnia, Croatia and Herceg-Bosna signed a peace accord, brokered mainly by the USA and in part by Iran, that called for a joint Muslim–Croat federation in Bosnia, leaving an opening for the Bosnian Serbs to join. Under pressure from Washington and the threat of sanctions against Croatia the two sides made peace and Mate Boban, leader of Herceg-Bosna, was replaced. The war in central Bosnia between the HVO and government forces stopped almost overnight. The territories that Bosnian Croats and the Bosnian army currently control will be joined in a Muslim–Bosnian Croat federation, probably linked to Croatia, while the majority-Muslim part of Bosnia juggles its western and Islamic heritages.

That spreading Islamisation called for a delicate balancing act by Bosnian commanders, and other officials. One morning we drove from Kiseljak to Visoko, a stronghold of government forces also facing the front-line, shelled daily by the Bosnian Serbs. We took the only safe way in, across a winding mountain track that cut behind the front-lines. Ice crackled under the tyres as we climbed through the mountains outside Sarajevo past the Bosnian army checkpoint. The scenery was breathtaking: clumps of trees hugged the steep hills as the winter sun reflected off the snow. The boom of artillery echoing again around the valley reminded us this was a war-zone.

Visoko greeted us with the usual panorama of Bosnian destruction: buildings with roofs like collapsed soufflés, houses with massive holes punched through their walls, and streets empty apart from the frantic barking of stray dogs. A small picture of the Ayatollah Khomeini was taped to a cabin outside army headquarters and nobody was available to talk to us. Visoko's hospital had gone underground because of the constant bombardment and boxes of Iranian Red Crescent aid were piled up at the entrance. Two wounded Algerian soldiers lay on their beds in the basement. 'I came here for the idea of Islam,' said one, but as soon as he started talking the doctors quickly stopped the interview, fearful that if we reported his presence it would trigger a fresh Serb bombardment of the hospital.

Ultimately it was this deep sense of betrayal that Europe had

53

deserted Bosnia, more than the Muslim aid convoys or the Mujahideen, that was helping create a vacuum steadily being filled by Islam. Nor was this confined to Bosnia proper. The ripples of Islamisation also reached the hundreds of thousands of Muslims forced from their homes, listlessly passing their days away in the network of refugee camps over Europe.

In places such as the Nagyatad centre in southern Hungary, just a few miles from the Croatian border, and home to dozens of mainly Muslim Bosnian refugees, young women such as Mirsada spend their days studying the Quran and praying. One room there has been converted to a mosque, its white walls covered with Arabic inscriptions and carpets on the floor. In Yugoslavia, Mirsada, an eighteen-year-old from Visegrad, could not easily live as a religious Muslim, she said, but the war has provided a curious form of liberation. 'In Visegrad I could not talk about my religion or practise it this much, but now I have learnt a lot more about it. Because of my situation, like many young Bosnians, I am much more interested in Islam. The war has made me religious.'

Or as Dr Mustafa Cerić, leader of Bosnia's Muslim community, said one afternoon in his office at Zagreb's mosque, its entrance crowded with Bosnian refugees: 'They are doing this to us because we are Muslims. We are all Muslim enough to be killed. Muslims are coming together because their suffering is the same and no one wants to take them. But Muslim blood is not worth the same as Muslim oil.' He was eloquent in his anger at the West's inaction as his people were slaughtered. 'People feel they are not wanted in Europe as Muslims. But we are not Arabs or Turks. We didn't come here. People said "never again" after the concentration camps, but it happened again, in their neighbourhood, not in Africa, not in Asia, but here.

'Now Bosnian Muslims are witnessing a national transformation. The Muslims that were communists before know what power is. They are frustrated and they feel betrayed by Europe and they cannot ask Moscow [for help]. The people who have a faith have an explanation why this is happening. Now more people are turning to Islam. They feel betrayed by the West and by Europe. If Europe wants humanism and religious tolerance we are here and it should say we will not allow these people to be harmed. What is happening to us is a sin for Europe. No one can tell me that Europe can have a clear conscience over the Bosnian Muslims.

'What is happening to Bosnian Muslims is not war, it is not happening by chance. It was planned for us. No matter what we tried, the Serbs rejected every possible solution. This is why we are disillusioned with European values. We believed too much in Europe. I don't know a single Bosnian Muslim who wanted an Islamic state run on the Islamic religion. There are rules in Islamic laws, giving rules for life, but according to Islamic law nothing from Islam can be enforced on non-Muslims. Even if a Muslim wanted to make a Christian obey Islamic law he cannot do that. We have come to the bottom of the bottom. Now life for us is something else. What is better? To live in falsehood or die in truth? This war can continue to the day of judgment if necessary. We have no choice, no place to go and nothing else to lose.

'We are not a big united people who can create an Islamic state to threaten Europe. But the western world lost its chance to help us and get applause. By this inaction and by just observing it might lead us in a very dangerous direction. Some will look for revenge and they will have nothing to lose. We still control our people but I don't know how long anyone will be able to control them. We are asking please help us while we are still sane.'

Part of the tragedy of Bosnia's Muslims was they also believed too much in the Islamic world as they looked eastward for help. Considering the wealth of the oil-rich Arab nations, the response of many Muslim governments has been unremarkable, with more sound and fury than hard cash, apart from the Iranians and, to a lesser extent, the Saudis. Certainly the regular convoys of relief aid and ammunition helped many Bosnian Muslims stay alive and fight back against the Serbs. But the lack of political action, particularly by the Arab world, which has oil production as a powerful weapon, has left a gap readily filled by Tehran. 'I am a Palestinian from Gaza and I know what it means to leave your country,' said Kamal Mosleh, a relief worker based in Zagreb. 'The reaction of the Islamic world is very weak. They could have given more and done more. All the money has come from the people except from Saudi Arabia.'

Some Islamic countries have also offered UN peace-keepers, including Iran which said it was ready to send 10,000 men, but the UN rejected the plan. Most of the Islamic relief effort has been financed by private donations and Muslim countries have taken in just a tiny fraction of the refugees that poured out of Bosnia, although this is also due to Bosnian Muslims' reluctance to leave Europe and live in the Arab world. Money allocated to relief work is often squandered, on publications like *Sarajevo*, a thick glossy full-colour magazine printed in Arabic.

Muslim states see Bosnia as a recruiting ground for their own brand of Islam and spend as much time manoeuvring for advantage as actually helping refugees, said one senior Islamic aid worker with extensive experience of working in Bosnia, who must remain nameless. 'Muslim non-governmental organisations are run by amateurs, instead of doctors or people with experience. They are sitting on millions of dollars and they don't know what to do with them, so they produce a colour magazine. You can see the level of political commitment in the number of embassies in Sarajevo [in 1993]. Only Iranians and Turks are there, and not a single Arab country. Their involvement is to pour in relief supplies, and that's because the people in their own countries are clamouring for them to do something.'

Instead of uniting, Islamic countries were using relief aid as a weapon in the struggle to establish a bridgehead in Europe between competing regimes such as the Sunni Saudi Arabians and the Shiite Iranians, the aid worker said. 'It's not even effective. The Arab countries should have tremendous clout. In 1973 in the Yom Kippur War they cut off oil supplies. They could hold the world hostage, but instead aid has become a political weapon in Muslim relief organisations because there are so many different groups such as the Saudis and the Iranians. The Iranians will not work in an area where there are no [rival] Saudis.

'Don't think the Iranians are in Sarajevo to express solidarity with their fellow Muslims. That would be naive in the extreme. Once they are in the field they have the power to use aid as a weapon: "We will give you aid, but you must follow our line." As Bosnian Muslims become more politicised the different Muslim states will move in an organised way to get a foot in Europe. The

Saudis demand that women refugees wear the veil. This is the sinister aspect of the Muslim relief effort. Make them Muslims and then we will give them aid,' he said.

Iran has skilfully exploited the Bosnian war to try and build a bridgehead in Europe. By openly breaking the arms embargo and supplying arms, fuel and weapons-manufacturing equipment it has left the West with a dilemma. Now, after the Dayton accords, the arms embargo is lifted – a move also supported by many American politicians – and Iran is seen to have set the international agenda and gains kudos, in both Bosnia and the wider Islamic world. When the arms embargo stayed, Iran gained influence in Bosnia as the country's patron, ready to supply the embattled government with what the West refuses. Both Washington and Tehran regard each other with loathing, but on the issue of Bosnia they became de facto allies. Towards the end of the war, there were repeated stories of US-organised arms drops to Tuzla, always denied, of course, by US officials.

Either way Tehran has laid firm foundations for future influence in Sarajevo and also in Zagreb. After Iranian foreign minister Ali Akbar Velayati visited Sarajevo in May 1994 to open a new embassy there, he discussed setting up a joint economic commission with Bosnia and Croatia. Meanwhile Saudi Arabia promised to send two Jumbo jets to fly Bosnian Muslim pilgrims from Sarajevo to Mecca, a move that looked feeble in comparison. Once again the Ayatollahs of Tehran had outmanoeuvred the White House and the United Nations to set the Bosnian agenda, while Washington and even the Arab world looked on helplessly.

The very words western politicians and many reporters have used during the Bosnian war have also accelerated this process of Islamisation and realignment away from the West. The mainly Muslim Bosnian government army, with its significant minority of Serb and Croat soldiers and officers, especially in and around Sarajevo, is inaccurately referred to as the 'Muslim soldiers'. The Muslim-led Bosnian government, with its Serb and Croat officials and ministers becomes 'the Muslims'. Land held by the Bosnian government, an internationally recognised sovereign state and member of the United Nations, becomes 'Muslim-controlled territory', and so on. No matter how many times Bosnian leaders such as President Izetbegović emphasised their commitment to a multi-ethnic society of Bosnian Muslims, Serbs, Croats and Jews – and the adherents of these faiths who stayed faithful to Sarajevo are testament to his sincerity – the language of diplomacy ghettoised their government.

The Bosnian war was described as a 'civil war', fought by 'warring factions', a description especially favoured by UN spokesmen. At times in Geneva during the many futile peace conferences UN officials could barely contain their impatience with the Bosnian government for refusing to surrender at least half their country to the Bosnian Serbs. Of course if they were only 'Muslims', their claim to the land was much weaker.

As the West sows, so shall it reap. As one soldier put it, referring to claims that Bosnian Muslims wanted an Islamic regime: 'Europe will bring about here the very thing it fears.' For young Muslims like Samir, a twenty-year-old soldier waiting outside the multi-coloured mosque, the West was doing nothing for Bosnia while Islamic countries were ready to help. 'Islamic countries will give us guns because there is no one else to help. We were waiting for Europe, but now there is no other way because we were betrayed by Europe.'

Both Izetbegović and Silajdzić have made visits to Libya and Iran, seeking financial and military aid for Bosnia. These links, which Bosnians defend as unavoidable given the West's failure to stop the Serbs and the continuing UN arms embargo, were being watched with concern in western capitals.

'Europe is accusing us of an Islamic fundamentalism that is a danger to Europe, but this notion of Islamic fundamentalism is very hard to defend yourself against,' said Dr Mustafa Cerić. 'It is a political category of conflict between Iran and the US. For the Serbs someone is an Islamic fundamentalist if he has an Islamic name. There are staunch communists who imprisoned Muslims and are now charged with being Islamic fundamentalists.'

In fact for Muslim activists like Melika Saliahbegbosnawi, jailed for two years under the Communists for her beliefs, Izetbegović's government was not Islamic enough. The former dissident was angry because a Bosnian soldier had reprimanded her in the streets of Sarajevo for dressing as an orthodox Muslim woman in headscarf and long sleeves.

'At the beginning of the war I was stopped on the street by a Bosnian soldier. He said, "I'm going to arrest you and Allah." He even had a Muslim name. I said you can arrest me but you cannot arrest Allah. The new government is doing the same as the communists against religious people. The Bosnian government is afraid to be seen as Islamic fundamentalist because then they won't get help from the West. The communist authorities did the same thing.'

A former party member and graduate of Zagreb university who also studied in Paris, Saliahbegbosnawi started wearing the chador at the time of the Iranian revolution in 1979. 'That's when I started to wear Islamic clothes, but that revolution had nothing in common with my revolution. I wear the chador because it keeps human morality and a law always gives a rule for society. Women are beautiful and if they adorn themselves they will attract someone from the street and they will try to get her. If a woman is uncovered she attracts men through her body as an object. If a woman covers herself she will force men to see her other possibilities and potential as a woman. Love from this kind of respect is more lasting.'

Like many Sarajevans, she had a narrow escape from death when a missile destroyed her house. 'I escaped three minutes before it came in. I just thought something was going to happen. I lost everything, my books, my manuscripts and my furniture. Now I write and try to live a normal life. I never run on the streets because I don't want them to destroy my dignity. I'm not an animal who is scared. I believe that if there is a missile to kill me it is my destiny.'

She was scathing about President Izetbegović's poor planning for war. 'Izetbegović sparked the fire of nationalism among Muslims as that was the one chance for him to get a party and then get power. He used to say that Bosnia was three nations and now he exudes nationalism. He plays the role of Gandhi to establish and defend the country through diplomacy. He cannot do it through power but you need power to get the respect of your enemies. We knew that war started in Slovenia and Croatia. He didn't want to arm the Bosnian people and prepare but he is prepared for bleeding.

'I love and respect Ayatollah Khomeini but humanity did not get a chance to learn the truth about his deeds. But during his lifetime people from the Majlis [Iranian parliament] changed the objects and aims of the revolution. Muslim ladies were treated in communist propaganda as ignorant and repressed but I chose this. I know what is going on. I am very peaceful but unhappy. I would be happy if I could call people to light – Islam. But their ears are full of false promises from the government. Izetbegović has nothing to do with Islam. Everything in the flag comes from pre-Islamic times. But that is wrong because these people are Muslim in their way of life. Islam is composed of a culture and a life and that is nothing to be ashamed of. I would like to see a civil society and I would like to establish Islamic law and for God's law to rule the world, but it's too early, you have to call people back to God. I don't want the morality that prevails in the West. That's immorality if you want to plunder people or lie to them.'

Just as in Travnik and Zenica, the old idea of a multi-national Bosnia was also fading in Sarajevo as the Islamic wing of the SDA party began to gain strength in the capital. The shadow of a one-party state fell again on Bosnia, although this time it was Muslim and authoritarian, rather than atheist and communist. Even loyal Bosnian Serbs and Croats began to feel marginalised. The city too changed, its fabled cosmopolitanism fading as more and more sophisticated urbanites left, their places taken by refugees from the countryside who hated Serbs and Croats for killing their families and destroying their houses and were not impressed with talk of Bosnia's multi-ethnic heritage. Concern spread among the political classes at the growing influence of the SDA and in February 1995 five opposition members of Bosnia's collective presidency, Serb, Croat and Muslim, published a statement in the Sarajevo daily newspaper *Oslobođenje* warning that the future of a secular, multi-cultural Bosnia was under threat. 'Each weakening of multi-culturalism diminishes the prospect for liberating the country and establishing a new democratic society,' they said.

But if the city could live through over three years of war, it could cope with SDA Islamic activists. The new general manager of Sarajevo Radio and Television banned short skirts and leggings for female workers, reported Tom Gjelten in his book *Sarajevo Daily*, but Gjelten still watched an uncut version of

Basic Instinct, complete with Sharon Stone crossing her legs while free of underwear on television one night. When Džemaludin Latić, editor of the pro-SDA weekly *Ljiljan* wrote a series of columns condemning marriage between Muslims and other faiths as a 'catastrophe' he triggered an immediate broadside from Slavko Santić, a columnist on the city's *Oslobođenje* newspaper – whose ethnically mixed staff had never missed an edition throughout the war – attacking his intolerance.

This move away from a multi-ethnic Bosnia was a direct result of the logic of the international peace plans that sought to divide the country along ethnic and religious lines. Diplomats too opened the path for a Muslim national state. Under the Dayton accords, Bosnia is to be divided into two ethnic entities: one Serb and one Muslim–Croat federation, the former with 49 per cent of territory, the latter 51 per cent. The pretence of a unitary state is to be maintained, as Sarajevo keeps control of trade, finance and international relations, but the entities control their own armed forces and police. Dayton is a diplomatic figleaf that justifies Bosnian Serb ethnocide and the Serb entity will not have to wait long before fusing with Serbia proper, with the Bosnian Croats perhaps following suit.

Not surprisingly, just as Bosnian Serb and Croat nationalists sought their own states, some Muslims began to follow their example. In the winter of 1993, for the first time, Bosnian leaders formed a self-appointed Muslim assembly in Sarajevo, that excluded Bosnian Serb and Croat leaders loyal to the government. As they pounded the tables and waxed lyrical about Ottoman rule, they simultaneously called for a Muslim national state in Bosnia, and blamed the West for forcing them into an ethnic ghetto in the first place. By then President Izetbegović's SDA had already voted in favour of ethnic partition of Bosnia. But even then, with the multi-ethnic ideal in its death throes, while most of the delegates called for a Muslim Bosnia, they demanded one based on the idea of nationality, rather than religion.

This future Bosnia could be a Muslim national state, but largely secular, much as Israel is a Jewish state but a secular and democratic one where religious identity has fused with nationality to spawn a new nation. Most of the delegates at the Sarajevo Muslim assembly drank alcohol and few read the

61

Quran or attended services at the mosque, but their religion both formed and framed their embryonic nationality. This latest stage in the (not necessarily religious) Muslimisation of Bosnia was merely a continuation of events almost twenty years ago, when Tito's Communists gave Bosnian Muslims the status of a nation. Now, in the fires of war, that nation was defining itself. But whatever the final size and type of the so far still-born Bosnia – independent Muslim majority nation-state, Muslim-Croat federation or new mini-Yugoslavia – it is clear that once the war is over, the new Bosnia will in many ways be more Muslim than its predecessor, the Yugoslav Federal Republic of Bosnia, ever was. Economically if not politically, Bosnia will be a Muslim Bantustan in the heart of Europe, propped up in part by diplomatic and financial aid from the Muslim world.

It could also be a political springboard into Europe for Iran, and some Arab states as well, all of whose aid will long be remembered with gratitude, thus adding another perpetual destabilising factor to the Balkans, an already deeply unstable region. Its angry and resentful population scattered inside its borders, or exiled in their hundreds of thousands across Europe and the world, could provide ready recruits for any future Bosnian Liberation Front, ready to use force for Sarajevo's cause, their rage fuelled by militant Islam. As Croatian professor of philosophy Žarko Puhovsky, a former advisor to President Izetbegović, told me: 'There is a simple formula for the future of Bosnia. The smaller the territory, the more the regime will be drawn to Islamic fundamentalism.'

Bosnia will also be part of an arc of Muslim-majority states stretching from central Asia, through Turkey, to Albania, another former part of the Ottoman empire where Islam is being reborn, on the shores of the Adriatic. Even as the Bosnian war broke out, Turkish officials saw it as an opportunity to expand Ankara's political fiefdom. The UN security council deployed Turkish peace-keeping troops in Bosnia, to the anger of its traditional pro-Serb enemy, Greece. The decision reversed a long-standing policy that countries with a historic involvement in a war-zone should not provide peace-keeping troops. In January 1996 Turkish general Ersim Yaltsin signed an agreement with Bosnian army commander Rasim Delić to provide military training. For the Turks it will be a homecoming of sorts to a land now wrecked and shattered, where billions of dollars will be spent on reconstructing a country that need never have been destroyed in the first place. Turkey will be aided by the United States in beefing up the Bosnian army, as part of Washington's geo-political strategy to build an arc of allies stretching from Bosnia, through Albania, Turkey, Jordan and Israel.

And where Washington goes in Bosnia, Tehran soon follows. Few countries are currently receiving so much simultaneous attention from the USA and Iran, arch-enemies in so many other ways. In July 1996 a high-level Iranian delegation, led by First Vice-President Hassan Habibi, visited Sarajevo where its members pledged $50 million to help reconstruct the country, through financing companies and repairing infrastructure. It was a shrewd move by the Iranians to help Bosnian businesses, for that will give Tehran a foot-hold in the Bosnia economy as it steadily grows. The agreement also singled out a factory in Zenica, home of the remaining foreign Mujahideen and the all-Muslim 7th Corps of the Bosnian army, for Iranian economic assistance.

Now even *The Economist* carries advertisements for banking officials to work in Bosnia to help reconstruct the economy. Every country's war has left physical destruction and wreckage in its wake. What was unique about the Bosnian war was that it was the world's inaugural prime-time ethnocide, diligently reported, televised and watched for over three years before the West called a halt to the killing. For the first time in history, a country was laid waste, its people massacred and Bosnia's Slavic-Turkic culture was destroyed, much of it live on television. Muslims the world over believe, probably rightly, that had the Bosnian Serb guns been pointed at Christians the killings would have been stopped long ago. The Croatian war of independence, after all, didn't even last a year. The Slovenian war lasted ten days.

Not only mosques, houses and people, but also libraries have been destroyed, as Bosnian Serbs turned their guns on Bosnia's very history. In just one day, 17 May 1992, Sarajevo's Institute for Oriental Studies was destroyed. It held thousands of books, manuscripts and Ottoman documents, much of Bosnia's historical records, until they were incinerated in a hail of deliberately targeted rockets.

Every house, every field, every yard of Bosnian territory that was lost to the Serbs steered Bosnia's Muslims away from the West and their hopes of European intervention and towards the East and the Muslim world. In the fields of destruction, Islam was laying its roots, nurtured by Iran and the Arab world. 'Religion is the only stronghold we have, and the support we draw from it,' said Mustafa Bećirević, chief Imam for Croatia and Slovenia. 'The war showed Bosnian Muslims that they do exist as a people and the Serbs cannot tell them what is worthwhile in their culture. Even as victims they discovered this. Muslims have now become conscious of their force; politically, militarily, religiously and culturally.'

Even now, for me, the very word Bosnia still triggers a chain of images and memories. Of being stuck outside Novi Travnik with a column of refugees and the sudden flinch of shock and fear on a young woman's face as she crouched, suddenly shrinking into herself, when a mortar exploded fifty yards away from us, kicking up a plume of earth. Of a ridge near Gornji Vakuf and a turbanned Imam standing silently among the clutch of Muslim soldiers, like a scene from a Second World War partisan film, as they slowly advanced down the hill towards us. Of the Koševo hospital in Sarajevo where Kemal Karić, a four-month-old Muslim boy lay on his back in a hospital cot, the stump of his amputated leg waving uselessly in the air as he grinned and gurgled. Of a young Bosnian Serb soldier in hospital in Belgrade and the sheet lying flat on the hospital bed where his legs should have been. Of an old lady sitting screaming in the street in Sarajevo. And the black ski mask on the face of the Croat fighter in the hotel outside Vitez as he advanced up the stairs towards us, his Kalashnikov in his hand.

The West is now weary of images like these, as Bosnia slides down the newslists at newspapers and television stations. But they are images which the Muslim world will long remember.

Hungarians in the Rudas Turkish Baths, Budapest

Chapter 3

EUROPE'S FORGOTTEN ISLAMIC HERITAGE

'In the mosques there is no more prayer
In the fountains no more ablution
The populous places have become desolate
The Austrian has taken our beautiful Buda'
Seventeenth-century Ottoman song lamenting
the Austrian capture of Budapest

'I am the garden, I awake adorned in beauty: Gaze on me
well, know what I am like . . . What a delight for the
eyes! The patient man who looks here realises his
spiritual desires.'
Verse by the fourteenth-century poet Ibn Zamrak,
inscribed on the walls of the Alhambra,
Granada, Spain

The mosques and *hamams* (baths) of Bosnia have vanished
under Serb shells, or carefully placed explosive charges. But in
Budapest scattered jewels of Ottoman architecture remain.
Pashas and Imams, Sufi dervishes and Ottoman merchants, perhaps even Sultan Suleyman the Magnificent himself once
soaked in the sulphurous, slightly radioactive waters of the
Rudas Turkish baths' thermal springs, on the banks of the
Danube in Budapest. I spend every Saturday morning there,
one of a less illustrious group of bathers than our Ottoman
predecessors; foreign correspondents planning the weekend's
parties, Hungarian businessmen with clanking gold chains and
bracelets, their arms and backs covered with exotic tattoos, and
weary factory workers, soaking away a week on the shop floor.

But we all share in our enjoyment of one of Europe's finest remaining hamams. Budapest is dotted with thermal springs and four hamams still remain from the time when Hungary was ruled by the dictates of the Sublime Porte in Istanbul. Lazing in the hot water, gazing at the domed roof while sunlight cuts through the steam rising from the main pool, it's simple to reinvent yourself as an Ottoman tradesman who has just dismounted from a days-long Caravanserai trek from Istanbul up through Sofia and Belgrade. Built by Szokoli Mustafa, the sixteenth-century Pasha of Buda, who is still commemorated on a plaque by the tap dispensing sulphurous mineral water, the Rudas is an extraordinarily atmospheric place, that retains its original cupola, vaulted corridor and main octagonal pool.

Bathing in Budapest has been a tradition since the arrival of the Romans, but it was under Ottoman rule that the culture of the baths flowered. Islam demands that its followers follow a strict set of rules before praying five times a day, washing and abluting in the prescribed manner.

Every mosque must have a supply of clean running water for worshippers to cleanse themselves. Water, or more specifically, running water has always had a specific motif in Islam, partly perhaps because of the faith's origins in the deserts of Arabia, but also for its life-giving and sensual qualities. Paradise for believers, as described in the Quran, will be a garden of bliss, filled with crystal fountains and springs, fruits and sweetmeats, as verses 15 to 19 of Sura 56 describe:

(They will be) on couches
Encrusted (with gold and precious stones)
Reclining on them
Facing each other
Round them will (serve)
Youths of perpetual freshness
With goblets, (shining) beakers
And cups (filled) out of
Clear-flowing fountains:
No after-ache will they
receive therefrom, nor will they
Suffer intoxication

The previous Sura, 55, describes in detail the two gardens where the Blessed will be able to stroll in the afterlife, dark green in colour from plentiful watering, according to the Quran. Verses 66 to 67 outline the pleasures that await there:

> *In them (each) will be*
> *Two springs pouring forth water*
> *In continuous abundance*
> *Then which of the favours*
> *Of your Lord will ye deny*

There will be plenty of beautiful young virgins as well, among the fountains and ornate couches, as verses 70 to 74 describe:

> *In them will be*
> *Fair (maidens), good, beautiful*
> *Then which of the favours*
> *   of your Lord will ye deny?*
> *Maidens restrained (as to*
> *Their glances) in (goodly) pavilions*
> *Then which of the favours*
> *   of your Lord will ye deny?*
> *Whom no man or Jinn*
> *Before them has touched*
> *Then which of the favours*
> *Of your Lord will ye deny?*

None, obviously. The Islamic paradise is a far more sensual and exotic one than the Christian version, with its promises of fulfilling all of believers' sensual appetites. A hint of its spirit lives on at the surviving *hamams* but the Ottoman tanneries, mosques and *medresas* (schools) that once filled Budapest's streets have vanished, and only a few remnants of that era remain across central Europe.

Further east, Romania was once a bridge between western and Arab culture. Its provinces of Wallachia and Moldavia were by the eighteenth century important centres for the study of Arabic. The first Arabic typography appeared in Wallachia, before being transferred to Aleppo, in Syria. Romania even once boasted a centre for Sufis, Islamic mystics, on an island in the

Danube, long since submerged. In the Serbian capital Belgrade, once the former frontier city between the lands of the Sultan and those of the Hapsburg Emperor, hundreds of mosques and hamams have long since been demolished. Now only one mosque still stands, where nervous Muslims pray in a city home to many of those Serbs who strove to eradicate Bosnian Muslim culture.

Overlooking the Danube, at the top of Budapest's last surviving Ottoman street, a steep incline named for Gül Baba, is his tomb. The bustle of the capital and one of the main bridges across the Danube are just a few hundred yards away, but the tomb is one of the most peaceful places in the city. Perched on a ridge overlooking the river, the site of the tomb, the most northern place of pilgrimage for Muslims, is suffused with the sense of tranquillity that is the hallmark of Islamic places of worship.

Gül Baba was a holy man and a high-ranking member of the Bektashi Sufi order of Islamic mystics. His name means 'father of the roses' and according to local folklore, he was the man who introduced the flower to Budapest, thus giving the name Rózsadomb, Rose Hill, to the area around Gül Baba street. Several beds of roses surround the small domed structure. In fact he died during the thanksgiving service for the capture of Budapest on 2 September 1541, just after the King Matthew church had been converted into a mosque. Inside the mausoleum are verses inscribed by the Turkish traveller Evliya Çelebi when he visited the tomb in 1663, as well as antiquities and furnishings donated by Hungarian Muslims. Sadly, the adjacent hotel that once catered to Muslim pilgrims is no more, but Çelebi's writings on the Magyars remain. Çelebi was quite a fan, understandably preferring their company to those of the Austrians he had met:

> They are clean in their ways and in their eating and honour their guests. They do not torture their prisoners as the Austrians do. They practise sword play like the Ottomans. In short, though both of them are unbelievers without faith, the Hungarians are more honourable and cleaner infidels. They do not wash their faces with urine every morning as the Austrians do, but wash their face every morning with water as the Ottomans do.[1]

In fact the appearance of the first Muslims in Hungary preceded Gül Baba and the Ottomans by over five hundred years. But apart from mentions in specialist academic journals, Hungary's Muslim history remains largely unknown even to most Magyars, a representative and telling example of Christian Europe's rewriting of history in favour of the cross rather than the Islamic crescent. According to the Hungarian Chronicle known as the *Anonymi gesta Hungarorum*, a group of Muslims arrived, probably from Bulgaria, in the tenth century. During the tenth, eleventh and twelfth centuries Hungary's Muslims were granted several freedoms and given civil and military duties, serving the border guards. Other Muslim communities were settled by the country's then frontier, marked by a wooden stockade between the Danube and Lake Balaton. When the Tatars invaded in 1241, they laid waste to their settlements, and the rest of the country. A description of early medieval Hungary (whose territories then stretched much further than its present borders) survives in the writing of Abu Hamid, a Spanish-Arab traveller and writer from Granada who arrived in the region of the Slavs and the Magyars in the middle of the twelfth century. In his book *Tuhfat al-Albab* he describes what he found in Bashgurd, as the area was known in Arabic:

It has seventy-eight cities, each one of which is like Isfahan and Baghdad wherein is to be found (God's) bounty, favour and abundant blessing and a luxury and easiness of living that can neither be accounted for nor quantified. My eldest son, Hamid, there married two ladies from among the Muslim noblemen and he (by them) begat male offspring.[2]

Hamid's example has since been followed by many expatriates even now entranced with Hungary's luxury and easiness of living. But for all the centuries that the country was the crossing point between Islam and Christianity, and the cultural fertilisation that sprang from its mixtures of populations – who then included Muslims from Spain and Bulgaria, Arabs and native converts – its Islamic heritage has been in large part not only physically destroyed, but also deliberately ignored. Just as the Communists rewrote the past, according to the dictates of ideology, many Christian historians of Europe have ignored, or at best marginalised the role of the Ottoman empire and Islam in developing the continent. This is a Europe-wide trend. The inventions and discoveries of Muslim mathematicians and scientists, doctors and astronomers have been deliberately sidelined, their contributions often ignored in favour of a historiography that claims a seamless progression from the Dark Ages to the Renaissance, under the benign patronage of Italian and French nobility. This view is nonsense. In mathematics alone for example, two of the most important numeric processes and sciences, without which the present-day computer would never have existed, algebra and algorithms, were invented by Arab mathematicians. Both are Arabic loan words, that still retain the prefix Al (the), linguistic remnants of a rich and intricate culture that flourished while most Celts and Anglo-Saxons were still lurking in damp and freezing wattle and daub huts. Suggest to most Magyars, like most Europeans, that Islam has helped developed their continent and civilisation and they will shudder with horror, having been indoctrinated with the view that the arrival of the Turks was an unmitigated disaster. It was not, for the Ottomans brought a civic infrastructure, a network of schools, kitchens and public bath-houses in their wake, as well as religious freedom for Jews and Christians. Certainly Budapest's Jews knew what lay ahead when in 1683 the Hapsburg guns pounded the hills of Buda, where their community had flourished under Ottoman rule. They fought hard on the side of the Sultan's armies, for Muslim rule was always preferable to that of the Catholic church which often brought persecution and pogroms.

In one building, in the southern Hungarian town of Pécs, the cross has even physically displaced the crescent. This pretty town of sloping streets filled with tile-roofed houses was once an important Ottoman centre. Now its squares are filled with American soldiers in I-FOR, the NATO force in Bosnia, whose border is just a couple of hours' drive away. At the top of Széchenyi square stands the tall imposing building of the Gazi Kasim Pasha mosque. Unfortunately while the building retains its Islamic interior, including Arabic calligraphy, it has been turned into a Catholic church, and the resulting mutant hybrid is an unsettling and insulting attempt to appropriate a building designed to worship Allah for the cause of Jesus and Mary. Better preserved, and unaltered, is the Jakovali Hassan Mosque, with its surviving friezes, miner (pulpit) and white walls. That said, the Ottomans converted plenty of churches into mosques.

The idea of the rapacious Turk is encapsulated in books such as *Egri Csillagok* (*Stars Over Eger*), the story of a group of young Hungarians who make a trek to Istanbul to rescue their captured friend. The book is riddled with ethnic stereotypes of the cruel, lascivious Turk, all portrayed through the writer Géza Gárdonyi's narrow prism of nineteenth-century catholicism. *Stars Over Eger* is one of the most famous books in the country, required reading for every school-child, and has shaped several generations' perception of Muslims, Turks and Islam.

August 29, 1526, when King Lajos II and fewer than 10,000 Hungarian knights were routed by 80,000 Ottoman troops at Mohács, is commemorated by many Hungarians as one of the worst disasters to befall the country. It marked the start of Turkish rule and the era of the northernmost expansion of the Ottoman empire which at one time reached the gates of Vienna. King Lajos, who drowned in a stream when he was trapped by his armour, was mourned even by Suleyman the Magnificent who led the Ottoman forces. 'May God be merciful to him and punish those who misled his inexperience. I came indeed in arms against him, but it was not my wish that he should be thus cut off while he had scarcely tasted the sweets of life and royalty.'

Most Hungarians now view the start of the Ottoman occupation as the beginning of a dark age, of desolation and oppression when Christian Hungary fell under a cruel Muslim yoke. Undoubtedly cruel practices such as *devshirme* (boy tribute) ripped apart families across the Ottoman empire. But the arrival of the Ottomans also gave young foreigners across the empire undreamed-of opportunities in the capital Constantinople. It brought new ideas, new scientific discoveries and new ways of thinking to Europe. In fact the lives of many of the Ottomans' new subjects, whether Hungarian, Serb, Romanian or Bulgarian, flourished under the Sultan's rule. Hungarians such as Ibrahim Muteferrika, a Christian convert to Islam, wrote one of the first books to be published from the first Turkish press, which he had founded, a lengthy work outlining the necessary changes in Ottoman military strategy.

History records though that others fared less well, such as Murad, a teenager who was captured by the Turks at the battle of Mohács and converted to Islam. He became a successful interpreter in the Ottoman foreign service, composing a missionary treatise in Turkish and then in Latin and even translated Cicero for Suleyman the Magnificent. Unfortunately Murad remained more Magyar than Muslim and was sacked for persistent wine drinking. Turkey also provided a refuge for Hungarian refugees after the failed eighteenth-century revolution of Ferenc Rákóczi, when the independence fighters fled the rule of Vienna for sanctuary in Turkey. His memory is still commemorated in a museum at the eastern town of Tekirdag. A second wave of Hungarian refugees fled to Turkey after the failed revolution of 1848, and helped modernise Turkey's civil service.

Contemporary chroniclers, such as John Shirly, author of *The History of the Wars of Hungary (Or, An account of the muiseries of that Kingdom)*, published in London in 1685, record how, when it came to cruelty and religious persecution, it was the Catholic church, rather than the Ottoman Muslims that set the pace, especially when dealing with Protestants:

> Anno Domini 1605. Notwithstanding the former Defeat of Botscay, other intestine Troubles arose in the Kingdom, occasioned by the Bishops in their late assembly, passing a Decree, cruel and bloody, *viz.* That all of the Reformed Religion should be Burnt or Banished: Against which, notwithstanding the Nobility, as well of one Religion or another, Protested. Yet the Reformed Churches were Seized, publick and private Worship forbidden; also the reading of the Holy Bible . . . Such a desolation was made by the discontented Persons in arms, that the Turks stood amazed to see themselves out-done in cruelty.

The Hungarian Catholic bishops' call for the Protestants to be burnt or banished would find an echo centuries later in the Nazi puppet state, set up by Croatian fascists in alliance with the Catholic church in 1941. Its policy for Orthodox Serbs was:

'Kill one third, expel one third and baptise one third.' Perhaps not surprisingly, passing through Hungary in 1790, the Ottoman envoy Azmi Effendi records that Hungarians showed extreme good-will towards both him and the Ottoman empire.

Here then is the clash of cultures that is so often written about by the media pundits on Islam: not the supposed inability of Islam and democracy to co-exist, but the refusal or more likely inability of most Europeans to realise the contribution that Islam and Muslims have made to Europe, in every way from architecture to religious freedom, of which Hungary is an excellent example. Christianity, whether Catholic, Protestant or Orthodox, has claimed all of central Europe and eastern Europe and its history for its own, reducing the Ottoman empire and Islamic culture to a series of cultural stereotypes of ravagers of maidens and despoilers of land, when, if anything, the reverse is true, for the Catholic crusaders left a far wider and deeper river of blood in their wake than the Ottoman armies.

Over three hundred years after the fall of Budapest to the Hapsburgs, a small Turkish community has once again settled in Budapest, although none can trace their lineage in Hungary back to the Ottoman empire. Turan Aktas's Török Büfe (Turkish Buffet) at the city's Józsefváros (Joseph town) market is the meeting point for the city's nascent Turkish community. There Turkish businessmen drink tea from small gold-rimmed glasses, to be slowly sipped with the first cigarette of the day. Breakfast is lentil soup and lamb kebab, eaten to the accompaniment of Turkish pop music. The smell of roasting lamb fills the morning air while Turkish businessmen chat and joke over their food.

Most of the 1,500-strong community are businessmen, importing textiles, running restaurants or travel agencies. 'It is the best of friendship between Hungary and Turkey, in business, culture we are similar to each other,' says Sedat Harputluoglu, a 32-year-old businessman from Istanbul. But even now the Magyar–Turkish connection is an ambivalent friendship, even one-sided, say many Turks, who say their compatriots' warm feelings towards Hungary are not always reciprocated. 'In Turkey everyone sees Hungary not as a friend, but as a brother.

But Hungarians have a different view because of the 160 years of occupation,' said one Turkish diplomat. That some Hungarians take an unenthusiastic view of their distant cousins annoys some Turks now living here. 'We didn't spoil the country. We have been to a lot of places and we never touched religion or the land. We were here for 160 years but show me one Hungarian who speaks Turkish,' said one Turkish businessman.

As the Ottoman empire advanced up through the Balkans and into central Europe, however, Islam's western-most land, cradle of much of the Muslim world's finest achievements in science, culture and architecture, was rapidly collapsing under a Catholic onslaught. The last Islamic outpost in Spain, Granada, fell in 1492 to the armies of Ferdinand and Isabella, who allowed safe passage out of the city for those Muslims who could not live under the rule of the cross. The legend goes that at the final ridge overlooking Granada, Boabdil, the city's last Muslim king, turned back one last time to see his lost lands. 'You should weep like a woman for the land you could not defend like a man,' his mother taunted him as they stood on the outcrop now known as *El Ultimo Suspiro del Moro*, the Moor's Last Sigh.

The victory of the Spanish Catholics was a disaster for Iberian Jews and Muslims but led to an undreamed-of prize for the Ottomans. On 31 March 1492 Ferdinand and Isabella issued the Edict of Expulsion, that all Jews must leave Spain by the last day of July. Don Isaac Abravanel, leader of the community, pleaded in vain for the order to be rescinded. 'Thrice on my knees I besought the King. Regard us, O king, use not thy subjects so cruelly. But . . . the King hardened his heart against the entreaties of his supplicants,' he wrote.

In Istanbul, Sultan Bayezit II was amazed at the stupidity of the Spanish throne. 'Do they call this Ferdinand a wise prince who impoverishes his kingdom and thereby enriches mine?' he supposedly asked when he learnt that his adversaries were expelling en masse many of Spain's most skilled professionals, from doctors and scientists to traders and teachers. If Spain's Jews were not welcome there any longer, they could make a home in the Ottoman empire. The Sublime Porte was flung open to welcome the exodus, leading to a flowering of Jewish life in places as far apart as Salonika and Sarajevo, Cairo and Cyprus. Putting down new roots in the Ottoman empire, Jews spoke of the Sultan's tolerant realm in wonder. It was: 'A broad expansive sea which our Lord has opened with the rod of his mercy. Here the gates of liberty are wide open for you that you may fully practise your Judaism,' wrote one Jewish immigrant to his friends. Even now, among the remnants of the small Jewish community in the Bosnian capital, there are Jewish families with Spanish surnames, who trace their roots to the expulsion in 1492 and who still know some Ladino, the Judeo-Hispanic argot of Iberia.

For decades after 1492 Jews, dissident Christians suffering under Catholic rule, Muslims and Moriscos – Muslim converts to Christianity – poured into the Ottoman empire bringing a whole universe of knowledge and expertise to revitalise the Sultans' realm. When Granada fell Ferdinand and Isabella had promised to honour the religious rights of the remaining Muslims, but that promise was soon broken. Ten years after the expulsion of the Jews the Muslims were given the same choice: convert or go. Most went. A hundred years later the Moriscos were thrown out as well. Certainly there were some restrictions on Jews and Christians under Ottoman rule, but compared to life under the tutelage of the Vatican, the Sultan's lands were a paradise, especially by sixteenth- and seventeenth-century European standards. Jews and Christians were *dhimmis*, that is, people of the book, whose prophets are recognised as part of the series of God's messengers, of which, Muslims believe, Muhammad was the last. They were restricted in minor matters such as the weapons they could carry and the animals they could ride. *Dhimmis* also had to pay higher taxes. But as long as they recognised the ultimate supremacy of Islam, they were free to live and run their communities. It was a supremely sensible as well as a humane policy. Jewish refugees from Spain brought sciences and knowledge virtually unknown to the Ottomans until then. Their contribution was especially important in medicine, printing, and military science, and the Turkish armed forces began to incorporate western military techniques in their warfare manuals. By expelling his Jews King Ferdinand had invigorated the scientific, intellectual and military life of the Ottoman empire.

Among the massive exodus of skilled professionals were, of course, a good number of Jewish physicians, for in fifteenth-century Spain, as now, Jewish mothers liked to boast of 'my son, the doctor'. In his book *The Muslim Discovery of Europe*, the distinguished historian of Islam Professor Bernard Lewis details how the influx of Jewish doctors revitalised Ottoman medicine:

> By the sixteenth century, Jewish physicians, most of them of Spanish, Portuguese or Italian origin, were common in the Ottoman empire. Not only the sultans, but many of their subjects had recourse to these physicians, whom they recognised as representing a higher level of medical knowledge.[3]

Christian visitors were often dismayed at the influence that Jewish doctors had on the Ottoman sultans, who became so numerous that they soon formed their own corps of court physicians, separate from their Muslim colleagues. One of the first ever works on dentistry was written by Moses Hamon, a Jew of Spanish origin who became chief physician to Suleyman the Magnificent.

Islam's western bastion was founded in 711 when the Spanish city of Toledo fell to the Moorish – North African Muslim – armies. Under the leader of their commander Tariq – whose name is commemorated in the word Gibraltar, Arabic for Jebel Tariq, or mountain of Tariq – the Moors defeated the Visigoths at the battle of Janda and their adversaries' kingdom collapsed. City after glorious city soon fell to the advancing Moorish forces: Cordoba, Granada, Seville, Valencia. Cordoba became the jewel of Europe, where learning, art and culture flowered under Muslim guidance. 'Islam was overextended in Spain; it thus made its accommodation with its habitat, ruled with a light touch,' writes Fouad Ajami:

> At its zenith in the tenth and eleventh centuries it was to fashion a society of tranquillity and brilliance. Its cities thrived. Cordoba's population approximated a quarter of a million people; it was unmatched by any European city of the time. Its only rivals were the cities of Baghdad and Constantinople.[4]

The finest monument from Spain's Islamic era is the Alhambra in Granada. Built by the Nasrids in the fourteenth century, it was not so much a fortress as a mini-metropolis. Inside its walls were gardens, palaces, fountains, a mosque, houses and shops. For Victor Hugo it was a 'palace that the genies have gilded like a dream and filled with harmony'. Even Granada's blind beggars boasted of its glories, lamenting a cruel fate that deprived them of the chance to see its marvels, as a means of eliciting sympathy and bigger donations. There was nothing like the Alhambra in the Christian world, no palace that could compare to its light and tranquil series of patios, courtyards and gardens, where the sound of water gently rippling through fountains was a permanent backdrop. Even the walls are bedecked in Arabic poetry, prayers and praise for God. Thankfully, the Alhambra never fell in battle and survives still, as a monument to a civilisation now almost vanished.

But the scientific achievements of Islamic Spain and the eastern Muslim empire live on. Medicine, mathematics, astronomy and navigation, all these arts flowered from Toledo to Baghdad, as Muslim scholars followed the prophet Muhammad's injunction to study and seek knowledge. The *hadith* (sayings) of the prophet include:

> To seek knowledge is obligatory on every Muslim.
> Seek knowledge even unto China.
> The ink of a scholar is holier than the blood of a martyr.
> Those who go out in search of knowledge are fighting in the
>   way of Allah until they return.

The great age of Islamic scientific discovery began, according to legend, with a dream. The ninth-century Caliph al-Ma'mun, who ruled the lands of Islam from his palace in Baghdad, dreamt he met a man with a fair and ruddy complexion, a broad forehead, joined eyebrows, a bald head and a generally pleasant appearance. It was the Greek philosopher, Aristotle. A short dialogue followed.

'What is good?' asked the Caliph.

'That which is good in the mind,' replied the master of philosophy.

'And what comes next?'

'That which is good in the law.'

'Then what?'

'That which is considered good for the people.'[5]

Aristotle also advised the Caliph to guard the doctrine of *tawhid*, or oneness of God. It was all useful advice. Under al-Ma'mun's reign reason and a spirit of scientific enquiry triumphed, and the work of the world's first great international multi-lingual and multi-disciplinary scientific academy, Baghdad's House of Science, reached its zenith. Al-Ma'mun invited linguists, doctors, astronomers and scientists of every discipline from all over the world to Baghdad and provided them with lodgings, financial support and facilities to allow them to carry on their research. The results were astonishing. Works were translated from Greek, Syriac, Hebrew, Sanskrit and Persian into Arabic, triggering an explosion of ideas as the heritage of the great cultures of the Mediterranean, the Arab, Persian and Indian worlds flowed across the academy's busy corridors. For the first time, an international body of knowledge was being shaped into a single corpus, in one language. As this vast corpus of science germinated and cross-fertilised in ninth-century Baghdad Arab scientists leapt ahead of their European counterparts in fields as diverse as optics and astronomy, medicine and, especially, mathematics.

Arab mathematicians had of course never seen a laptop computer such as the Apple PowerBook on which this book was written. But the works of al-Khwarizmi and al-Kashi, in which they developed our current system of numbers, drawing on Indian mathematical systems based on units of ten and zero, laid the intellectual foundations for the mathematical calculations that would, centuries later, result in enormously powerful computer chips and the whole revolution in information technology that flows from that. It is ironic that some Muslim regimes now seek to control the flow of that information in and out of their countries and try and censor the Internet. Caliph al-Ma'mun would not have approved. But he might have welcomed the state-of-the-art technology used by the Islamic Saudi dissident Dr Muhammad al-Mass'ari as he runs his anti-government campaign from his base in north-west London. There banks of fax machines and computers send his message all over the world, the latest manifestations of intellectual advancement in mathematics that began in Baghdad a millennium ago.

Even now our system of numbers is referred to as Arabic numerals, in contrast to the ungainly Roman system, which has survived only on Roman monuments, watches and the credits at the end of film and television programmes. Like every scientist then and now, Arab mathematicians drew on what had been discovered before, and drew on Indian and Chinese numerical ideas. But while it's unclear who exactly invented the zero – the Arabic word for which, *sifr*, has become the Latin cipher – it was Muhammad ibn Musa al-Khwarizmi who was responsible for its systematic introduction into mathematics. The word Algebra comes from the title of al-Khwarizmi's great work *Al-Jabr wa Al-Muqabala,* written during the reign of Caliph al-Ma'mun. It drew on Indian, Euclidean and Babylonian methods but was unique in its systematic cataloguing and rendering of mathematical problems and the accompanying proofs and solutions. Al-Khwarizmi also developed the idea of logarithms, a corruption, in fact, of his name. Knowledge soon begat knowledge and from this small stream of mathematical discoveries a great waterfall of scientific advancement quickly burst forth.

As well as being a mathematician al-Khwarizmi was also a geographer and a philosopher. In 830 he translated Ptolemy's epic work on geography. Under Caliph al-Ma'mun's tutelage he drew up a map of the world, adding the Muslim lands, that divided the world into seven zones in accordance with climatic changes. His work was used for centuries by western geographers. Together with his colleagues he developed an astronomical counting table by which the earth's distance and width could be surveyed, with the logical conclusion that the planet was not flat, but round. Al-Khwarizmi's work was later translated into Latin by Adelard of Bath, and helped shape western European astronomy.

The Key to Arithmetic, by Jamshid ibn Masud al-Kashi, written in Samarkand in 1427, is one of the finest works of Arab mathematics. A manual for the use of everyone who needed to understand numbers, from astronomers to clerks and surveyors, it also included a comprehensive examination of the workings of decimal fractions. In fact these had already appeared in the works of al-Uqlidisi, a mathematician based in tenth-century Damascus. 'Al-Kashi's novel treatment of the subject thus anticipated similar developments in Europe by about two hundred years,' writes A.I. Sabra in *The Scientific Enterprise*, part of *The World of Islam* compendium.

But if one man embodies the spirit of Islamic scientific enquiry and discovery, it is Hakim Abu Ali Abdullah Husayn Ibn Sina, known in the West as Avicenna. Centuries before the Renaissance that began to drag Europe out of the dark ages, Avicenna, born in 980 in Bokhara, central Asia, was the ultimate Renaissance man, preceding Leonardo da Vinci by almost half a millennium. He is perhaps better described by his Arabic honorific: the Sheikh of the peak of knowledge.

Avicenna was already a Hafiz – one who has memorised the entire Quran – by the age of ten. Six years later he turned to medicine, in which field his achievements would be best remembered and which still influence western doctors today. At sixteen he cured the Samanid Sultan, Nuh ibn Mansur, of a serious ailment and was then appointed his court physician. Other doctors were frequent visitors at his rooms, discussing his new discoveries and formulae. Like Caliph al-Ma'mun he was strongly influenced by Aristotelian ideas and served as a bridge between Greek and Islamic thought. His output was prodigious: he wrote over 200 works covering everything from medicine, physics, chemistry, mathematics, music, economics and religious and moral philosophy. In his book *Kitab al-Insaf* (Book of Impartial Judgment) written when he was twenty-one, he poses and answers 28,000 questions on the nature of Divinity. But it was his two great medical works, *Kitab ash-Shifa* (the Book of Healing) and *Al-Qanun fi'l at-Tibb* (the Canon of Medicine) that remain his greatest legacy to medical science, the latter, according to the *Encyclopedia Britannica*, 'the most famous book in the history of medicine, in both East and West'. His achievement was to codify a work that would serve as the basis of medical science in European universities for centuries.

Over a million words long, the five volumes of the *Canon of Medicine* utilised every medical knowledge from every system of health and healing in the then known world, including Tibetan, Greek, Chinese, Arab, Persian and Chinese. It is the single most influential work of medicine in medical history. Avicenna also codified the scientific principles that led to the development of modern botany and pharmacy and invented the process of distillation, extracting oil from roses. His ideas of the importance of a balanced metabolism still influence practitioners of homeopathy today.

The twelfth-century Syrian writer Usama ibn Munqidh has left us a vivid description of the different approaches of European and Arab doctors, quoted in Professor Lewis' *The Muslim Discovery of Europe*. The words are those of Thabit, a Syrian Christian doctor, who was called to treat some patients by a Crusader baron. He was away for only ten days, for his diagnoses were overruled by a European doctor, with gruesome results for the patients:

> They brought me two patients, a knight with an abscess on his leg and a woman afflicted with a mental disorder. I made the knight a poultice, the abscess burst and he felt better. I put the woman on a diet and kept her humour moist. Then a Frankish physician came to them and said to them: 'This man knows nothing about how to treat them!' Then he said to the knight: 'Which do you prefer, to live with one leg or to die with two?' And the knight said: 'To live with one.'
>
> Then the physician said: 'Bring me a strong knight and a sharp axe,' and they brought them. Meanwhile I stood by. Then he put the sick man's leg on a wooden block and said to the knight: 'Strike his leg with the axe and cut it off with one blow!' Then, while I watched, he struck one blow, but the leg was not severed; then he struck a second blow, and the marrow of the leg spurted out and the man died at once.

The unlucky knight at least died quickly. Next in line for the European's brutal attentions was the woman with a mental disorder, as Thabit describes:

> The physician then turned to the woman and said: 'This woman has a devil in her head who has fallen in love with her. Shave her hair off.' So they shaved her head, and she began once again to eat their usual diet with garlic and mustard and such like. Her disorder got worse and he said:

'The devil has entered her head.' Then he took a razor, incised a cross on her head and pulled the skin in the middle until the bone of the skull appeared; this he rubbed with salt, and the woman died forthwith.

Then I said to them: 'Have you any further need of me?' and they said no and so I came home, having learnt things about their medical practice which I did not know before.[6]

Jewish culture too flourished under Muslim rule, especially in Islamic Spain. Far from the academies of Baghdad, Spanish Jews developed their own western European intellectual ideas, that drew on Judaic, Muslim and Christian thought. Jewish academies opened in Granada, Toledo, Barcelona and Cordoba. It was a golden age, still referred to by that title by Jews, an era when thought flowered and Jewish life enjoyed a renaissance of freedom and civil rights that was unrivalled in history.

Even now few Jews know that the greatest intellectual of medieval Judaism, Moses Maimonides, put many of his original thoughts to paper not in Hebrew or Spanish, but in Arabic, the language of the Quran. Known as Rambam, Moses ben Maimon was born in Cordoba in March 1135. Like his Muslim philosophical predecessor Avicenna, he was a doctor as well as a religious thinker, for it was symptomatic of intellectuals under Islamic rule that they specialised in several disciplines, their knowledge advancing through the symbiosis of subjects. Like Caliph al-Ma'mun, founder of Baghdad's House of Science, Maimonides believed that reason should be a guide for life, without sacrificing the Bible's tenets. His *Guide to the Perplexed*, written in Arabic, draws on rationalist ideas and led to major disputes within the medieval Spanish Jewish community.

But as he pored over his text the shadow of the cross fell over Muslim Spain: the *Reconquista*, and the Catholic advance was proceeding. Toledo, Tudela and Saragossa had all been lost to the Muslims. Cracks appeared in the edifice of Muslim tolerance. In 1159 Maimonides' family fled to Fez in Morocco from Cordoba after suffering persecution from Islamic extremists. In Fez too they could find no peace and they finally settled in Fostat, near Cairo. There he practised medicine and eventually became court physician to Sultan Saladin, precursor of the

Spanish Jews who, centuries later, would bring their medical skills to the court of Sultan Suleyman the Magnificent.

Ghosts and customs still remain scattered across southern Spain, remnants of a unique Muslim–Judaic–Hispanic civilisation, destroyed by Catholic royal edict and burnt on the pyres of the Christian Inquisition, a civilisation whose harvest of science and culture flowers still to enhance our lives. Catholic families who for centuries lit candles on a Friday night, the start of the Jewish Sabbath; Spanish lyrics sung to Arabic rhythms and the jewels of Islamic architecture. That Hispanic–Arab connection has also been given new life by ventures such as the new Euro-Arab Management School, in Granada. Promoted by the EU and the Spanish government, the school aims to train a generation of Arab managers and teachers of management. Spain proudly promotes its Islamic heritage through its vigorous tourism industry marketing. An exhibition of Islamic art in Granada entitled *Al-Andalus*, the Arabic word for Spain, in 1992, the 500th anniversary of the expulsion of the Jews, attracted over two million visitors.

And did not the Moorish Sultan Boabdil's last sigh echo through the centuries across the streets and plazas of Madrid, when in October 1991, Arabs and Israelis met there for the slow start of the Middle East peace process? The Spanish capital was an apt venue for the talks. For if Jews and Muslims could flourish together there a millennium ago, perhaps Israelis and Arabs could once again learn to live together in peace, starting on Spanish soil.

If medieval Baghdad, Cordoba and Granada were the sites of the zenith of Muslim civilisation, then 1990s Sofia is – apart from the wrecked cities of Bosnia – its near nadir. A swastika marks the wall of the sixteenth-century Bani Bashi mosque in the downtown city centre, and on a sticky summer's afternoon the inside of the building is almost deserted, apart from a few worshippers staring contemplatively at the building's white walls. Trams trundle by outside on the hot dusty street as vendors sell beers and chocolates to passers-by, while the idling men that are a permanent feature of every Balkan city sit on a low wall nearby, barely visible beneath plumes of cigarette smoke.

In Bulgaria, as across all of eastern Europe, the collapse of Communism has triggered an upsurge in nationalism and a search for a spurious pure ethnicity, in a region that for centuries has been home to a myriad of peoples. Just as in Bosnia, Slavic orthodox nationalists have made Muslims their new *bête noire*, although this small south Balkan country is not about to erupt in a Muslim–Christian war. Bulgaria's Muslims are mainly ethnic Turks, with a small minority of Pomaks, Slavic Muslims. Both are an easy target for the country's small but violent neo-Nazi movement.

'Now we have problems with skinheads, you can see outside on the wall. In the last four or five years the situation for Muslims is worse. It's the same as in Germany. The police do nothing,' says Bilal Halil-Darcan. At twenty-five, Halil-Darcan is young to hold the post of Imam, but Islam in Bulgaria is a long way from re-establishing itself from the neglect of the Communist era, let alone enjoying any kind of renaissance. Halil-Darcan's wife is reluctant even to venture outside alone, for her covered head marks her as a Muslim and she has been abused and intimidated, he explains. 'If I go outside on my own, I don't have any problems, because nobody knows that I am a Muslim. But if I go outside with my wife, her head is covered, it is very dangerous. Once at 8.00 pm, we were coming to the mosque, some nationalists attacked us both. Now my wife is always with me. People look at me with dirty looks, although very occasionally people are nice.'

As one of just two European countries to share a border with Turkey, Bulgaria was a natural first stop on Islam's northward and eastward expansion. Ottoman cultural influences still linger. As in all of the Balkans, Bulgarian coffee is served thick and strong in small cups, Turkish-style – which itself came from the Bedouin method of preparation – and Turkish influence is evident in the country's cuisine, a mix of fish, kebabs and salads. Like Albanians and Bosnian Muslims, other former Ottoman subjects, Bulgarians are also proud of their country's history of religious tolerance and co-existence, in part a legacy of Ottoman policies. Back in the thirteenth century these lands were once the site of the adventures of the legendary warrior saint Sari Saltik, a leader of Muslim Turkic nomads, whose name is still revered across the southern Balkans and the Middle East. The subject of many epic tales of conquest and miracles, Sari Saltik was a prototype for the super-hero of today's comic books and his adventures draw on the fantastic events related by Scheherezade, narrator of the *One Thousand and One Nights*. His feats denote an intricate culture of story-telling, part of an Islamic cultural mosaic that in Bulgaria is now much reduced and dilapidated. Saltik takes to the air on a giant bird; he is anointed with salamander grease that becomes a winged horse that is both heat-proof and fire-proof; he flies over water on his prayer rug; he converts the prince of Christian Georgia to Islam and cuts the head off a seven-headed dragon in Kalagria (now known as Kilgra, near the Bulgarian city of Varna). He is even credited with leading a band of seventy disciples into Russia and Poland, eventually reaching Gdansk, where, the story goes, he killed the patriarch and set about converting the locals to Islam.

But for Bulgarian Muslims today, reality is more prosaic. Imams travel to outlying villages to give crash courses in Islam and its five pillars, for many have forgotten the principles of their ancestral faith. 'Only a very small minority come to the mosque. For the last fifty years, under time of Communism, religion was forbidden, especially Islam. But now people are starting to come, a new generation, more young people. All the teachers in the Islamic school are from other countries, there are no Bulgarian teachers. Some Bulgarians have gone abroad to study Islam in Arab countries and will be able to help. But now it is very difficult,' says Halil-Darcan.

Of all the countries that claimed to be Communist, it was the Bulgarian regime of Todor Zhivkov that showed itself most willing to use nationalism for political expediency. In 1989, in a last desperate bid to shore up the crumbling Bulgarian Communist system the Zhivkov government launched a political blitzkreig against the country's million or so ethnic Turks. They were protesting against attempts to make them adopt Bulgarian names, and a wave of bans against Turkish-language newspapers and even conversations in Turkish. Thousands of Muslims poured across the border, seeking refuge in Turkey, with tales of being given just a few hours to pack, before being expelled. Just as in Bosnia, European Muslims were being ethnically cleansed, although the term was not then in common

87

use. And just as in Bosnia, most of western Europe reacted slowly and with great reluctance against the deportations.

Over seven years later, a key figure in the 'assimilation' process, as the anti-Turkish policy was known, Ilcho Dimitrov was once again stalking Sofia's corridors of power, this time as Minister of Education and Science in the democratically elected government. Now Bulgarian Muslims fear not a new attempt at 'assimilation', but a more subtle clampdown on their rights and national identity. 'I am worried that Turkish television will be forbidden. In many towns it is already forbidden for muezzins to call people to prayer from the mosque, although not in Sofia. They are all small steps,' says Halil-Darcan.

For Mehmed Beytulla, an MP in the ethnic-Turkish Party of Rights and Freedoms, the presence of Dimitrov in government is bad news. 'We have misgivings about him, because during the Zhivkov regime when the assimilation policy was going on he had the same position. We are afraid the government will start a policy of limiting the rights of the Turkish minority in Bulgaria. We don't believe they will start changing names again, but some things they have done seem to indicate a process of restricting the rights of the Turkish minority. I'm meeting the vice-minister of education, because they sent letters to regional inspectorates instructing them not to hire full-time Turkish language teachers.' At the same time the government has reinstalled its own place-men, who held office under Communism, as leaders of the Muslim religious community, said Beytulla.

Like most Bulgarian Muslims, Beytulla, 62, is not religious. Rather Islam is for him a badge of cultural and ethnic identity, part of his Turkish heritage. 'My father and grandfather were deeply religious although I am not and I don't go to the mosque. There were some difficulties during the "assimilation" process. We could not bury our dead according to the Muslim rights, during 1984 to 1989. My father and mother died then so I could not bury them according to Muslim rituals. It was forbidden. I am a Bulgarian citizen, but my nationality is Turkish. My home country is Bulgaria, I love Bulgaria, and will do everything to help my country. But my nationality is Turkish because I love my mother tongue, my culture, I keep my traditions and the rituals, they are very precious to me.'

Like ethnic Hungarians in Slovakia and Romania, Bulgaria's

ethnic Turks seek not political or territorial self-determination, but a form of linguistic, and cultural autonomy. Much as the Ottoman empire granted its subject peoples. As Beytulla says: 'We want the conditions to develop Turkish culture in Bulgaria, we don't have book printing, theatres or folk troupes. Also we would like the Turkish language to be studied as a mandatory subject at school for children belonging to the Turkish minority instead of as an option.'

On the other side of the Balkans, in Albania, Islam is enjoying a renaissance, but this is a very particular rebirth. This spectacularly beautiful country, the only European state to join the international Islamic Conference organisation, was once the most isolated corner of southern Europe. It was virtually sealed off for decades under the rule of the Communist dictator Enver Hoxha who in 1967 outlawed religion, closing or demolishing many mosques. Now money is pouring in from the Middle East, in an attempt to build a bridgehead in Europe for Saudi and Iranian-style Islam. Nominally at least 70 per cent of Albanians are Muslims, but while they welcome the chance to rebuild their mosques and revitalise their Islamic culture, they often have radically different ideas about how to live the life of the faithful to their Arab and Iranian co-religionists.

Organisations such as the Abu Dhabi Welfare Organisation (ADWO), based in a large house in the back streets of Tirana, have set up a nationwide network of aid projects, such as repairing houses and sponsoring orphans. Money for many Muslim aid projects is funnelled through a joint Arab–Albanian bank, but it's a touchy subject. Muslim aid workers deny that their groups are active in Albania only because it is a Muslim-majority country. 'There is no difference between us and Christian organisations. We have no Islamic aims, for us there is no difference between Muslims and non-Muslims,' said the ADWO's Osama Lila. But posters on the office wall explain how to pray according to Islamic ritual, and the Arabic writing has been covered over with instructions in Albanian. I ask Mr Lila where else his organisation is active. 'We have branches in other countries,' he explains. 'Somalia, Pakistan, Kashmir, Bosnia and Macedonia for example.'

A couple of miles away from the ADWO's office a present

from King Fahd of Saudi Arabia sits on the sideboard in Bashkime Korca's house. She has never met the Saudi Arabian monarch, but the Quran she received from him, via an Islamic relief organisation, is one of her greatest treasures. Like many Albanian Muslims, Korca and her husband Shafiq have received aid from Islamic welfare organisations based in Saudia Arabia, Kuwait and Britain, often gifts of sugar and flour when Islamic holidays occur.

And with the food and clothes comes the message that Islam, specifically Arab Sunni, or Iranian Shiite Islam, is the answer for Albania. Tirana airport is crowded daily with bearded Arabs from the Gulf states, flying in and out. Over 400 new mosques have been built in Albania since the end of the hated Communist regime, mostly financed by foreign Muslim countries. Under the old system mere possession of a Quran, or a Bible, brought a prison sentence of several years. But now almost every village has a new Muslim prayer house and travelling across Albania, it's a common sight to see a concrete shell of an almost finished mosque dotting the landscape.

'Now there is freedom in Albania I go to the mosque every Friday. When I am at home we pray five times a day. Under the old system religion was illegal, but now there is a place in our souls to know peace,' said Korca, an activist in the Tirana Women's Islamic Organisation. 'For fifty years there was no faith here, because it was taken away. Now I have entered the Islamic faith and we have to start again from the beginning. My life has changed since I became a Muslim. The faith is in our soul and I feel more at peace. I am satisfied that I see this and the change in our family. Even my daughter prays in the morning.'

Islam was established in Albania under Ottoman rule which lasted over 400 years, from the late fifteenth century to 1912, when Albania declared its independence. Albania supplied a stream of Grand Viziers to the Ottoman rulers in Istanbul and Albanians rose to prominence all over the empire. An Albanian even led the defence of Buda against the Austrians. Vizier Abdurrahman Abdi Arnaut Pasha, the last Turkish governor of Buda, was killed still fighting at the age of seventy as the advancing Hungarians and Austrians took the Castle in 1683.

Islamic officials say there is now an Islamic renaissance in Albania as more young people turn to the ancestral faith of their fathers. 'There is a renewal of Islam in Albania, because the young people are free to come to the mosque and more and more are coming. But that is natural, because over seventy per cent of Albanians are Muslims,' said Ramazan Rusheku, vice-chairman of the Muslim community.

One of these young people is Adam Nelku. Dressed in wrap-around sunglasses, black jeans and matching t-shirt and a reversed baseball cap, Nelku, 21, who rides a pink and white bicycle, does not fit the stereotypical western view of what a Muslim should look like. 'I accepted Islam two years ago after I studied the Quran and saw that it was the word of God. To be a Muslim is the best life in the world, to love people and to worship. Islam says that all Muslims are brothers. People in the West have the wrong idea about Islam, they should study it.' I met Nelku at the Kokonozit mosque, a few minutes' walk from the Muslim community offices. The Kokonozit mosque was named for a grand old Tirana family, but its glory days were long gone, its extreme dilapidation testament to the destruction and neglect of the Hoxha regime. A thick layer of dust covered the mosque's floorboards and the once intricate and colourful floral motifs on the walls were peeling off. Its plaster was cracked and pitted and its window frames bent and collapsing. The minaret had been demolished and still lay outside in a pile of rubble and the ceiling was full of holes. But it was still a mosque, and as Nelku knelt to pray a sense of serenity filled the room.

For Hafiz Shaban Saliaj, the mosque's Imam, the grimy room was full of memories. It was at a ceremony at the Kokonozit mosque in 1952 that he became a *Hafiz*, one who has memorised the entire Quran. 'We learn the Quran by heart, in case it ever gets lost. Then we can get it back in a few hours,' he explains happily. A genial man in his early sixties, Imam Saliaj is very pleased to see western visitors at the mosque that means so much to him. 'Even in these conditions Muslims carry on their faith. We waited for this day, because it says in the Quran to be patient. When religion was banned I carried on secretly, and even in the workplace I gave hints about religious questions. I was very careful in the beginning. I worked in a laboratory with eighty women and I would drop extracts from the Quran and other sayings into the conversation, and they liked it because they had never heard them. I secretly kept a copy of the Quran in my room. The director told me: "If all the workers were like you we would have Communism now!" But Allah protected me.'

I first visited Albania in March 1989, back when the 'Land of the Eagle', as Albanians refer to their homeland, was an isolated Balkan backwater in the grip of the world's most maniacal Marxist regime, apart perhaps from North Korea. The only way in was to pretend to be a football fan, visiting for the England versus Albania game, as foreign journalists, like virtually everything else, were banned and whatever was not banned was compulsory, as the old Communist joke had it. In Albania though, it was true. Religion, private cars, private tourism, western books and newspapers, all these were illegal. The Land of the Eagles seemed more of a bizarre curiosity than a proper country, where the best-known film star is Norman Wisdom, where a nod means 'No' and headshake 'Yes'. Even beards and flared trousers were outlawed at one time. Looking out from my hotel at ten o'clock in the evening I saw a cleaning lady sweeping the deserted streets outside the Edhem Bey mosque, one of the few to survive Hoxha's campaign of destruction.

Now Tirana is a city transformed into a buzzing Balkan minimetropolis. The main square is jammed with cars wandering across intersections, new hotels are springing up and bars and cafés are crowded into every corner. Downtown is jammed every night with Albanians of all ages strolling up and down and chatting to their friends, as in any Mediterranean city. Small kiosks and stalls jam the pavements, selling everything from bananas and shaving cream to beer and chewing gum. Tirana still buzzes with the heady air of freedom. Everywhere there are friends talking, gesticulating, and loudly greeting each other, sipping thick coffee from tiny cups and blowing plumes of smoke into the air as they light the next in a chain of cigarettes. The streets are filled with the sounds of hooting cars as a procession of battered old Mercedes, Audis and BMWs meanders up and down the boulevards. Tirana by night is an engaging slice of Balkan disorder.

It is hard to reconcile this relaxed chaos with the image many have in the West of life in a Muslim country. But to be a Muslim in Tirana is something quite different to being a Muslim in Tehran. The roots of Albanian Islam are Ottoman. In Albania, just as in the rest of the Ottoman empire, religious denominations enjoyed a good measure of freedom under the rule of Constantinople. Albania was also for centuries an important centre for Sufism, Islamic mysticism, and when Kemal Atatürk closed the Sufi centres in Turkey, the headquarters of the Sufi Bektashi movement moved to Albania.

The Bektashis, as part of Islam's heterodox tradition, incorporated many of the traditions of pre-Islamic central Asia in their rituals. By their wanderings and easy-going emphasis on spirituality – in contrast to Arab formalism – they played an important role in the spread of Islam through the Ottoman empire. They emphasised spiritual communion with God through prayer and meditation, rather than the importance of orthodox Islamic ritual. Women are admitted to the *tekke* (prayer house) without a veil and are recognised as having equal rights to men. A Bektashi meeting might include a meal where a sheep will be slaughtered, and washed down with wine – forbidden for Muslims – before the start of religious discussion. Under Enver Hoxha Albania's Bektashi heritage was almost wiped out. Of fifty-three *tekkes*, only six were left standing. In the mid-1940s there were about 285 Bektashi Babas and dervishes, both grades of membership in the Bektashi hierarchy. By 1993 there were five Babas and one dervish left alive. The Bektashis met their deaths in prison, or at the hands of Hoxha's executioners. Their beliefs though, live on. In March 1991 the Bektashi headquarters in Tirana, formerly converted into an old people's home, reopened. Speakers from all of Albania's four main religious traditions spoke at the opening – Bektashi Sufis, Sunni Muslims, Catholic and Orthodox. Each led the crowd in prayer, and each paid homage to Albania's multi-faith heritage.

This tradition of tolerance of different faiths and a liberal interpretation of the Quran has helped ensure good relations between Muslims and their Orthodox and Catholic neighbours for hundreds of years and still continues today. 'There is no danger of Islamic fundamentalism here. Many Muslims think that all this talk of fundamentalism comes from people who are hostile to the Quran. Albanian tolerance could be an example to other Islamic countries, but this is something that comes from the Quran. Europe is afraid of Islam because Islam preaches equality between people, and says do not obey other people, only God,' says Ali Hoxha, a teacher of Islamic studies.

But now many Albanian Muslims fear that their country's tradition of tolerance is under threat from foreign missionaries. Bahai travel teachers, Evangelical Christians, Muslim emissaries from the Gulf States, Mormons, Jehovah's Witnesses, representatives of virtually every faith, major and minor (except Judaism, which does not believe in proseletysing), are all pouring into Albania. For them the country is now a supermarket of souls, where a naive and unsophisticated population that was sealed off from the rest of the world for almost fifty years offers easy spiritual pickings.

On a sticky summer night, in the lounge of Edward Isufi's flat in a crumbling apartment block in central Tirana, a dozen or so young and middle-aged Albanians are earnestly grappling with the theological intricacies of the Bahai faith. Isufi was born a Muslim but has now adopted Bahaism. 'My life has changed since I became a Bahai. I am more optimistic about my new life. Bahais are working for a new world, for peace, for unity. In origin I am a Muslim but religion was forbidden and for a long time we had a space in our heart. My friends and colleagues have a very good impression of the Bahai faith, they told me this is the religion for the future of the world,' says Isufi, a professor of civil engineering at Tirana University.

The Bahai faith was founded in the nineteenth century by the Persian Bahaullah, a.k.a. Mirza Husayn Ali. Liberal and humanistic, Bahais, who claim believers in virtually every country, reject slavery, polygamy, religious prejudice and call for equal rights for both sexes, world peace and harmony. Krishna, Buddha, Moses, Zarathustra, Jesus, and Muhammad are all recognised as prophets, a divine chain culminating in, say Bahais, Bahaulla himself. But the Bahai claim that another prophet followed Muhammad drives Muslims into a fury, including Albanian ones. 'Bahaullah is an Indian deceiver who wants to revise the Quran. He was just a normal man. I'm not angry about him, I'm just revolted by the ignorance of people who accept his word as truth,' says Ali Hoxha. 'Bahaism is not a true religion, they are just deceivers. Because religion was forbidden here many people have minds like a *tabula rasa* and the Bahais take advantage by giving material things like gifts or scholarships.'

Isufi is hosting a 'fireside', a sort of multi-lingual informal chat where, in a babble of Albanian, Italian, Spanish, French and English, new Bahai converts are discussing their faith that preaches love, peace and universal brotherhood. Trays of bananas and peanuts are passed round together with glasses of fizzy orange juice as the foreign 'travel teachers' – missionaries by any other name – from Iran, birthplace of the faith's founder Bahaullah, Italy and the United States discuss the religion's precepts. 'This is the most common way that the Bahai faith becomes known, through personal contact,' says Iraj Sabet, who fled his homeland in Tehran for Switzerland after the Islamic regime launched a wave of horrific persecution against the country's Bahai community. Sabet is now a regular visitor to Albania, where, say Bahai officials, about 12,000 Albanians have converted in the last few years.

A mile or so from the Bahai centre, at the Haxhi Hafiz Dashi mosque, I get a more guarded welcome from some worshippers. This is where the emissaries from the Arab world, bearded young men with sunglasses, come to pray after parking their new four wheel drive cars outside. Upstairs on a balcony sits a middle-aged Egyptian Sheikh, who lives and sleeps here on a mattress on the floor. He ushers me in, and politely serves cold drinks, while beckoning me to sit down. He is neither friendly, nor unfriendly, but he won't tell his name and turns all my questions back on me, turning my attempt at an interview into a tutorial on Islam which is a complicated business, as he speaks in Arabic which is then translated into Albanian and then English.

Here I feel that same sense of distance and suspicion that radiates from many radical Islamists towards the West and westerners. The Sheikh has met my type before: 'I travel to all Muslim countries on my own expenses. This is the third time I have met journalists and they always ask when did you come and why?' He does have some thoughts on the *jihad,* or holy struggle, that is a duty of every Muslim. *Jihad* can be interpreted as covering a range of obligations, from spiritual self-purification to waging a holy war. 'During the Communist regime the *jihad* was mixed with mud, but now it can shine again and the light from this *jihad* will never fade away.'

The Sheikh's ambivalent welcome annoys many of the Albanian Muslims at the mosque, who assure me that in their country everyone is welcome to visit and ask whatever they want. In fact the Albanian liberal interpretation of Islam has led to several disputes between local Muslims and Arab emissaries, just as has happened in Bosnia, where foreign Muslim fighters were shocked to see Bosnian Muslims drinking alcohol and women fighters on the front-line. 'There are some who try and make Albanian Muslims more religious, but the desire and the facts are sometimes different,' says Bardhye Fico, a Muslim official in the Department of Religion. 'They try to make more Albanian women wear a scarf, but that is not Albanian. There is too much speculation on this.'

Many Albanian Muslim women, especially in the cities, such as Bashkime Korca, refuse to cover themselves, seeing the veil as a retrograde step. 'We have our rules that when women go to the mosque their heads and arms must be covered, so we do. But when we have finished praying we take the coverings off. We want to be good Muslims but European Muslims, not Arab ones. There is a big difference between European and Arab Muslims. We cannot be like them and we don't want to be. In the past women here were covered and followed the rules like Arab women, but then we changed. There is nothing to be scared of in Islam. There is peace in our soul but nothing more.'

Budapest, Pécs, Belgrade, Sofia and Tirana. All were once important Ottoman cities, where Islam and Muslim culture flowered in the mosques and *medreses, tekkes* and *hamams.* In Hungary and Serbia, those countries' Islamic heritage has been demolished and marginalised, apart from a few scattered remains. In Sofia, Bulgarian Muslims fear a new wave of oppression from the former Communists still in power. But perhaps it will be in the ramshackle mosques and dusty streets of Tirana, and other Albanian cities, that a new Balkan Islam can flourish, synthesising and drawing on everything from Ottoman tolerance, Bektashi eclecticism, liberal Sunni orthodoxy and secular feminism. Europe's least developed country could yet spawn a modern Islam that combines the heritage of the Sultans with the demands of the modern age.

Mosque, Brick Lane, London

Chapter 4

LONDON: BEIRUT-ON-THAMES

'Living here means you are influenced by British culture, British democracy, British traditions, that unconsciously seep into your character. There are many things about being here which have given me a fuller and rounder understanding of the world and of myself as well. As far as I am concerned London is a very good place to be.'
Dr Ahmad Khalidi, Palestinian author, academic and adviser to the PLO leadership

'London is very bound up in the affairs of the Middle East. Look at the al-Mass'ari affair. Britain is not run on the principles on which he wants Saudi Arabia to be run, but he needed Britain to be the way it was in order to carry on an Islamist cause from here.'
Dr Rosemary Hollis, Middle East Programme Head, The Royal Institute of International Affairs

The world's first Islamic cyber-revolutionary chose an unlikely base for his international campaign to topple the desiccated and increasingly fragile edifice of the Royal House of Saud, but the beauty of cyberspace is that location matters far less than the quality of the telephone lines. Even quiet, pedestrian London, NW10, has no shortage of these. And should Dr Muhammad al-Mass'ari, Secretary General and spokesman of the Committee for the Defence of Legitimate Rights (CDLR), ever return home in triumph to Saudi Arabia from his exile in a north London suburb, then Willesden will finally be assured of its place in the history books.

Its quiet streets of 1930s houses, with their middle-class Indian, Afro-Caribbean and Jewish communities, have few claims to fame. But events in at least one residence were watched avidly by virtually every player in the Middle East, both in the public sphere and the shadow world, from the CIA and MI6 to the Saudi Arabian embassy and the Foreign Office. From there al-Mass'ari ran his campaign through telephone calls, faxes and e-mail – he also has a site on the Internet's World Wide Web – to remove the monarchy from power in Saudi Arabia and replace it with an Islamic democracy, a movable feast of a political concept, and one which is perhaps best described as being in the eye of the beholder. Information and intelligence on events in Saudi Arabia pours out of the fax machines every hour, sent in by sympathisers and supporters of the CDLR across the whole spectrum of Saudi society, from officials in the military and intelligence services, to businessmen and Islamic clerics. All are keen to see the moribund monarchy replaced by a government better able to respond to what they believe are the national and international needs of Saudi Arabia and its population.

Al-Mass'ari – whom the British government has repeatedly, and unsuccessfully tried to deport as a hindrance to British–Saudi relations – is proud of his technology. 'We use the telephone and fax. We use a system of safe calls, which works very well as long as the telephone is not under surveillance. They can call us and there is no way the call can be traced, we use an 0800 number in the USA, through the British Telecom operator to make collect calls, or on credit cards. We have e-mail but we don't use that so much because many people in Saudi Arabia only use computers for games or word-processing or education, and are not yet computer literate,' says the man who was formerly one of Saudi Arabia's top theoretical physicists, and eminent scholar of the *Shariah*, Islam's code of law.

Al-Mass'ari's rows of state-of-the-art computers contradict the stereotypical views that many in the West have of Middle Eastern Muslims, portraying them either as roaming camel-traders and indolent oil-rich sheiks, or dour nonagenarian Ayatollahs passing *fatwas* (judgments) on the dusty plains of

Persia. And unlike in Iran, Mass'ari's concept of Islamic democracy has no special place for the Islamic clergy as a separate and powerful political class. The Islamic revolutionaries of Saudi Arabia, in fact across the Middle East, draw on professional technological and scientific backgrounds that firmly root them in the 1990s. Although while they are happy to benefit from a western scientific education, many Islamists maintain a visceral hostility to the liberal values of the societies that trained them. But just as science flourished under the reign of Caliph al-Ma'mun in ninth-century Baghdad, under scientists who saw their experiments as part of a holistic unity that combined God's will with the expansion of knowledge, Islamists such as al-Mass'ari embrace new technology as part of Islam's mission. To see Islam as not scientific is to have the eyes of a fool, he believes.

'People who think that must be idiots, this is absolute nonsense. They think this because of misconceptions and because of the demonisation campaigns against Islam, through the centuries, that it is anti-science. It is not only not true, it is a joke and should not be discussed. Now in Saudi Arabia the most pro-regime people are the classical clergy. They think in terms of Islamic law which has been developed over the centuries, but they are unable, because of their limited scope of thinking, to go back to the original sources in the Quran which must be applied to the current situation and analyse other points of view. They don't have a critical attitude.' Now Islam is enjoying an intellectual renaissance, he says. 'We are coming out of a deep time, a very low time in Islamic culture and civilisation, with no critical thinking and analysis. Most of the scholars and clergy of Islam are quite backward in the sense they are supporting these regimes out of fear. But the ones who are not overloaded with historic rubble of old ideas, who have sharpened their analytical tools, and studied physics, mathematics, they are now accepting change and improvements.'

It is in London, rather than Cairo or Beirut, Damascus or Riyadh, that these 'changes and improvements' are being fashioned. Positioned halfway between the Middle East and the United States, with easy access to Europe, the hub of a global communications network, and with decades-old ties to Islam's lands, London has now become the *de facto* intellectual capital of the Middle East. Speech is free, no British government hand censors newspapers or television reports – although Saudi-backed London-based newspapers such as *Ash-Sharq Al-Awsat* (*Middle East*) cannot criticise their paymasters – and opposition groups enjoy the sort of freedoms here they could never exploit at home.

As long as exiles do not break Britain's laws, or advocate violence or terrorism, there are no legal restrictions on political activities for Arab opposition groups in London, whether their members arrive as tourists, students or claim political asylum. London's large community of Arab exiles makes the city a bridgehead between the Levant and the West, bringing substantial amounts of capital and investment, and adding a vibrant patch of colour to the city's multi-cultural mosaic. Britain's tradition of Arab scholarship gives the many analysts watching events in the Middle East an open window onto the Arab world. But every benefit has a cost as well, and the downside was never more evident than in July 1994 when two bombs exploded outside the Israeli embassy and the office of the Joint Israel appeal.

Two major international Arabic language newspapers *Ash-Sharq Al-Awsat* (*Middle East*) and *Al-Hayat* (*Life*), are published in London, and the city is also home to an Arabic satellite television station and, of course, the BBC Arabic service, respected across the Middle East for its impartiality and accuracy. The English–Islamic media arc extends also to Pakistan, with the Urdu-language newspaper *Jang* and the English language *The News*, both published in London and Pakistan. Many exiled Muslim dissidents take ready advantage of British freedoms that they would never allow their own citizens, should they ever take power. Radical nationalists, pan-Arabists, Islamists, democrats, liberals, Baathists, monarchists, every shade of Arab, Kurdish, Turkish and Iranian political opinion can be found in Britain's capital. The newsagents in the central London streets of Queensway and Edgware Road, tucked between the Arab cafés, restaurants and estate agents, are crowded with piles of newspapers, magazines and bulletins, all calling for everything from parliamentary democracy, to Islamic theocracy, or a revival of

Baathism, that hybrid ideology of socialism and Arab nationalism. Every major and most minor opposition groups have a presence in London.

They include: Algeria's Islamic Salvation Front; the Palestinian Hamas; the Tunisian An-Nahda (renaissance) movement, led by Raschid al-Ghannouchi; secular Iraqi opposition organisations such as the Free Iraqi Council and even Pakistan's Altaf Hussain's Mohajir Quami Movement, based in the north London district of Muswell Hill, as for some reason radical Muslim groups feel quite at home on the capital's quiet suburban streets. Most of these are banned in their mother country and the presence of so many Muslim revolutionary organisations, many of whom are in regular close contact by telephone, fax and e-mail has even prompted talk of London being the base for a new 'Fundamentalist International', a sort of Muslim Comintern, where Islamic revolutions are planned and emissaries despatched with secret orders. These organisations are tolerated for several reasons, although many in the Home Office and the Foreign Office would like to see them expelled because of the difficulties they can cause to Britain's domestic security, and the way they disrupt trade and diplomacy with the Arab world. To change the laws and outlaw political activity would be a legal quagmire, because there is, after all, still a tradition in Britain of giving asylum to foreigners seen as trouble-makers at home; they provide useful intelligence from their networks of supporters at home and also, there is always an outside chance that one or other group may come to power in what is still an unstable region, and hopefully will then remember who its friends were in the wilderness years.

As well as a flourishing Arab community – of businessmen and women, students and holiday makers, as well as Islamic activists – London is also home to a large Jewish community, among which I grew up. I was born in London, grew up and went to school there. As a child I first saw Arabs in Edgware Road and Oxford Street, shopping or chatting in one of the many Arab cafés around Marble Arch, and at Speaker's Corner at Hyde Park, where I sometimes spent Sunday afternoons watching the passionate and ferocious arguments between Jews and Palestinians. My ancestors are Jews from Lithuania and

Belarus, on one side, mingled with English, Scots and Irish on the other. My paternal grandparents left the Czar's lands at the end of the last century, heading west for a better life, where no Cossacks on horsebacks would thunder past their doors, heralding the latest pogrom. Like many Jews of that great migration, they settled first in London's East End, before moving westwards across the capital to greater comfort and prosperity.

History laid its hand lightly on us, compared to those left behind in eastern Europe. My grandmother lived in White-chapel's Sydney Street, where as a young girl she witnessed the siege, when Russian anarchists holed up in a house nearby fought a gun battle with the police, an operation directed by the young Winston Churchill, then Home Secretary. Some relatives became capitalists, running small factories making clothing or opening shops, others, communists and ardent socialists, demonstrating for Spain during the civil war and throwing bricks at Mosley's fascists as they marched in Cable Street in the East End. Britain has been good to my family, and all have prospered to some degree, living there in peace and safety. The Holocaust passed at least my immediate relatives by, as everyone had left in time. Still, I am sure that old family friends of my great-grandparents and unknown distant relations must have taken that final walk to the trenches outside town before tumbling into the mud and the bodies, or into the gas chambers of the German concentration camps. Now that same immigrants' path across London on which my grandparents travelled is filled by Muslim arrivals. The streets and squares of Whitechapel and Spitalfields that once resounded to Yiddish and Polish are filled with Urdu-speaking Pakistanis and Bangladeshis and the smell of chicken soup has been replaced by curry.

My first school was the North-West London Jewish Day School, the second the Jewish Free School, in Camden, London. Not surprisingly Islam, apart from the Golden Age of Spanish Jewry, did not figure greatly in the syllabus at either, although at both we were taught plenty about Israel and Zionism. But even among the Yiddish-speaking Ashkenazi Jews of north-west London cultural bonds remained with the Middle East and their distant estranged cousins, the Arabs. The Yiddish greeting *Sholom Aleichem* (peace be upon you), derived from Hebrew, is virtually identical to the Arabic greeting *Salaam Aleikum*. On trips to Israel I picked up a few words of Arabic, learning that many were identical or extremely similar to Hebrew, such as the word for house, *beit*, or one, *wahad* in Arabic, *achad* in Hebrew. Theologically, culturally, and linguistically, Islam and Judaism have far more in common with each other than Christianity, even though that religion was also spawned in the Middle East and was for a long time an alien implant in white Europe, which many Europeans seem to forget when they decry Islam as something strange to this continent.

Both Islam and Judaism are monotheistic and recognise the oneness of God, expressed as *tawhid* in Arabic (which takes its root from the word *wahad/achad*), and repeated assertions of God's unity in Hebrew prayers. The concept of the trinity, or praying to an individual, even a deity in human form such as Christians believe Jesus was, is anathema to both. However, Islam recognises all the major prophets of Judaism, such as Abraham and Moses, as well as Jesus and Mary as prophets of God, a chain of revelation culminating in Muhammad, the last and final messenger. Both faiths emphasise the timelessness and holy revelation of their scriptures, the Torah and the Quran respectively. And like Judaism, Islam evolved through a system of interpretation and intellectual questioning, in its case of the meaning of the Quran, and the *hadith*.

Muhammad made quite stringent efforts to convert the Jews of Arabia to Islam, although he failed, Jews then as now being a stubborn bunch, and the Jewish community of Medina was eventually killed, the first stage in the elimination of the ancient Jewish presence in Arabia, apart from Yemen. At the birth of Islam the first Muslims even prayed toward Jerusalem, not Mecca. Both faiths share strict dietary laws, and the laws of *halal* (for Muslims) and *kashrut* (for Jews) are so similar that even the extreme radical Islamist Sheikh Omar Abdul-Rahman, no friend of Jews and now imprisoned in the United States, exhorted his followers to buy kosher meat if no *halal* was available. The family too, of paramount importance for Jews, is the centrepiece of Islamic society. Parents are respected, their wishes obeyed. Aurangzeb Iqbal, a Muslim lawyer in Bradford, told me that when his young clients were arrested and came to him for help, the first thing they asked was not what will happen to them, but 'What will my Mum and Dad say?' No wonder that on my travels I felt far more at home in Muslim Bosnia than in Bavaria, shelling aside.

Growing up in London, immersed in Jewish culture, for some paradoxical reason by my late teens I wanted to know more about Arabs and Islam. A few years later I realised that this was quite a common reaction – on my bookshelves stand several books about the Middle East and Islam by Jewish authors. At school I was not exactly taught that the Arabs were my own personal enemy, but it was understood that our interests were diametrically opposed. I grew up in the 1960s and 1970s, at the time of the Six Day War in 1967 and the Yom Kippur War in 1973. The aim of the Arab armies was simple: to eradicate the state of Israel and throw the Jews into the sea (no distinction was made between Jews and Israelis). The Holocaust was still fresh in my parents' and grandparents' minds. The Arab armies were the heirs of the wartime Mufti of Jerusalem, Haj Amin El-Husseini, good friend of Hitler. They were the soldiers of Nasser, who had hired Nazi German rocket scientists to try and destroy Tel Aviv. Once again it was us against them, although this time 'them' spoke Arabic instead of German. Actually many of us didn't like the Israelis at school very much. They stuck together, spoke Hebrew all the time, and worse, always got to go out with the prettiest girls in class.

But slowly I began to realise the tangled relationship between Jews and Muslims was a bit more complicated than Nasser and Sadat *v* Golda Meir and Moshe Dayan. At school we learnt about the Golden Age of Spanish Jewry, one of the transcendent moments in Jewish history, when culture, religious life, philosophy and science flowered in medieval Spain, all under Muslim rule. And then there was Auschwitz, the very nadir of Jewish life, or rather death. We studied the Holocaust in depth, watching grisly but necessary films of stick men and women in striped pyjamas peering out from behind barbed wire, bodies lying starved on the pavements of the Warsaw Ghetto, bulldozers shoving piles of wasted bodies into trenches. 'Never again!' we cried before singing the Israeli national anthem.

But why were we singing the Israeli national anthem? We weren't Israelis, we were British. If Israel was so great, as our teachers kept telling us, then why didn't they go and live there?

Looking back, it seems almost our whole education, and our developing identities as Jews, were refracted through a prism of Israel and Zionism. Either way it seemed to me that the logic of hating all Arabs was slightly faulty. True, the Arabs wanted to annihilate Israel, and all its Jewish inhabitants, or at least they said they did, repeatedly, their bloodthirsty rhetoric a substitute for their inability to do so.

Still, several millennia of by no means perfect, but nevertheless reasonable – in comparison to Christian Europe – co-existence showed that such virulent hatred between Arab and Jew was a comparatively new phenomenon, dating more or less from the evolution of political Zionism at the end of the nineteenth century and the establishment of the State of Israel. Across the Middle East, just as in Serbia, the lack of a democratic, pluralistic culture, the absence of a free press and political repression combined to shape a population easily susceptible to hate campaigns and demonisation of a supposed enemy. For the Serbs, the devil was Bosnia's Muslims. For the Arabs it was, and for many still is, the Jews. Even now, the sales assistants at the Muslim bookshop on Charing Cross Road will happily sell customers works purporting to outline the mechanics of the mythical 'International Jewish Conspiracy'. In Belgrade and Baghdad, Damascus and Tripoli, the ruling élite well knows how to transfer their subjects' anger and alienation onto an outside enemy, instead of their own governments. For Arabs Israel was an alien implant in the Middle East, the ultimate symbol of their impotence in the face of the West, that had sliced up the Ottoman empire like a Sunday roast, drawing arbitrary borders to create states such as Jordan and Iraq to suit imperial interests, deposing and imposing monarchs and leaders on a never-ending merry-go-round of place-men and stooges.

But who had so far killed the most Jews in history? It was not Muslims or Arabs who built the death camps of the Holocaust, but Christians, Catholic and Protestant Germans, with their copies of Goethe in one hand and the gas chamber lever in the other. It would make more sense to go to war against Germany.

If Israeli is a colonialist implant, so are most Arab regimes, which is in fact the position that many radical Islamists take, denouncing everyone from Saddam Hussein to Shimon Peres as the lackeys of western imperialism. They have a point. Until

Winston Churchill invented – and I use the word advisedly – Iraq, for example, at the post-war carve-up of the Middle East, there had never been such a country. Present-day Iraq comprised three separate Ottoman provinces: Mosul in the north; Baghdad in the centre and Basra in the south. The area was under British military rule, an army which included my paternal grandfather. There is a picture of him at home, sitting proudly on a horse outside Baghdad railway station. The provinces were home to substantial Kurdish, Assyrian, Shiite and Jewish minorities but Winston Churchill ignored advice that the arbitrary unification of such a diverse area would eventually lead to disaster. The Gulf War dispute over Kuwait proved the naysayers correct. T.E. Lawrence, better known as Lawrence of Arabia, was in Cairo with Churchill, and later boasted that he was one of a small group who had designed the modern Middle East over dinner. They did a bad job. It was a faulty structure, with serious inherent flaws whose consequences are still with us now.

I also learnt that across the Arab world, in Egypt and Syria, Morocco and Iraq, Jewish communities had thrived for millennia, tracing their roots back to the Babylonian exile, all once an integral part of the Middle East's ethnic mosaic, but now vanished apart from a few remnants. Their lives then under Islam were not perfect, but the institutionalised discrimination of the Islamic world was far more benevolent than in Christian countries. It was far easier, and pleasanter, to live as a Jew in sixteenth-century Cairo or Baghdad than, for example, Venice or London. Venetian officials then forced Jews to live in an area known as the *ghetto nuovo*, a cannon foundry – the origin of today's word ghetto – surrounded by high walls, with ten watchmen paid for by the Jewish community. In England Edward I had expelled the Jews en masse in 1290, and while a few individuals remained, no sizeable community returned until the mid-1650s after the English Civil War.

It was not too fanciful that I sat next to some of the descendants of Babylonian Jewry in the sixth form common room. Some of my schoolfriends' families had left Arab countries such as Iraq or Yemen, to live in Britain. They even spoke Arabic among themselves, rather than English. It took me a while to realise that when we played poker at lunchtime the muttered conversation in Arabic behind me was my opponent's cousin telling him what my hand was. But how could you be a Jewish Arab, I wondered? One schoolfriend, whose family had left Baghdad, once confided to me that he didn't know what nationality he was; not English, because he was born in Iraq, no longer Iraqi, because he was a Jew living in London, and certainly not Israeli, because he had no desire to move to Tel Aviv. It was my first experience of the dispossession of exile, although at the age of sixteen I didn't really understand its subtleties, or its power. Fifteen years later, in the refugee camps of Bosnia, I would do.

That is my background. But if this book has any specific genesis it was a spring morning in 1980, when I was working in a wood factory on a kibbutz in northern Israel, before starting university. We stopped for breakfast and I noticed that workers split into two groups: Jewish Israelis, speaking Hebrew, and Muslim (or Christian) Israeli Arabs, speaking Arabic. There was no mutual animosity, but the division was clear and, it seemed, natural there, in the sense that this was the correct order of things. But why? This was a kibbutz after all, an outpost of radical socialism and communitarianism, almost Communism, in fact. An Arab though could not join the kibbutz, because that option was only open to Jews. The Arab workers were hired hands, wage-slaves in the Marxist ideology to which the kibbutz still professed to adhere. There was a contradiction here. There seemed only one way to try and solve the contradiction, for with whom do you make peace, if not your enemies? I decided to learn Arabic, that language that was grammatically and linguistically so similar to the Hebrew that I then spoke reasonably well, and to study Islam, as I did at Leeds University. I also took a summer course in colloquial Palestinian Arabic at the Hebrew University of Jerusalem in August 1982.

From there I took a bus to Cairo, where I first heard the call of the muezzin to prayer. I still remember the sound now, as it reverberated through my room at the Anglican Hospice, on the island of Zamelek in the cool of an August morning. The long, stretched-out consonants of classical Arabic, and how they filled the dawn silence of Cairo, soaring across the Nile, summoning the believers to the mosque. Here you are no longer in Europe, with its bland safe certainties, the muezzin said to me, here you sleep and awake in the *Dar al-Islam*, the House of

Islam, where other values reign. Something deep inside me shiv-
ered and stirred when I heard him, an ancient ancestral memory,
stretching across the millennia, to a time of deserts and exile, of
miracles and patriarchs, and an awesome God who shepherded
his troublesome people out of Egypt across the Sinai desert to
Israel.

Islam and Judaism: so similar but somehow so separate, two
tongues, two cultures, two religions; entwined for centuries but
now split asunder, like a once married couple who have lived
together for years, know each other's every characteristic, but
are now divided by a legacy of mutual acrimony and bitterness.

My half-remembered Arabic came in useful at the CDLR's
headquarters in Willesden. The door was opened by a sleepy
teacher of Arabic from Saudi Arabia, who lets me use the telephone to find al-Mass'ari, as our arrangements became
muddled and he is not there. Eventually he arrives, a bearded,
extrovert man, dressed in a long white jelabia that reaches
almost to the floor. For dissidents such as al-Mass'ari, even
though he has an American wife, London, home to foreign correspondents from all over the world, is the ideal centre of
operations. 'For the international media I need to be in an
English-speaking country, so what other English-speaking countries are there? The choice was down to Britain or America.
Frankly we would not feel safe in America. We were following
the case of Sheikh Omar Abdul-Rahman, which was a frame-
up, and America has a very clear agenda in the Arab peninsula,
to keep the puppet Saudi regime in power. My wife is American,
she had a very bad experience when I was in jail, from the
embassy who were very uncooperative. They neglected her. But
here we have all the facilities to speak out, and we don't have to
worry too much about a frame-up. Britain has been quite tolerant, maybe they have an agenda for this, but Britain is the safest
place.'

It's well known across the Middle East, and among many
London-based Arabs, that al-Mass'ari's enemies would like to
see him silent and or dead. Criticising Arab regimes can be a
perilous business. Arab diplomats here, he claims, have been
involved in plans to silence him. They even asked Mossad, the
Israeli intelligence service, to help, he said, but Mossad declined

to get involved. 'Mossad so far has refused to cooperate with such extreme measures as assassination. They said they didn't want to get involved, and that they had their own problems. But one Arab official told them, "But you did assassinate [PLO official] Abu Jihad in Tunisia," and the Mossad said, "Yes we did indeed assassinate Abu Jihad, but we regret that we did that, it would have been better not to do it." Even the Mossad is wiser.'

The late Ayatollah Khomeini was reported as saying that 'there is no fun in Islam', which might be true under the reign of the Ayatollahs but al-Mass'ari takes a radically different view. He is articulate, learned and loquacious, entertaining even, his conversation spinning off on tangents, peppered with *hadith*, verses from the Quran, ranging from musings on Islamic history and theology to the duty of married couples to satisfy each other sexually, adopting whichever position takes their fancy. No wonder he drives the Saudi royal family into such a furious frenzy, for he runs a slick PR operation and knows what the international media need for a story: human interest, a sense of outrage at injustice and amazement at the cravenness of the British government in bowing to Saudi demands to try and expel him. But the al-Mass'ari case is significant as more than just a simple black and white deportation trial. It highlights London's role as the epicentre of events in the Middle East, it shows how decisions made in Riyadh and Jeddah to push for his deportation from Britain reverberate across England and it also illustrates how, despite many Muslims' claims of a widespread Islamic bias in Britain, even an unlikely candidate such as a Saudi Islamic dissident can become a *cause célèbre*, with support across almost the whole political spectrum, even be invited to appear on the television programme *Have I Got News For You*.

Dr Muhammad al-Mass'ari's trek from Riyadh to Neasden began at 2.30 am on 15 May 1993. His American wife Lujain al-Iman, then aged 26 and seven months pregnant, woke next to her husband in the large house they inhabited on the campus of King Saud University in Riyadh, to the sound of bumps and banging. Writing in *Vanity Fair*, Leslie and Andrew Cockburn report what happened next:

Crashing through the garage entrance to the house, a dozen or so heavily armed *Mabaheth* – secret police – had entered the servants quarters, on the ground floor. They were Bedouin tribesmen from the Saudi interior; red and white checked *ghutrahs* masked their faces so that only their eyes showed. They held a maid at gunpoint until she waved them toward the study, where Mass'ari's eldest son eighteen-year-old Anmar was sleeping. They woke him and smashed his head against the wall, shouting, 'Where is your father?'

The masked Bedouin crashed through the bedroom door and dragged al-Mass'ari away. Lujain suffered an asthma attack while the *Mabaheth* dragged away books, pulled down the curtains and slashed the carpets. For good measure they confiscated her asthma medicine and her American passport as well. Al-Mass'ari's arrest received scattered publicity in the international press, but there was no hint of his future status as international *cause célèbre*. Earlier that month, he had, together with a group of lawyers, judges and professors, launched the CDLR after many meetings over a series of months that aimed to build an embryonic opposition. In a repressive monarchy that saw no role for independent political organisations, he and his colleagues had taken a brave and public stand: they demanded a measure of accountability from the House of Saud for its actions, and criticised King Fahd, the Keeper of the Two Holy Shrines (Mecca and Medina) on Islamic grounds. The members of the CDLR were not, to be sure, western liberals or democrats. They based their criticisms of the Saudi regime on their interpretation of the Quran. Which made them even more dangerous to King Fahd, and even more of a target, for they could not be dismissed as western interferers.

Before he was arrested al-Mass'ari had told his wife to go to the American embassy for help. None came, and Lujain was cold-shouldered. Her husband meanwhile was in Al-Hayer prison, outside Riyadh. He was imprisoned for six months and repeatedly beaten on the soles of his feet. Warned after his release that the government was planning to execute him on trumped-up charges, he was brought by the Saudi underground to Britain. In

London he started his bulletin, *Monitor*, cataloguing events in Saudi Arabia, which was faxed and e-mailed back to the Kingdom. In Mecca and Medina, Riyadh and Nejd, copies circulated through the underground opposition movement passed by hand to hand, or faxed to offices and universities. *Monitor*, available on the Internet's World Wide Web, is a mixture of polemic against King Fahd and the Saudi royal family, facts and analysis. It is extremely anti-western in tone, implacably opposed to the Arab–Israeli peace process, and presents a different shade of the CDLR to the one al-Mass'ari gives to western journalists. Here are some extracts from number 19, published in March 1995, addressed to the Saudi Royal family:

YOU HAVE TURNED US INTO A NATION OF BEGGARS, OUR LAND IS A WESTERN COLONY

The whole nation has been deprived of its Islamic character – deprived of its mastery of the land. You have reduced their country into a colony of Superpowers. Their wealth and resources are daily being looted by monsters whose greed knows no bound. You have created animosity between their neighbours and weakened the ability of the military to defend their own land and security.

. . . Despite the disinformation, our people are only too well aware of your immoral relations with your genocidal Zionist friends. You are protected by the Americans and continue to sustain the illusion that they will protect you permanently. Think what happened to another American-lover, the Shah of Iran. There is no one left with any interest or conviction in your leadership!

THE LAST STRAW – EL AL TO FLY IN SAUDI AIR SPACE

The Zionist Minister of transport declared that the Saudis would soon allow the airplanes of El Al airlines to fly in Saudi airspace. This is considered an important step in the normalisation of relations between the two countries, the result of open and secret meetings. In yet another treacherous development, Bandar Ibn Sultan was accompanied on one of his trips to the Kingdom by a group of Jewish business men who are being persuaded to invest in the Kingdom.

That al-Mass'ari was free to publish and distribute *Monitor* from London drove the Saudi royals into a frenzy. Riyadh quickly piled on the pressure to expel him, twisting the arms of the British weapons industry. Arms manufacturers were warned that vital arms deals between Britain and Saudi Arabia, worth hundreds of millions of pounds, were being threatened by his continued presence in London. The industrialists buckled quickly. A memo written by the Chief Executive of Vickers, Sir Colin Chandler, a former head of arms export at the Ministry of Defence, published in the *Guardian* in January 1996, cast a revealing light over the shadowy web of finance and armaments that binds Britain to Saudi Arabia. Dated 6 September 1995, it said that Britain passed secret intelligence on Saddam Hussein to Saudi Arabia to appease Riyadh's fury. More ominously, it referred to 'direct Saudi intervention' against him, warning that it would be difficult as 'he is, as you probably know, the son of a leading cleric'.

The later revelation that Andrew Green, Britain's ambassador to Saudi Arabia, had been a non-executive director of Vickers since April 1994 surprised few with any knowledge of the links between Britain's arms industry and the palaces of Riyadh.

Government ministers flapped and flailed under Saudi pressure, claiming a plethora of excuses as to why al-Mass'ari must leave, for, of all places, the Dominican Republic. Prime Minister John Major said al-Mass'ari was an illegal immigrant who had sought to create an 'unsettled relationship' with Saudi Arabia. Home Office minister Anne Widdicombe was more honest when she said: 'We have close trade relations with a friendly state which has been the subject of considerable criticism by Mr al-Mass'ari.'

By attempting to deport him the government forged an unlikely alliance between left and right, says the Saudi dissident. 'They didn't understand how much it would backfire. It united the imperialists who cannot live with the idea that the empire is gone, and the humanists who cannot live with the idea that basic freedoms are threatened. That leaves only a minority of arms manufacturers and the poor workers in the north-east, who really have a case. . . . Have you seen *Spitting Image*, the last one? It showed a cabinet meeting, and someone said and now for the al-Mass'ari case. One minister said: "Couldn't you have found a suitable lie, instead of telling the truth about balancing economic interest against human rights?" The other holds a bucket and replies, "No we couldn't. We have been in power for seven years and all our lies are gone now. Look in the bucket, it's empty!",' he exclaims, laughing uproariously.

The al-Mass'ari case has also complicated relations between Britain's Muslim community and their Christian compatriots. On one hand, everyone from crusty old peers to liberal *Guardian* readers has rallied to his Islamic standard, but at the same time, the government's attempts to throw him out because ministers fear the impact of his message are compared by many Muslims to the state protection given to Salman Rushdie. The talk now in the mosques is that the British government supports free speech to attack Islam, but not to criticise trading partners.

'Many Muslims in Britain felt very negatively about my story, compared to Salman Rushdie. They wonder what the British believe, whether freedom of expression is a British right, or a universal one. Salman Rushdie was defended on UN conventions that guarantee basic human rights, not because he is British. So tell us clearly what you mean, if these are basic human rights, then al-Mass'ari should enjoy them, if not, if they are only for British people then shut up. You have to be consistent. Rushdie insulted Islam, al-Mass'ari insulted the [Saudi] royal family, so what does freedom of expression mean? Because if you only allow what you like and prohibit what you don't like, this is not freedom of expression, this is a dictatorship. This is a very difficult argument to overcome. Salman Rushdie also cost the taxpayer money. The broken relations with Iran must have lost hundreds of jobs in cancelled contracts. But those workers have not been considered. Are they less worthy than the people working at Vickers? They are all worthy human beings.'

Which brings us to the Rushdie case. Most Muslims believe that Rushdie, in *The Satanic Verses*, set out deliberately to insult Muhammad and court controversy and publicity in what they see as one of the basest ways possible: by apparently both satirising Islam in general and insulting it in specific ways as well, such as giving a clutch of prostitutes the same names as Muhammad's wives. If that was the author's tactic it worked, not wisely but too well. Unfortunately for Rushdie events spun out of control, for he was caught up in an intra-Iranian power struggle as various factions jostled for position and influence as Ayatollah Khomeini lay on his death bed. That he was born into a Muslim family only increased his peril. Briefed by his son Ahmad, Khomeini issued a *fatwa* (judgment) that Rushdie was an apostate, one who has renounced the Muslim faith, an act punishable by death under Islamic law. Tehran radio carried a report of the ailing Ayatollah's pronouncement:

The author of the book *The Satanic Verses*, which is contrary to Islam, the Prophet and the Quran, together with all those involved in its publication who were aware of its content, are hereby sentenced to death . . .

I call on zealous Muslims to execute them promptly on the spot they find them, so that no one else will dare to blasphemise [*sic*] Muslim sanctities.

To underline the seriousness of the threat, the Iranian 15th Khordad Foundation offered a reward of $2.6 million to anyone who killed Rushdie. He has been under police protection ever since, although he appears with increasing frequency at London literary parties. Understandably fearful for his life, he converted to Islam, but then appeared to backtrack, further inflaming Muslim anger. So, I ask al-Mass'ari, is there an Islamic justification for the *fatwa* on Salman Rushdie? The answer, as I have grown to expect, is complicated.

'The question is whether or not he is in the Islamic domain. There you may punish him because it is prohibited to attack God and the prophets who are mentioned in the Quran. But you have to distinguish between Muslim and non-Muslims. In the case of Muslims, he will be regarded as an apostate, depending on your interpretation of the apostasy law. One school says that his family relations will be severed and so on and he will not be executed. This is a minor school, very minor, but it does exist. The other is that he should be executed. But if he is a non-Muslim, this has been a problem for Islamic thinkers all through history. For example there is the question of what to do with a Jew who says Mary, peace be upon her, was an adulteress. The first thing is that we believe there can be no compulsion in religion. So if that is his belief, for us it is a disgusting belief, but he has it. Others say no, she enjoys the protection and the dignity that the Quran guarantees for its prophets. The other school says no, he enjoys the protection of his faith and religion and we cannot force him not to say that. For me the answer is that is his point of view, you cannot punish him if he is non-Muslim, if he is in the Islamic domain.

'Outside the Islamic domain you could condemn him. I don't think Salman Rushdie was an apostate, because he was never a Muslim in the beginning, and he is entitled to his point of view. My view is that if you insult certain personalities, there may be some punishment, not necessarily up to death, to keep public discussion away from insult and degradation. You may very well believe in the immaculate conception, maybe Mary was married, maybe it was from Joseph the carpenter, or maybe from something else. If I say that it is not insulting, but if I say she was an adulteress, that is insulting. But I don't think the punishment should go to death, maybe some jail term, whips or lashes, whatever the Islamic state adopts. In his writings now Rushdie is insulting Hindus, so he seems to be a specialist in outraging other people. I can express my point of views respectfully. Consider the Pope: I have respect for the man, but I don't believe in his infallibility. I would not call the Pope a dog or a *schwein-hund*, the dog which cares for pigs, the worst kind of dog. That's very insulting.'

As our discussion ends he asks if I have a faith myself. 'Yes, I am Jewish,' I reply. Not for a nano-second does he pause.

'Ah, Jewish, oh yes, I was walking down the street the other day and I saw this lovely old Jewish couple coming towards me and the man asked if I knew where the Jewish cemetery was. I said of course, which one do you want, liberal or conservative!'

But a few months after our meeting, the good Doctor was taking a less ecumenical position on Jewish–Muslim relations. Press reports quoted an article in his newsletter *Al-Huquq*, that described Jews as 'a nation of cowards' and reportedly claimed, 'Their annihilation is not difficult for Muslims'. Furious MPs, including Greville Janner, *de facto* parliamentary spokesman for the Jewish community, demanded the Crown Prosecution Service rescind its decision not to prosecute al-Mass'ari for what Janner regarded as incitement to racial hatred. The Saudi dissident then claimed in an interview with Chrissy Iley of the *Sunday Times* – who summed him up as 'an Islamic equivalent of a wide boy' – that the whole furore had erupted because of a mistranslation, and the *Al-Huquq* article referred only to those Jews living in Israel. Quite.

A few miles from the CDLR's headquarters in Holborn, central London, are the offices of the Saudi-supported *Ash-Sharq Al-Awsat,* one of the Arab world's most important newspapers, whose pages are a forum for debate on almost every issue affecting the future of the Middle East, except anything critical of the House of Saud. A picture of a smiling Queen Elizabeth greeting the Saudi King Fahd is proudly displayed in the newspaper's foyer, a pictorial remnant of Britain's long ties to the Arabian Gulf.

Britain still has a special place in the Muslim world, says Ayad Abu Chakra, a senior editor at the newspaper. That influence is based on several pillars: an imperial legacy as one of the powers who dismembered the Ottoman empire to create new states such as Jordan and the Gulf Emirates; the works of writers such as Richard Burton, translator of *One Thousand and One Nights* and military adventurers such as T.E. Lawrence, who helped lead the Arab revolt against the Turks. British schools and universities have also educated a generation of Muslim leaders and politicians, such as Muhammad Ali Jinnah, founder of Pakistan, who studied law in London and practised for several years. 'Britain enjoys a unique position in the Muslim world. As a mandatory power in Asia and Africa Britain interacted with the Muslim communities, and with the intellectual trends in the Muslim world. You cannot underestimate the influence Britain had on the Indian sub-continent. Jinnah was a lawyer in the Temple and the head of the Muslim League. In the First World War the British promoted the idea among Arabs (of Arab nationalism) that "you are Arabs, why should you obey a Turkish sultan, he is not a Muslim sultan, he is a Turkish sultan". It created a legacy of goodwill until 1948, when the state of Israel was created.'

The orientalist view of the 'noble bedouin', untouched and uncorrupted by the modern world, still widespread among certain parts of the British upper-classes, has also helped Britain's cause in the Levant. 'The British are easily charmed by the East, British travellers like Burton were fascinated by the East, they were fascinated by its sentimentality and the spiritualism. Look at the way they dealt with the beauty of their surroundings, the romanticism of Lawrence. He was sitting in a tent with an old bedouin sheikh, explaining how advanced our modern observatories are, all the stars you can see and the poor old sheikh said, "that's great, I'm very impressed, but we see someone you don't see, beyond the stars, and that is God". For someone like Lawrence, an intellectual, he thinks this man has something, he is not dumb.'

As a journalist and self-described 'semi-academic' Abu Chakra represents a different breed of Arab intellectual to al-Mass'ari, still Muslim of course, by birth, culture and belief, but tending more to modern secularism than Islamic revivalism. For him Islam, as a religion of about a billion believers spread across the world, is a mosaic of cultures, each with its own colours and textures. A Shiite Ayatollah in Iran, an African Muslim musician in Senegal, a Turkish businessman in Istanbul, an Arab journalist in London, all may share the same core religious beliefs, but their lives are a reflection of their own national cultures as well, which may not always include the idea of universal brotherhood.

'You cannot simplify Islam, just as you cannot simplify Christianity. You cannot say that Christianity is the brand that I define as Christianity. Christianity for a monk on Mount Athos in Greece is his brand, but if you go to the Bible belt in America, it is about baptism and evangelical Christianity. Islam is a world culture, it is a huge culture, a global religion. Someone in Bradford, involved in the mosque with a puritanical approach to Islam, does not behave in the same way as a secular Muslim in Istanbul, or as an Arab nationalist who thinks that Arab nationalism is based on Islam in Syria and Egypt. They are all totally different. What Islam means to X is not necessarily what it means to Y. To me, I believe that Islam is a global religion, it can encompass many trends, you cannot tighten it up to the extent that it suits your own definition. I perhaps am a very bad example, I am a very secular man myself, but I don't believe that you serve the interest of your religion if you try to make it narrow, narrow its scope and make it exclusive. Inclusivity is the source of greatness of every religion.'

As an international capital, home to a large Arab community of exiles, dissidents, businessmen, students and tourists, London can be host to a cultural symbiosis between the West and the Middle East, says Abu Chakra. Arabic language newspapers, television stations, cafés, restaurants, clubs and mosques bring a new facet to London's ethnic mosaic. 'In the West there is enough social flexibility to accept these things. I believe that multi-cultural societies thrive. Take America for example, the top scoring students in the universities are Chinese or Indian or are from outside America. It is not a source of bringing these cultures down. It is creating more diversity, enriching the culture and bringing a multi-faceted angle and face. The problem that we have in the West today is that some politicians are charlatans and they play the race card all the time.'

But this must also be a two-way process, he says, and Muslims must give as well as take, if they wish to be accepted. 'What is required is understanding by both sides. The Muslims might not like this, but I think I have to be realistic, you don't expect people to accept you in their culture if you are not ready to concede something. I for one have no right to impose my values on the British. I am gaining from them, I can give to them if they want to get something from me, but I don't impose myself on them. But if they want to know more about my culture I am ready to give them, to give them the best I can. We need concessions from both sides. A civilised society has to be open-minded.'

But not every import from the Middle East to London is welcome. The cycle of violence in the Israeli–Arab conflict spilled over onto the streets of London in July 1994, when a car bomb exploded outside the Israeli embassy in Kensington. Fourteen people were injured in the attack, which followed repeated rumours of an impending operation against Israeli targets and Jewish organisations. Four more people were hurt the next day when a bomb exploded outside the offices of the Joint Israel Appeal in north London.

For Middle East expert Hazhir Temourian, an Iranian Kurdish exile now living in London, the increasing Saudi dominance of the Arabic-language international media, and the presence of so many Arab journalists, indeed a substantial Muslim minority at all, is not healthy for Britain. 'The Sheikhs of Araby want to use London to set up newspapers to spread propaganda among the other Muslims who live in Europe, and London is a good communications centre for that. Britain allows this. It is supposed to have a tight immigration policy, but every year it allows hundreds of Arab journalists to be recruited by Saudi Arabian Sheikhs and princes who own the Arab press here, and after four or five years working here, they all become British citizens, because they don't want to go back. They like life here and I don't blame them. I have met some of them, who have taken me out to lunch and have begun to trust me. They admitted that they are Muslim revolutionaries, passing themselves off as moderates, in order to be brought to Britain by the Arab press. London is now the biggest television satellite centre for the Arab world. I believe that Britain is just storing up trouble.'

I met Temourian, who is a regular contributor to the BBC and *The Times*, for tea at the Athenaeum, one of the first division English gentlemen's clubs where crusty old bastions of the British establishment meet to bemoan the state of the world over tea and cakes, or an excellent dinner washed down with vintage claret. Pink-faced gentlemen seated in leather armchairs dozed off around us in the large lounge or perused the day's newspapers, while white-jacketed waiters brought a pot of tea. It was a quintessentially English scene, and for all his background as an Iranian Kurd, Temourian looked very much at home. For him, like many Middle Eastern exiles, Britain is still the home of democracy and democratic values. And those values, he believes, are threatened by the influx of a large Muslim minority, many of whom, he says, do not agree with western liberal values or mores and seek to impose an Islamic lifestyle.

'The Muslim intellectual, or person of Muslim background, who has a constructive manner, he is not going to be a source of trouble. But the ones who are culturally very Islamic, they could be. The Muslim who comes here, who believes that his own society is superior, he comes here to take advantage of prosperity,

but keeps his militancy. In my opinion liberal Muslims are
cheats who are trying to endear themselves to western society.
The liberal argument about multi-culturalism is naive, it
assumes that everybody is going to be as good as you are. I
don't believe in a multi-cultural society, they all come to grief. I
don't believe that in the name of tolerance you should tolerate
intolerance.

'I've told Muslims in Britain that if you really believe that
Muslim society is superior to this society, then why did you
come in the first place? They become angry, they become abusive, I say really you owe it to yourselves and your children to go
back, you can never turn this into a Muslim society by force, but
they do have such dreams. Once I was in hospital, visiting an
Iranian friend, who was here for heart treatment. Because this
man had received government-subsidised currency, the local
Mullah from the Iranian embassy came to see him. This Mullah
was quite new in Britain and he had never seen me. He asked me
what my name was and I had to give a false name in case this
patient was in trouble for meeting me. The Mullah became quite
complacent and he asked me how many children I have. I said
two, he said, "Is that all?" I said why, what do you mean. He said,
"We cannot conquer these people with tanks and troops, so we
have got to overcome them by force of numbers." He was very
sincere and I don't blame him. He is commanded by his God that
it is better for the world if everybody turns into a Muslim.'

As an immigrant himself, Temourian says he can articulate
what he believes are the secret fears of many in the liberal
middle classes, who are scared to speak their mind for fear of
being accused of racism. 'The answer is for people like me, especially immigrants who care about liberal values, to be more
active, to write about it. It's easier for us to say this, if you wrote
you would be described as a fascist. I cannot be accused of
being a white supremacist, or a racist. I believe, and I think lots
of people in Britain believe, although because of political cor-
rectness they won't write about it, especially if they are British,
that Muslims are unlike the previous waves of immigrants. Even
in their own countries, these Bengalis and Pakistanis are
regarded as hillbillies. They are not even from the capitals, but
from the backward countryside, they come without a word of
English and the British allow them to bring their own Mullahs

who are extremely hostile to the spirit of enlightenment. They discover themselves as a minority, they feel rejected and so they grow more attracted to the only thing they have in common together, Islam.'

London has also played a pivotal role in the burgeoning Arab–Israeli peace process. Some of the first meetings between the two sides took place in the British capital, and it was there that the early tentative feelers toward a rapprochement of the decades-old conflict were extended. Both Israelis and Arabs say that it is often more productive for them to meet in the British capital than in Cairo, Amman or Tel Aviv. For Palestinian intellectuals such as Dr Ahmad Samih Khalidi, born in Beirut in 1948 and a scion of an ancient Jerusalemite family, London is the place where Israeli and Arab could talk freely.

'London was the place where they met for the first time, it began in London, when Hanan Ashwari met an Israeli university professor, after it was suggested to him that he meet a senior PLO figure. Much of the debate does take place here. London and England are the venue for many other kinds of meetings from places such as St Anthony's College, where Arabs and Israelis meet and talk, to Chatham House, and studies, conferences, lectures. There is a whole environment which has been here for a long time. The British role in the Middle East was absolutely paramount, and for the Palestinians it was absolutely crucial. People come here for serious academic work on the subject, because you have all the state archives here, partly because there is a cultural affinity and respect for British education.'

The British capital is also a place where the many currents of contemporary Arab thought meet and coalesce. 'In many cases the Arab world is not really conducive to serious thought. If you think of yourself as a free thinker, and you want to practise what you preach or write what you believe it's much easier here. The atmosphere in much of the Islamic world today and in the recent past is not only repressive but pretty much closed. In my case it's not just that, I studied here in Oxford and London. One of the main factors in the last decades has been the demise of places like Beirut, especially for the Levantine Arabs. Physically Beirut is being rebuilt, but I don't think that intellectuality will return.

123

'From the mid 1980s, there has been an accelerated migration to the West to London and Paris, for people like myself and other categories – for want of a better word, intellectuals – the Palestinian and Lebanese business communities, which thrived in Beirut, many of them have moved to London. It is the closest major capital to the Middle East and a crossing point where you get the currents from across the Atlantic. In many senses London has become the intellectual capital of the Middle East. If you go to Queensway, and walk up and down the road, go to the newsagents and look at the very wide array of newsletters, magazine and journals, about 60 or 70 per cent will be printed in London.'

In one way it is a telling comment on the intellectually stifling atmosphere in much of the Arab world, rather than the inherent merits of London, that has led many Muslim thinkers such as Khalidi to base themselves in Britain. But personal considerations as well play a part, and a move back to Israel/Palestine would entail a massive upheaval for him, his wife and four children. But somehow, by retaining a geographical distance from the Middle East, Arab intellectuals also retain a more critical perspective on their homelands. 'In an ideal sense I suppose it is sad that the centre of intellectual life is in Europe, but in a real sense, given the situation in the Arab world, it probably isn't, because at least you have some focal point for all this cross-fertilisation for all these ideas. And they do, in one way or another, percolate back, such as in the case of al-Mass'ari, who is a very interesting man. You can see that at a distance, a relatively small outfit, with a relatively modest means, can have a major impact, possibly in a way they would not, if they were there.'

Just as events in Turkey or Algeria rebound through immigrant communities in Germany and France, the twists and turns of the Arab–Israeli struggle reverberate across London. Speaking at the Sharm el-Sheikh anti-terror summit in March 1996, that followed a wave of Hamas suicide bombings in Israel, John Major promised to clamp down on British-based groups that he said provided support for Hamas, the Islamic Resistance Movement in Jordan, Gaza and the West Bank. MI5, Britain's domestic intelligence service, had for several months been investigating support groups for radical Islamists based in London, partly at prompting from Israel that London was the 'focal point' for Hamas fundraising, with over £6 million a year being supposedly funnelled to its underground networks through charitable fronts in London. (That Israel had, not so long ago, encouraged the build-up of Hamas as a counterweight to the PLO in the Gaza Strip and occupied West Bank was conveniently forgotten.)

What followed the Sharm el-Sheikh gathering was not a wave of arrests, or the discovery of caches of arms and explosives, or even a list of Jewish or Israeli potential terrorist targets, but a single frozen bank account. It seemed a poor haul, but then the logic of politics and diplomacy is that something must be done, and preferably in public. The Charity Commissioners took over the funds of Interpal, a Palestinian charity based in north-west London, that in 1995 raised half a million pounds for humanitarian work in Palestine. Interpal's Vice-Chairman Essam Mustapha strongly denied that his organisation had any connection to Hamas, or engaged in any political activities either in Britain or abroad, and pointed out that its work on the ground was coordinated with both the Israeli government and the Palestinian National Authority. 'We do go through local authorities, whether that is the Israeli authorities or the Palestinian authorities. We have good relations with all of them and we have had no allegations from them against Interpal,' he said in an interview with the Muslim weekly newspaper *Q News*. Muslims dumped the blame for the Interpal affair into the laps of Israel and British Jews. For many Muslims across the political spectrum the Interpal affair was an excuse to lapse back into hoary old stereotypes about the supposed influence of the 'Zionist lobby', code for British Jewry, and fuel the anti-Semitic conspiracy theories that still hold considerable sway among Muslims.

Ahmed Khalidi does not give money to Interpal – which was eventually cleared of any wrongdoing – or the many other new Arab and Islamic welfare organisations, preferring other, older charities such as Medical Aid for Palestine. 'Muslims in Britain give money to charity and the funds are transferred to social projects; mosque X in Gaza or mosque Y in Kabul. But you don't always know where the line between social welfare and political activism begins and ends. If you feed a family of someone who will be sustaining a suicide bomber then you are sustaining him. The Israelis have put enormous pressure on Britain, but it's very difficult to prove that welfare organisations are engaged in military activities. I don't think they are. It's not a problem to get weapons there, you don't need to buy them in London and send them out. The Israeli policy is to uproot Hamas and go after the infrastructure, but it's wrong and unachievable because you cannot find the right legal mechanisms. The answer, as always, is political. Hamas is not a law and order problem and will not be resolved by military means. The answer is to provide Arafat with the means to co-opt Hamas into some form of co-existence with the peace process.'

For Palestinians such as Khalidi the next few years present a unique challenge, more than for any other Arab thinkers living abroad: that of building a new independent state, of Palestine. That challenge could yet see him return to his ancestral homeland as his people build up their own country. A signed photograph of PLO leader Yasser Arafat sits on the wall of Khalidi's study in his house in west London. His credentials are excellent for some future role in the new Palestine. Now editor-in-chief of the Arabic edition of the *Journal for Palestine Studies* quarterly, and a research fellow at the Royal Institute for International Affairs, Khalidi served as an advisor/delegate to the Palestinian delegation to the Washington Peace Talks in 1991–93 as well as senior advisor on security issues to the Taba/Cairo PLO–Israeli negotiations until December 1993.

'I have a very active relationship with the Palestinian leadership, I have been there five or six times since Oslo, I maintain close contact, but also some distance. I have access and I can talk to anyone I like. For the intellectual and political exiles the return will take much longer, but the Palestinians could be drawn in because of the state-building, a specific challenge. Personally, I'm fairly rooted here, I have children here and I would have to completely uproot, it's paradoxical because that's where I come from and I suppose you shouldn't think of yourself of being uprooted from exile.

'Living here I have a more sanguine view of both the West and the East. I can see both the advantages and disadvantages of western and eastern societies. The clear kind of difference relating to issues of personal freedom you learn and observe from being here, but you also learn the limitations, of democracies, which are not always immediately applicable to other types of societies. I have learnt a lot but I think I have maintained a kind of distance from the extremes of the Arab and the western one. Obviously the fact that you are here gives you a necessary and healthy distance from the Arab world and you can observe it much better from a distance, that is my job, to observe it. London is far enough and close enough at the same time.'

Yet while Khalidi, whose wife is Scottish, is well assimilated into London life, many Arab visitors and residents stay in their own business and social communities, and never really take the pulse of their new host country, although admittedly that's partly because of traditional British insularity.

'One of the regrettable aspects is that by and large many immigrants, not just the Arabs, tend to stick together. In England a foreigner is a foreigner, very clearly, unlike the United States where everybody is different. In some respects I am anglicised, I am not a religious Muslim, I don't spend too much time cultivating or addressing the Arab community. Culturally I consider myself a Muslim and if you ask me I would say I am a Muslim, but I haven't made very strong or conscious efforts to convince my children to be Muslim. I have a broad network of connections, some professional, some social. I haven't encountered much racism, or come across overt racism. The other day I was in a cab and I was giving him directions, when I got to the door he said: "It's good to hear an Englishman speak with such perfect diction." I just smiled to myself.'

Which is, of course, a perfectly English reaction.

The Satanic Verses *on fire in Bradford*

Chapter 5

BRITAIN: THE EMPIRE
STRIKES BACK

*'People are looking for an Islamic identity. You find
someone called Muhammad, who grew up in western
society, he concedes a lot so people accept him. He
changes his name to Mike, he has a girlfriend, he drinks
alcohol, he dances, he has sex, raves, rock and roll, then
they say, "You are a Paki". After everything he gave up to
be accepted, they tell him he is a bloody Arab, or a
Paki.'*
Omar Bakri Mohammad, leader of the radical group
Al-Muhajiroun

*'We call ourselves British Muslims. Whether or not
anybody acknowledges us or accepts us, we have decided
that this is our country, this our home and that is where
our children and grandchildren have decided to live.'*
Sher Azam, Muslim community leader in Bradford

There is no spiritual hierarchy in Islam, for it has no ordained
priesthood. Any male Muslim may lead the five daily prayers.
Just as there is no ecclesiastical system of Muslim rank, there is
no grade of mosque importance, or equivalent of the division
between church or cathedral. The front-room of a small terraced house in Bradford, the grand mosques of Istanbul or
Riyadh, wherever Muslims gather to pray five times a day, all
are equal in the eyes of Allah.

But if one mosque in Britain is first among equals, it is the
Central Mosque and Islamic Cultural Centre by Regent's Park
in central London. The struggle for control of this complex has

played a vital symbolic role in the evolution of British Islam, specifically in the battle for power and influence between the two main opposing currents of Muslim thought in Britain. In one corner, the outward-looking modernists, who want Islam to be engaged in a dynamic debate in British society, allied to Christians and Jews on issues of common concern such as morality, religion and education. These are thinkers and theologians such as the centre's former director Dr Zaki Badawi, who are trying to build a British Islam and develop a Muslim theology that responds to the needs of a minority community living in a late twentieth-century industrial society, and Pakistani-born Professor Akbar Ahmed, of Cambridge University. In the other, the strident radical Islamic activists, such as the late Dr Kalim Siddiqui, leader of the Muslim Parliament, arch-exponent of the *fatwa* on Salman Rushdie, and one of a vocal minority of Muslims who foment confrontation politics based on what they believe to be an unalterable enmity between the Muslim and non-Muslim world, an enmity that sustains them in their intellectual hostility to many western values. And somewhere in the middle, the majority of Britain's more than 1.5 million Muslims.

The Regent's Park Mosque is probably the most important site of British Islam, attracting thousands of worshippers on important Muslim festivals such as *Eid al-Fitr*, the feast which celebrates the end of the Ramadan fast. So, I thought, it was clearly the best place to start investigating the state of Islam in Britain today. I phoned the mosque to arrange a meeting, but the man to whom I eventually got through, Mr Bashir (he never would tell me his first name), one of the mosque's administrators, was not very encouraging. He was, it must be said, pretty rude at first, for he took it for granted that I was out to do a hatchet job on the mosque, on Muslims and on Islam in general, but eventually I persuaded him to meet me. He later warmed up and we parted, I hope, on good terms. He even gave me a rather beautiful copy of the Quran in Arabic and English, with a blue and gold cover and an inscription inside announcing it was a gift from King Fahd of Saudi Arabia. Mr Bashir himself is an educated and sophisticated man, who has studied at London University and is an industrial chemist. Born in Mauritius, he is now a British citizen. But like many Muslims he gives credence to the idea of a world-wide anti-Islamism, that is not exactly a co-ordinated campaign, but certainly a sequence of events against Islam and Muslims. Many more Muslims across the world think like he does than would disagree with his analysis.

Why, I ask him, are there so many misconceptions in the West about Islam?

'I would like to think that it's all just a coincidence, whenever you see so many bad things said about Islam and the Muslims. I honestly don't believe in a conspiracy because I don't think that anyone can harm Islam. But then again all these incidents took place in such a way that to put it down to just coincidence is a bit hard to accept as well.'

What are these incidents?

'Anything to do with Islam. Salman Rushdie. The Gulf War. Bosnia. You name it. Chechnya. Algeria. It's nothing new. The world is manipulated by certain individuals and certain countries for their own use . . . sadly.'

Which countries and which individuals?

'Primarily all the western countries. There is an order, the United States, UK, France, Germany, and Israel and all these. They are dictating events for their own benefit. They don't give a damn about the ordinary people . . . about their own people. Let alone show concern for anybody who is different from them, who is a different religion or a different colour to them.'

So what did he think of the claim that Islam and parliamentary democracy, as practised in Britain, France or Germany for example, are not compatible?

'I certainly can understand certain Muslims when they say that there is no place for democracy in Islam. What they mean by that is the western form of democracy that is being thrown at them throughout the colonial contact that they have with the western world and the western way of life. If you look at democracy, how many UN resolutions have been passed against Israel and never been upheld? When the UN resolutions were passed against Iraq and Saddam Hussein every single word of these hundreds of pages were adhered to. Now do you expect that an ordinary Muslim living in a remote region in an Arab country who for years has had his territory, his village, his house bombarded by the mighty Israeli gun power, will he say to you "Yes, I'm in for democracy?" You say democracy is a change of government by the ballot box. So why did the West suspend the Algerian elections?'

The western powers don't want an Islamic regime in Algeria, I reply.

'So that is why some people are saying that democracy as we term it has no place in Islam? I would have thought that this kind of democracy has no place whatsoever in any society, if you have this kind of conditional approach that you can select whoever you want as long as it's the one that we are all agreed on . . . If people want to decide for Islam then let them, that is their right. Why is it that we can decide any form of government except Islam?'

It's a hard point to argue against, and when Algeria is added to the list of Muslim grievances, from Bosnia to Palestine, via Chechnya and Kashmir, it's easy to see why many Muslims truly believe a small cabal of powerful countries dictates events across the globe.

We move on to life in Britain. How can Muslims keep their Islamic values in a society which so often seems diametrically opposed to those beliefs? By sticking to the precepts of Islam, says Bashir. 'I recently attended a meeting with the Chief Medical Advisor entitled "The health of the nation". They were concerned with certain aspects of young people's lifestyle causing concern. Drugs, marriage breakdown, things like that. Now you are saying to us, "How can Islam with all the things that we stand for find a place in that society?", yet the same government is trying its best to address these problems. But where we differ with them is they are reacting to the problems. We say that rather than reacting to the problems, which condemns them and us as well, we must proact to the problem and address it at its very core.'

At the core are Islam's moral precepts, of prohibitions against drugs and alcohol, and bans of pre-marital sex and homosexuality. There can be no compromise, he says. 'For example, the question of AIDS, the norm in British society is "a condom culture". This is the message that is being portrayed. But, no matter how careful you are, there are bound to be mistakes. So rather than saying to me, "Do whatever you like, but be careful", what we are saying, and what Islam is saying, is "No". Islam says there is no sex before marriage. The same thing with drugs and alcohol. Why do you have this fantastic campaign during Christmas, "Don't drink and drive"? Islam doesn't say "Don't drink and drive", Islam says "Don't drink at all" because there is no benefit whatsoever in drinking. You can only have problems. But western society is saying we cannot implement it so therefore forget it. Or we are dictated to by the big brewing and whisky companies.'

Like Islam everywhere, British Islam is a mosaic, a complicated pattern of different components. Mr Bashir represents one influential political strand, which takes a radical anti-western perspective on global issues. British Muslims are all united in their observance of their faith but they differ widely socially, culturally, economically and, perhaps most importantly, in their interpretation of Islamic theology.

British Muslims are Arabs and Iranian businessmen in London's Kensington and Bayswater. They are Turkish and Kurdish factory workers in the north of the capital and Bangladeshi snack-shop owners in the East End. They are Yemenis in Sheffield, Pakistanis in Bradford and Birmingham, Malaysians in Manchester and Somalis in Spitalfields. Most are Sunni, with small minorities of Iranian Shiites and Turkish Alevis. They speak half a dozen Arabic dialects as well as Farsi, Urdu, Bengali, Pashto, Dari, Hausa, Swahili, Turkish, Kurdish and, of course, English. But even among the Sunni majority there are deep divisions. The first division, political and ideological, is between the modernists and the radicals, but that distinction is useful only for evaluating the range of Muslim attitudes to life in a modern western secular society.

The theological gulf between the different traditions too is deep and wide, even among otherwise homogenous ethnic and national groupings. British Muslims with origins in the Indian sub-continent, for example, have brought with them en masse the ancient tension between the two groupings of Barelvis and Deobandis. Barelvis give the prophet Muhammad a superhuman status, seeing him as a figure who is everywhere at all times, who is not mortal flesh and blood, but light itself. Deobandis too revere the prophet Muhammad, but only as a mortal man, even though he was the *insan-i-kamil*, the perfect person. The emergence of the Barelvi tradition is an interesting example of how Islam, often wrongly viewed in the West as a monolithic homogenous faith, is in fact highly syncretistic and has evolved across the world by absorbing and adapting local traditions.

The Barelvis' particular veneration of Muhammad has its roots in the South Asian and Hindu tradition of myths and legends of fantastic gods who can perform miracles. Barelvi reverence for, and perception of, Muhammad, was shaped by the pre-existing polytheistic Hindu culture that accorded superhuman status to religious figures. This might be just an interesting footnote in the development of Islam in Britain, except the Barelvis' veneration of Muhammad explains why they were so angered, hurt and infuriated by Salman Rushdie's *Satanic Verses*, why they led the campaigns against it and why, ultimately, they were driven to publicly burn the book. Many Arabs and Turks, for example, took a much more sanguine view of the whole affair, saying that far more insulting works about Islam than *The Satanic Verses* are available on the bookshelves of their own countries.

Several foreign Muslim political parties are also active in Britain, of which the two most influential are probably Hizb-ut-Tahrir and Jamaat-i-Islami. Both enjoy only minority support, but their presence as activists gives them a voice and a presence, and they set an agenda to which mainstream leaders must respond, if only to dismiss their claims and demands. Hizb-ut-Tahrir, about which more follows later in this chapter, was founded in east Jerusalem in the early 1950s. Jamaat-i-Islami was founded in Pakistan by Sayyid Abu'l Ala Maududi, one of the most important thinkers of modern Islam. 'Maududi's primary aim is to present Islam as an absolute and self-sufficient ideology, completely distinct from and opposed to both the western way of life and its eastern socialist equivalents,' writes Malise Ruthven in *Islam and the World*. Maududi's legacy of visceral anti-westernism can still be heard among Muslims everywhere from Mecca to Manchester. Jamaat-i-Islami does not enjoy wide support among the Pakistani electorate, but is influential in Britain.

Like Maududi, the majority of British Muslims have their roots in the Indian sub-continent, perhaps as many as two-thirds of the total, who were either born here or whose parents arrived in the great waves of immigration during the 1950s and 1960s.

They altered for ever the ethnic and social makeup of large swathes of London, as well as a string of cities across the country, but nowhere more so than the mill towns and cities of Yorkshire such as Bradford, Batley, Dewsbury and Leeds. Decades later it would be Yorkshire, rather than London, that would see the first outburst of Muslim rage, against *The Satanic Verses*, and one of the first examples of successful Muslim political activism, the campaign for the provision of *halal* meat in schools.

In fact Britain has played host to Muslim traders, travellers and envoys for centuries, and the southern port of Hastings was known to Arab cartographers. One of the first Muslim travellers to record his impressions of Britain was Mirza Abu Talib Khan, who was born in Lucknow in 1752 and was employed as a revenue officer by the British. He travelled in Europe between 1799 and 1803 and on one of his journeys he visited Dublin. He was not impressed, for in all the city he could find only two ramshackle bath-houses, and they were used solely by the very ill. In the summer, he writes, Dubliners wash their bodies in the sea, in the winter, they don't bother at all. The bath-house itself was a great disappointment, and lacked the specialist staff, such as a barber or masseur, that make a visit to a Muslim *hamam* such a relaxing and invigorating experience. But it seems there was no pleasing Abu Talib, for while the Dubliners didn't wash enough, the English gentlemen he met were too fussy about their appearance. Number six in his crotchety list of Englishmen's defects are 'their wasting much time on sleeping and dressing and arranging their hair and shaving their beards and suchlike'.

But it was the opening of the Suez canal in 1869 that marked the start of the first substantial Muslim presence. Indian, Yemeni and Somali seamen landed in Britain and Yemeni boarding houses opened in Cardiff and South Shields. Sufi Sheikhs arrived soon after, to meet their religious needs, opening *zawiyahs*, or centres which soon became the focus of those early Muslims' social and religious life. Many of the sailors married British women and stayed on, the start of Britain's first Muslim communities.

Unlike Christians and Jews, British Muslims have no organised national communal leadership, whether temporal or spiritual. Just as in France or Germany, they speak with many voices, which weakens their case on issues such as reform of the blasphemy law or the provision of halal meat in schools. Those same differences of ethnic origin, culture and theology that make Islam in Britain such a many-splendoured faith also mitigate against unity. Many Muslims argue for the establishment of a body along the lines of the Board of Deputies of British Jews, a quasi-parliament, representing different strands and factions, as the best solution, but so far the community has failed to agree on a framework.

But if there is no one voice of British Islam, British Muslims do have several leaders to represent them. Dr Zaki Badawi, now principal of the Libyan-funded Muslim College in west London, is often described as Britain's foremost Muslim cleric. Born in Egypt, Dr Badawi studied in London University, taught at Al-Azhar university in Cairo, the Muslim world's foremost theological academy, as well as in Malaysia and Nigeria before becoming Imam and director of Regent's Park Mosque. Dr Badawi took a strong stand against Ayatollah Khomeini's *fatwa* of death on Salman Rushdie, and was involved in the author's short-lived adoption of Islam, taking a brave public stance in favour of free speech which contrasted sharply with the public equivocation of many Muslim thinkers, who well knew how far back the *fatwa* would set relations between Islam and the West, but still kept quiet. It was a stand that then weakened Badawi's position in the community.

Demonstrations against the book were organised by Saudi Arabia, working through Jamaat-i-Islaami, he says. 'The presence of Jamaat al-Islami is one of our main disasters here . . . The Saudis were pouring money into them. I tried very hard to reconcile Salman with the Muslim community, despite the fact that I knew it was a thankless task. He wrote a document saying he was a Muslim, signed it and gave it to us. But he relented very quickly. He wanted to be a Muslim out of fear and I accept this is a legitimate approach, if you are under pressure you can become anything. I thought his opponents, if they had any sense, which they don't, should have encouraged him. He would have lost his liberal constituency very quickly. I thought he was an asset, he is a good writer and many of his opponents are ignorant illiterates. The Muslim community could gain a lot by having people of talent on their side.'

Bruised but not disheartened by the Rushdie affair, Dr Badawi is now among the vanguard of British Muslim modernists who believe that Islam must develop in line with Muslim life in a western secular society and evolve a new theology to meet those needs. His progressive beliefs have often brought him into conflict with the more obscurantist trends in British Islam, and their paymasters in Saudi Arabia and other Gulf States. Dr Badawi has been in the vanguard of inter-faith work, and Christian priests and ministers and Rabbis lecture at the Muslim College, but perhaps nothing he did was more controversial among Muslims than to introduce an Anglican priest and a Rabbi into Regent's Park Mosque to discuss religion and theology.

'We three thought that as religious leaders it's time we tried to make headway in bridging the gap between the communities. It was a risk because suspicion and hostility between them is always present . . . Muslims said, "How dare you bring a Rabbi and a priest into the mosque to speak?" Many Muslims then saw the mosque as their moral territory, something extra territorial, that we are not living in England, somehow when we enter the mosque it does not count under the British jurisdiction.'

But Dr Badawi persisted, and slowly the stereotypes, on all three sides, began to peel off and die. Those early meetings were perhaps the germ of an idea, now spreading in sections of both the Jewish and Muslim communities, that relations between Jews and Muslims should not be dependent solely on events in Israel/Palestine, when the two faiths have so many common concerns in 1990s Britain. 'At the beginning there was hostility, people tried to embarrass the Rabbi or the priest by saying, "You people hate Islam". But what was very heartening was the growing attendance and interest. And what really astonished many of them was how similar Jewish law is to Islamic law. So the people who came to be hostile and to embarrass the speakers gradually became accustomed to listening to other views. More importantly, for the first time Muslims frequented the synagogue and also the church. But the most important thing was people from different religions went to another place of worship, and were sitting there respectfully and participating politely in discussions.'

With the departure of Dr Badawi in 1981 from the Regent's

Park Mosque inter-faith work there has been much reduced, but the broader trend continues. The Jewish Board of Deputies, for example, does much work behind the scenes advising Muslim leaders on issues such as political lobbying, education and provision of *halal* meat. 'At the time this dialogue was sort of heretical, but suddenly it dawned on the Muslim community that it was really the way forward. It's really the convention that dialogue is not something to be accepted, particularly with the Jews, after Israel's creation. But the whole idea of dialogue, even with your greatest enemies, is something that is enshrined in Islam. But somehow people developed the idea that if you don't like someone then you don't talk with them. Ignore them. Don't learn about them. Don't even read about them. This is what I call the philosophy of ignorance, sanctified ignorance. If I don't like a book I burn it, which is a terrible thing. It is spreading.'

So where, I ask, does this originate from?

'From a contingent still living in medieval times in our local Muslim circles. We do not tolerate different opinions. We find someone who has a different opinion to be threatening and frightening. And rather than debate, we say, "You are no longer a Muslim" . . . Much of this comes from the Gulf states and their money. They exported a vision of Islam which was contrary to the development of what was taking place in Egypt, with a school of law and a school of thought that was tolerant, dynamic, and was moving forward, trying to adapt Islam to modern conditions and to incorporate modern science and technology. But its leaders were accused of being more or less heretical. That is what has happened, and now any new idea is regarded with suspicion.'

The answer, says Dr Badawi, is to deal with things as they are, and not as some Muslims would like them to be. 'To find a solution first, and then to theorise about it later. To live in the modern world and accept the modern world as it is. We cannot act like King Canute, demanding that science and technology must retreat at our command. It is there. No one lives without this, television, radio, the airplane. People can no longer escape the consequences of modernity.'

At the opposite end of the spectrum to the modernists such as

Zaki Badawi are the radical Islamists, who believe in, and work for, the eventual global triumph of Islam. They are not the same as the conservatives, described above by Dr Badawi, although they share their visceral hostility to western liberal values. In Britain the loudest voice for radicalism is that of Hizb-ut-Tahrir (Party of Liberation). Founded in east Jerusalem in the early 1950s by Sheikh Taqiuddeen al-Nabahani, the party calls for a new *Khilafah*, a pan-Islamic state based on the *Shariah*. Its members have been linked to several coup attempts in the Middle East, where it is banned but still maintains a secret cell network in most Arab countries as well as in Turkey, Pakistan and Sudan. It operates more or less openly in Britain. It is implacably opposed to the Arab–Israeli peace process and calls for the creation of an Islamic army to eliminate Israel, claiming that after the destruction of the Zionist state Jews will live in peace under Islam's guarantees. Hizb-ut-Tahrir publishes Arabic-language magazines across the Middle East as well as an English-language *Khilafah*, which is distributed at mosques in Britain and the United States. In Europe Hizb-ut-Tahrir has, or has had, bases in Denmark, Belgium, Germany and Austria.

Hizb-ut-Tahrir's growth is being watched with concern by a range of observers, including M15, which carefully monitors the activities of radical Islamists in Britain, especially those with connections to the volatile Middle East. Mainstream Muslim leaders fear, rightly, that the party's rhetoric of confrontation will further alienate middle-England and marginalise Muslim causes. Jewish organisations accuse Hizb-ut-Tahrir of virulent anti-Semitism. The National Union of Students accuses the party of intimidating Jewish, Hindu and gay and lesbian students, which it denies.

Judging from the many stories about Hizb-ut-Tahrir in the *Jewish Chronicle*, its student members seem ready enough to resort to verbal intimidation, although none has ever been arrested and charged with physical attacks. Either way Hizb-ut-Tahrir is also banned in dozens of British colleges and universities, where it now operates under cover names such as the 1924 committee, commemorating the year when Turkey's leader Kemal Atatürk abolished the Ottoman Caliphate. Hizb-ut-Tahrir supporters were accused of whipping up ethnic hatred in February 1994, after Ayotunde Obanubi, a twenty-year-old

African student at an east London college was stabbed to death in a clash between African and Muslim students. Four days before the killing, Omar Bakri Mohammad, then the party's leader in Britain, had spoken at a meeting for Muslim students.

The party's biggest triumph was the *Khilafah* Conference in August 1994, held at Wembley Arena. Thousands of Muslims jammed the aisles to hear the usual rhetoric against radical Islam's *bêtes noires*: Israel, the Middle East regimes – condemned as creations of imperialism – the World Bank, the United Nations, the International Monetary Fund, as the speakers verbally rounded up all the usual suspects. Despite the dire warnings from Jewish organisations of disaster if the *Khilafah* conference went ahead the main disturbance was the arrest of gay activist Peter Tatchell demonstrating on behalf of 'Queers Against Fundamentalism', as Islam forbids homosexuality.

But the question many, both Muslims and non-Muslims, were asking, was where had Hizb-ut-Tahrir suddenly appeared from, and more to the point, who was paying for extravaganzas like the *Khilafah* conference? 'Hizb-ut-Tahrir's presence is amazing, how they emerged so suddenly, they must have had some finances to appear so rapidly,' says Dr Badawi. 'When I was in Regent's Park Mosque in the early 1980s, they were not there. They appeared after the Gulf War, after the obvious and open delegitimisation of the regimes in the Gulf, which all appeared to be paper regimes, unable to defend themselves. Al-Mass'ari would never have happened without the Gulf War. I think Gulf money is behind Hizb-ut-Tahrir. Not the Saudis, they dislike them, almost all the governments dislike them, because they are revolutionaries, saying all the regimes are illegitimate. But just as all roads lead to Rome, all finances lead to the Gulf. There are people in the Gulf who will encourage any radical movement, because they hate the regimes and they want to get at them, but they cannot do that openly, so they sponsor any movement that is anti-establishment.'

Until January 1996 Hizb-ut-Tahrir's leader in Britain was Omar Bakri Mohammad. Bakri Mohammad, who arrived in London in 1985, was born in Syria in 1958 and describes himself as 'a leader on the ground', travelling across the country to speak at mosques everywhere from Barking to Bradford. Now based at the School of Shariah, a large scruffy house in Tottenham, north London, Bakri Mohammad has applied for British citizenship and receives welfare benefits. 'I am a very active person. I am not like Kalim Siddiqui, a nice sincere Muslim but who writes articles behind his desk, I am not like Zaki Badawi, who is funded by Libya, who has nobody to listen to him and doesn't give any talks, anywhere. There are people called leaders on the ground, there are many of them, we know each other very well.'

Hizb-ut-Tahrir's radical Islamic theology is the very antithesis of Marxist atheism, but it operates on classical Leninist lines. Core activists such as Bakri Mohammad travel the country, setting up closed cells in towns and universities, whose members are indoctrinated in the party's beliefs and worldview. The activists move on, but the new cadre-members are left behind, to infiltrate the Muslim establishment, such as established student Islamic Societies and try to take them over. For many young British Muslims Hizb-ut-Tahrir provides a set of ready-made answers to both political issues and the questions of personal identity that often draw alienated individuals to extremist organisations. And of anger and alienation, they have plenty. The party's millennarian message of proud self-reliance, rejection of the West, and unyielding Islamism has brought it growing support both in the backstreets of Bradford and Batley and across university and colleges campuses. 'If I was the Home Office I would be worried about the increasing anti-western sentiment among Muslim youth,' says one analyst watching developing trends among British Muslims. 'The idea of conspiracies against Islam, of Christian/Jewish/Zionist anti-Islamic cabals all working against Muslims are dealt with very casually, as accepted facts and this is a matter of great concern.' For some young British Muslims anti-western and anti-Semitic stereotypes are not myths, but facts.

Omar Bakri Mohammad has for several years been demonised as a hate figure in the British media, starting in the Gulf War when he was reported to have called for the assassination of John Major, which he strongly denies. He is a bearded, somewhat excitable man, who, like Arthur Scargill, has the slightly unnerving habit of referring to himself in the third person, and he plays a delicate game of working for the global triumph of Islam, but fighting his battles verbally or in print, while his lawyer supporters advise him of the correct legal parameters in which he may operate. Bakri Mohammad explains how he set up Hizb-ut-Tahrir: 'Omar made a small group of brothers, I started to culture them, I moved with them from campus to campus. We divided the country into three areas: the community, society, universities, campuses or organisations. I played a role in all three of them. We started at the beginning moving from place to place. Wherever I go, I put one or two brothers there, and they convert other brothers. All the chocolate Muslims, they reject that. They don't want Islam to be introduced as a political or economic system.'

For Bakri Mohammad, 'chocolate Muslims' are Islamic Uncle Toms. Just as Uncle Tom is a term of abuse in the black community for someone who has black skin but is considered white inside, a 'chocolate Muslim' is someone who believes in Islam, but fails to live what Bakri Mohammad says is a truly Muslim life and struggle for its triumph. 'Definitely there is a struggle between western civilisation and Islam. The Muslims who say there is not are chocolate Muslims, who don't want to change reality. A chocolate Muslim is the one who does not believe Islam can change reality, who believes "I can let Islam fit with reality". But I believe that God sent a messenger, Muhammad, in order to change reality, not to find if he can live with existing reality, that is what Islam is about. Any Quranic text says God is the only creator, the only commander, that means sovereignty for God. Man-made law says sovereignty for Man. Remember I don't believe Islam is only a religion, the way you think about Islam, or the way many chocolate Muslims think about Islam. It is a system of life, therefore it is impossible to think like this mentality among certain intellectual Muslims, who say "Oh yes, we can live together", no, we cannot live together.'

I ask him what form this struggle between Islam and the West will take. 'It is an intellectual struggle. We do believe we must convince people about the new way of life. We struggle to change society . . . But when we have a debate on the campus they go to the NUS [National Union of Students] and say we are fundamentalists. If you reject the peace with Israel you are anti-Semitic, if you reject western civilisation you are a fundamentalist. If you reject the existing regimes in the Middle East you are an extremist. So they label you as they like. But we are living in the Muslim community and they know us. If I did this in the Middle East I would be arrested or killed. But here there is a facility. The environment of freedom of speech helped us a lot, to convey the message to the Muslim community.'

Many mainstream Muslim British leaders and thinkers are desperate to marginalise Bakri Mohammad and dismiss him as an irrelevance, for his rhetoric is a public-relations disaster for those Muslims who wish to work within British society. 'Kalim Siddiqui and Bakri Mohammad, what is their long-term impact?' asks Professor Akbar Ahmed, Pakistan-born author of several books on Islam, and fellow of Selwyn College, Cambridge. Just as Lenin, that arch-strategist once asked 'who benefits', when trying to gauge a rival's support and tactics, Professor Ahmed queries who is behind the sudden appearance of groups such as Hizb-ut-Tahrir, who, he believes, serve only to discredit Islam and British Muslims, most of whom, after all, merely seek to live their lives in peace and raise their families in the laws and culture of Islam.

'They have come from nowhere, and they go nowhere. Why is the British media encouraging them? Because they can damage Islam. The natural ally of the Muslims here would be the traditionally oppressed classes, such as the Jews, or the Irish. These are the very people who they [Hizb-ut-Tahrir] are targeting. They have alienated the traditional allies, the majority population, the mainstream Muslims, and who have they ended up with? This is an important question that Muslims don't ask in public, but there is not enough critical self-analysis in Muslim society.'

For Professor Ahmed, groups such as Hizb-ut-Tahrir have absorbed the worst of British yob culture. 'They have had their fifteen minutes of fame, which you have given them through the press, with the sensation of them threatening this, and threatening that. They are playing the game, for whatever reason, personal, to propagate their version of Islam, or to satisfy their ego. The damage they are doing to Islam, which is a very rational, balanced system, which encourages dialogue, and all sensible Muslims want this, a much more serious interchange of ideas, the damage is incalculable. People just assume that Muslims are mad fanatics.'

143

But for Bakri Mohammad, Professor Ahmed, seeker after tolerance and co-existence, is merely another Uncle Tom, courting the western establishment. 'Chocolate Muslims will say that. Go the community and tell me which chocolate Muslim is the leader of the community. We have an Islamic law school here with top barristers and lawyers. Why don't they go to the chocolate Muslims like Zaki Badawi? Or Akbar Ahmed, he admires western civilisation more than Islamic civilisation. There is no respect for him in the community. He is a sincere Muslim, but sincere is not enough.'

In fact Professor Ahmed – unlike Bakri Mohammad – enjoys widespread respect among many British Muslims, particularly those originating in the Indian subcontinent. He made headlines in May 1996 when he preached at evensong at Selwyn College, Cambridge, one of the first Muslims ever to address a Christian congregation. His address was a call for mutual understanding and tolerance between Christian and Muslim faiths and peoples, and he quoted the speech given by Muhammad at Arafat: 'God has made you brethren one to another, so be not divided. An Arab has no preference over a non-Arab, nor a non-Arab over an Arab; nor is a white one to be preferred to a dark one, nor a dark one to a white one.'

It was a speech not universally welcomed among British Muslims and reaction to it followed the traditional dividing lines: while the radicals denounced him, the liberals rallied around. Dr Ghayasuddin, the new leader of the Muslim Parliament – itself dismissed by many Muslims as the arm of Tehran in Britain – was quick to attack Professor Ahmed as an 'apologist' who sought the approval of the West. '. . . Muslims have always been oppressed by the West. And to try to merely sweet-talk to them in churches is neither here nor there. Such dialogues have hardly any implications on creating "understanding between religions", if that is the idea,' he told *The News*. That triggered an immediate salvo in Professor Ahmed's defence, from Dr Abduljalil Sajid, Imam of the Brighton Islamic Centre and Mosque, who was present at the lecture. He pointed out that Muhammad himself had invited Christians from Najran to Medina mosque and said Muslims who criticised Professor Ahmed were 'ignorant'.

As well as providing more ammunition in the intra-Muslim

war of words, the debate over Professor Ahmed's address illustrated that Britain's Muslims are a dynamic group, with different voices competing for the hearts of a maturing community. Professor Ahmed himself described his church speech as part of a much-needed 'jihad of understanding', a battle for heart and minds, both among Muslim and non-Muslims. 'For us Muslims this is happening on two fronts. Between Muslims, to understand the real nature of Islam, its message of peace and compassion, and at the same between Muslims and the West, so the West understands that Islam is not a religion of monsters and Muslims don't behave like monsters.'

All that said, I believe it is a mistake to dismiss Bakri Mohammad as an unrepresentative extremist. He has written over half a dozen books on Islam, such as *Political Struggle in Islam* and the *Hidden Force of the Muslim ummah* (world community). He is an intelligent and articulate public speaker who well knows how to play a Muslim audience and how to fashion and exploit the anger of much of Britain's unemployed and alienated Muslim youth. Talking with Bakri Mohammad, I was reminded of Dr al-Mass'ari, which is not surprising for the two are old friends, and al-Mass'ari too is a former member of Hizb-ut-Tahrir.

In his book *Postmodernism and Islam*, Professor Ahmed quotes the writer Fazlur Rahman on the 'postmodern fundamentalist' position, and points to Rahman's argument that this group concentrates on those components of Islam, such as the ban on bank interest, collection of *zakat* (charity) and so on, that will 'most *distinguish* Muslims from the West'. This, it seemed to me, was Bakri Mohammad's outlook. His book *Essential Fiqh* (jurisprudence) outlines the framework for living as a Muslim in 1990s Britain, with chapters covering the laws governing dress, buying meat from non-Muslims, imitating non-Muslims and the prohibition on bank interest, in short how to live in a society without being *of* that society.

So much for the theory. But the practice, say a range of groups from the NUS to the Jewish Board of Deputies, is one of abuse and intimidation. Not so, says Bakri Mohammad. 'We are in Britain. We are not in Zimbabwe. Britain has a government, has a police, authorities. Why has no one ever reported us to the police? I challenge them. It is against my intellectual dignity as a member of Hizb-ut-Tahrir to intimidate somebody. If he defeats me in an intellectual debate, I will lose everything. If I use my hands, or intimidate you, that means I failed.'

But it is Hizb-ut-Tahrir's public questioning of the Holocaust that has drawn the most attention, outraging Jewish groups and dismaying Muslim ones trying to build a common front to fight racism and discrimination. I asked Bakri Mohammad if he believed the Holocaust happened.

'I condemn the killing of women and children by the Nazis. The issue of the Holocaust, I have never seen it [and] I don't believe in something I did not see. But if somebody does not believe that Muslims were killed in Sabra and Chatila, I would never say they are racists . . . If the Holocaust means a political weapon to justify the existence of the Jews in Palestine, killing the Palestinians and the Muslims there, I do not believe in this Holocaust. If the Holocaust means the killing by the Nazis of innocent people of the Jews, women and children, of course we condemn it.'

Do you believe that six million Jews were killed by the Nazis?

'I don't believe so. Is it illegal if I don't believe that? It is not illegal. If somebody believes that a massacre happened to his own people, and someone else does not believe it, does that mean he is a racist? . . . Israeli leaders have said many times that their real defence weapon is not the nuclear bomb, it is the Holocaust and nobody should doubt its existence. So that put a lot of doubt in the minds of the Muslims in the Middle East. It has justified the killing and torturing of many people in Palestine. That's the way we think. Remember I am an Arab from the Middle East, I am talking about somebody growing up there, all my culture is from there . . . I condemn the killing of Jews because of their race, but if you use the issue of the Holocaust to justify something else we will never accept it.'

By the winter of 1995 the increasing media attention on Hizb-ut-Tahrir in Britain was causing disquiet among the party's underground leadership in the Middle East. Its aim, after all, was to rebuild the *Khilafah* in Islam's ancient lands, not engage in public bust-ups with Jewish and Hindu students in British universities. Bakri Mohammad was replaced. In January 1996 he launched Al-Muhajiroun, taking many members of

Hizb-ut-Tahrir with him, as well as former supporters of Jamaat-i-Islami and the Muslim Brotherhood. He won't say how many members the new group has but claims a presence in the United States, France, Pakistan, Malaysia and Mauritius. 'We don't want to talk about it, but we have a lot of members. Many people are Sufis, they can gather a million, but one million Sufis they just dance. But four or five people, politicians and statesmen, they can make more of a difference.'

That a Syrian political exile, a radical Islamist, is free to live in Britain, claim benefits, apply for citizenship, all the while working for the global triumph of Islam, enrages many. I asked Bakri Mohammad how he replied to the argument that, while here, he should shut up and keep his ideas to himself? 'If they said that, we will leave this country, we will never fight. But they have never said that. We political asylum seekers have never been told that our political activity is illegal. Where is the law – I have lawyers here – which says political refugees cannot run any political activity? There is not, and I am not breaking any laws. If they say I cannot, it is my duty to leave and I will leave the next day. I don't want to challenge you. I will leave.'

The Egyptian Dr Zaki Badawi and the Syrian Omar Bakri Mohammad. Both Arabs from the Middle East, both practising Muslims and influential leaders expounding their versions of Islam, but two men with radically different worldviews. Most British Muslims though are not from the Levant, but the Indian sub-continent. They live in the cities and mill towns strung out across the Dales and the Pennines, where even the first-generation immigrants have Yorkshire accents as flat as caps.

It was time, if I wanted to properly take the pulse of British Muslim life, to leave the metropolis. So I went to Bradford, home to one of Britain's biggest Muslim communities, nearly all from Pakistani Kashmir, northern India and Sylhet in Bangladesh. By the year 2000, Muslim leaders say, fifty per cent of Bradford school-leavers will be of Asian origin. Bradford, with its twenty-eight mosques and fourteen Islamic religion schools, is where British Muslims first found their political voice and discovered the power of the media. It was there that the image of a flaming copy of *The Satanic Verses*, nailed to a stick like a literary crucifixion, tongues of fire charring the pages as it burned in front of a crowd of angry Muslim demonstrators, rebounded around the world. This is Muslim life in the postmodern age: where the Image – instant, powerful and permanent – defines the Message, a snapshot tableau that lives on for ever. And for many non-Muslims that picture symbolised every atavistic fear they had about Islam: that it was a faith irrevocably set on a collision course with the West, a religion of fury and rage, intolerance and censorship. The resonance with Nazi book-burning that triggered a deep shiver of repulsion among western Europeans struck no chord in Muslims from small villages in Sylhet and Kashmir.

Burning a book, any book, also horrified many Muslims. Not just because they knew what a public relations disaster it would be, setting back relations with non-Muslims by several years, but also because to burn a book is a deeply unIslamic act. To learn, to read, to study and perhaps most of all, to understand, is incumbent on every Muslim. The librarians of Cordoba, in medieval Spain, who guarded 400,000 volumes, or of ninth-century Baghdad, would have been aghast at setting the written word on fire. As Muhammad himself said: 'The ink of the scholar is more holy than the blood of the martyr.' But the spirit of enlightenment is sometimes absent in Bradford. It was there, that as a Jew writing about Islam, I encountered the single incident of anti-Semitism in the many months I spent travelling across Europe, Turkey and the United States. I was chatting happily with a taxi driver until he asked me what religion I was. I told him, and something hostile glittered in his eyes as he turned to look at me and the atmosphere changed. 'I think we have got a lot of problems then,' he said, as we bumped down the hill towards an almost-completed mosque. These 'problems' he could not well articulate, but they included, of course, Israel/Palestine. He was not exactly deliberately intimidating, but I was glad to arrive at my destination.

In Bradford, they would burn *The Satanic Verses* again, explains Sher Azam, former president of the Bradford Council of Mosques. 'We were quite clear that we do not want to upset anybody, or ridicule anybody, so why should somebody upset and insult us? We are in an environment where there is enough misunderstanding of Islam and when young people start studying this type of book, it will create further alienation and misunderstanding. We were asking for a ban. I supported that. I must make it clear that the Muslim community, and Islam, is as much a champion as anybody else, if not more so, of freedom of expression, but freedom of expression with responsibility. You are free to swing your arm around, as far as you can, as long as you don't touch my nose. Where your arm ends and my nose begins, that is the boundary.'

For many non-Muslims though *The Satanic Verses* came nowhere near Sher Azam's nose. Here two worlds, one western and secular, the other Muslim and religious, collided. The scars on both sides still run deep, still shaping perceptions, strengthening stereotypes and entrenching mutual acrimony. The Rushdie affair erupted over six years ago, but its legacy still poisons relations between Muslims and non-Muslims. There is no solution that could satisfy both sides, but if the long list of British Muslims' grievances had been considered with sympathy and understanding the Rushdie affair would never have become an Islamic standard behind which the community rallied.

'We are not powerful, we are a minority, a very powerless community,' says Azam. 'We hope that the people in power will understand our plight. You say we haven't succeeded, but we have at least brought it to the attention of the people, we have put forward the Muslim point of view and this has created a debate. You can burn pornographic material – we are not against books as books – when it is confiscated.' Before the book was burned Bradford's Muslims wrote to the publisher, the Home Secretary and the Prime Minister. They were, says Azam, fobbed off, or ignored. 'You could see the powerlessness of the community, that we were trying our best, without making an issue of it, and the number of complaints was growing day by day, people were worried, and angry and upset . . . If the circumstances which I have explained to you were similar or the same, we would do exactly what we did.'

Born in north-west Pakistan, Sher Azam, now in his middle-fifties, arrived in Britain in 1961. We met in his house in Bradford, where a Quranic inscription hangs on the wall, and the local paper is neatly folded by the sofa. The narrow streets of terraced houses resound to the sounds of Urdu as much as English. Shops signs are in both languages, the long curved consonants of that Asian language sloping down over more prosaic

English proclamations offering halal meat or basmati rice. Azam is a softly spoken man, much esteemed in the local community for his learning and stature as a community leader, dressed, like many Asians, in a baggy *shalwar-kameez*, long shirt and trousers. British Muslims are here to stay, he says, but they want their rights.

These include: state aid for Muslim schools; extension of race relations legislation to cover Muslims (there is no law outlawing prejudice against Muslims on religious, rather than ethnic origin); and the extension of the blasphemy laws to cover Islam. The Commission for Racial Equality (CRE) has so far maintained that religious discrimination falls outside its brief, which is based on enforcing the 1976 Race Relations Act. But after criticism from Muslim groups, the Commission has begun a series of consultations to begin countering religious discrimination. And groups working against racism such as the Runnymede Trust have appealed to the United Nations Committee on the Elimination of Racial Discrimination, based in Geneva, to press for the inclusion of Muslims in anti-racist legislation. Sher Azam gives an example of why new legislation is needed to protect Muslims: 'A precision engineering company in Bradford decided that their jobs were open to everyone except women or Muslims. The Commission for Racial Equality took them to court, and a very articulate Muslim presented our case, but we lost. The tribunal decided that the employer was found guilty on the first charge, but said that discrimination against Muslims was not an offence. This leaves the Muslim community very vulnerable and angry as well.'

But is there not a legitimate argument though that when an immigrant community comes to Britain it should conform to British values and not expect the host society to change? 'When you go to a place, you accept that country and you accept that land's laws. Muslims are expected and obliged to respect the law of Allah and of the land. For example, this is my house, and I have arranged the furniture according to my needs. If I accept you or someone else on an equal basis, it is a partnership. I expect you to pay the bills of the house, and contribute to the expenses. If this lampshade always catches you on the head, because you are a bit taller than I am, it's not unfair to ask me to raise it up a bit,' says Azam, gesturing towards the ceiling. 'I should do my best to accommodate you. That is what we are asking for, not special favours. The needs are different and it is not too much to ask if we, as an immigrant community, can be accommodated.'

Their campaign against *The Satanic Verses* failed, but Bradford's Muslims still learnt a lot about how to lobby, organise and campaign. 'I learnt a great deal about the misunderstandings we have about our perception of the community at large and the level of misunderstanding which does exist about the Muslim community. We had bags of letters, most of them were hostile. Our office was broken into and ransacked, nothing was taken, but a paper was left saying: "leave Rushdie alone", those sorts of things. I received hate mail, threatening phone calls. My little daughter answered the telephone and somebody said, "I'll cut your father's throat", I had to calm her down. You could see from these calls the hate that does exist in some people's minds. But we have learnt a lot about how British politics work.'

Beyond the media furore, Bradford is now home to a new and hardy plant, one putting down roots wherever Muslims live in Britain: British Islam. This is a hybrid but sturdy strain, born out of Mecca and Medina centuries ago, but now cultured in Manchester and Macclesfield. 'The trend is changing now towards a British system of Islam. The people who have grown up here and have been brought up in this environment, they understand the local language, the culture. They have not been brought up in an Islamic environment as we were. They have seen Islam practised by their parents or grandparents, they read about Islam, they have their own experiences together with the indigenous population. Western civilisation and psychology is more towards secularism and materialism than spiritualism, but they see that these are not the answers. So they are returning to the faith, a faith which is not my faith, but their perception of faith. A few years ago we were scared that our children would go away from faith, we were more worried about secularism. That feeling is not there now.'

Islam evolves in the environment in which it exists, says Azam. 'Islam is a tablet. In the Middle East, or the Far East, or eastern Europe, we have coated Islam with our own particular culture. British Muslims are coating that tablet with a British

Islam which is different from ours, very different. At the time of the Rushdie crisis the young people wanted to assimilate and were moving towards the local culture. That was really worrying, not because we don't want our children to be as British as anybody else, we want all the good habits of Britain to be in our children, but we don't want the bad habits. Parents were worried, but since the Rushdie crisis those people who were drifting away have come back. The Muslim booksellers said that they sold many times more books on Islam to young Muslims and non-Muslims after Rushdie.'

As well as spiritual problems, British Muslims, especially from the Indian sub-continent, face more mundane difficulties. Unemployment is over fifty per cent in some parts of Bradford, say Muslim leaders; racial attacks mean that some families are afraid to venture out, and young Muslims especially say they are regularly harassed by the police. Anger, alienation, racism, joblessness, an uncertain identity in a society that seems to have no place for them: all the ingredients in a literally explosive mixture. In the summer of 1995 it ignited. Bradford's Muslim youth – Hindus and Sikhs stayed at home – rioted and hurled petrol bombs at shops and cars, causing about £1 million worth of damage. The spark that lit the flame was reportedly rough handling of a Muslim woman by police in the course of two arrests. Muslim honour was defiled, Muslim pride was running high after a moderately successful campaign that spring to run local prostitutes out of town. So Muslim youth took to the streets, venting their fury.

And when Bradford's Muslim youth run into trouble, they call Aurangzeb Iqbal. Born in Mirpur, Pakistan, Iqbal, now in his early thirties, arrived in Britain in his early childhood. A flamboyant lawyer with a flair for snappy suits and controversial publicity – one campaign featured the Kama Sutra with the slogan 'We'll defend you in difficult positions' – Iqbal has set up his own firm of solicitors with offices in a former converted chapel. The waiting room is crowded with both British and Asian clients, asking for help with everything from divorce to criminal prosecutions. His clients are often young second- and third-generation Muslims, British citizens who lack the immigrants' deference that shaped their parents. Four of them, accused of threatening behaviour and assaulting the police during the Bradford riots, walked free after the prosecution case against them collapsed.

'British-born Muslims' aspirations are different. So far as they are concerned, the hunger that associated with the first generation, to take any menial job, is not there,' says Iqbal. 'They say why should we do that? We've gone to the same schools, colleges and universities, we are just as good, why aren't we getting the jobs? The authorities need to address this issue, there are parts of Bradford with sixty, seventy per cent unemployment in private residential areas, not council estates, and those kids have no channel, nowhere to go. With unemployment that high, one is asking for trouble. As far as I know not a penny has been spent to set something up for the kids, such as a leisure centre, job centre or training and skills centre.'

For Iqbal, a football fanatic, part of the answer is to bring young Muslims to sport. His greatest sporting achievement to date was helping organise the match between a UK Asian XI and Bradford City. The Asian XI lost 3–1, but that wasn't the point, says Iqbal. 'Muslims and Asians need to be involved in every sphere of activity. We don't just want Asians to be lawyers and dentists, we want them to become microbiologists and sportsmen. Sport has a unique ability to break down racial barriers. Ten years ago they said that black players will never make it because they will feel too cold in the winter. Now they say Muslim players will never make it because they will want to start praying in the middle of the match, when it's prayer time. I don't know where they get this from, I really don't. In five or ten years' time I want to see a situation with footballers wearing the names Khan and Abdul on their back. The Muslim community needs role models, to help bridge with the host community. Sports personalities can do that.'

I imagine that should he so desire, Iqbal could win a seat in Parliament in a few years. A graduate of Salford University and founder member of the Asian Business and Professionals Club in Yorkshire, he seems a natural spokesman for a community that surely needs young voices in 1990s Britain. Iqbal is in the vanguard of the British Islam that Sher Azam says is growing in Bradford. His religion is an integral part of his life. He prays five times a day, not always on time, for court cases wait for no man, not even Muslims, and reads the Quran every day. 'Islam gives you discipline, you never give up. You say your prayers, you don't say, "Oh, I don't feel like it today." No, you feel like it. You always look at the positive side, never the negative. The prophet Muhammad said never say "if", in your dealings in life. If something goes wrong you say it doesn't matter, I will learn from it and I will carry on. But Islam allows for flexibility, if you don't have time you read the Quran later. Because during the day I am involved in things, I pray in the morning before I come to work and the other four I say before I go to bed.

'If you see a Muslim you are supposed to have a very good idea that person is a Muslim, by the way he talks, the way he dresses, his demeanour, his manners, that shows he is a Muslim. So what good is it if somebody prays five times a day, wears tatty clothes, with rotting teeth. That is not living your life in the spirit of Islam. Islam tells you to dress smartly, to spend upon yourself, you are not supposed to hoard money. It's wrong to have a big bank balance or build a massive house in Pakistan that nobody lives in. That's wrong. Spend that money on your kids, on private education, don't hoard it. Have a nice house, invite your neighbours in regularly. Set yourself high standards, so that other people think, "I like that, I would like to be like that."'

But too many Muslims just sit back and complain, says Iqbal. 'The Muslim community needs more people like myself to get its views across. We can't always turn round to the local authority and say "it's your fault, your fault, your fault". The prophet Muhammad himself was a businessman, and there is no better example than him, his name was Amin, the truthful one. When any work was being done, he did it too. If it was building a mosque, he did it, if it was a battle he was involved in everything. Why is it up to the host community to provide us with jobs? To some extent we have done that. We employ thirty-two people, ten years ago you wouldn't have thought that a Muslim business could have so many people.'

British Muslims desperately need their own voice in the corridors of power, say Bradford community leaders such as Muhammad Ajeeb. When, in 1985, Ajeeb donned his ceremonial robes as Lord Mayor of Bradford, the first Asian – and

Muslim – to hold such a position, the city's Muslims glowed with pride, although many white locals were furious.

'I felt very honoured, very proud to achieve that, in a foreign country, I was from the first generation of immigrants,' says Ajeeb. 'Particularly coming from a country that was part of the British empire, where we were not regarded as equal human beings. Despite all these differences, prejudices, racist attitudes, I thought it was a remarkable achievement. Within the Muslim community and black community, they were elated. But within the white community there were mixed feelings. I got abusive letters, some very abusive.'

Now in his late fifties, Ajeeb arrived in Britain in 1957 from Kashmir. He trod the traditional immigrant's path, working for British Rail, and as a bus conductor, and has been an active Labour Party and union member for decades. He admits he has an eye on a possible seat in Parliament. 'When Muslims have their first MP it will be a watershed in British political history. It's vitally important the Muslim community gets a voice in British politics, every section of society should have representation. If you don't have any avenue to express your grievances or anxieties, other than lobbying, you feel disenchanted, left out, alienated, to the extent that you vent your frustrations on undesirable outlets such as riots. You become very bitter and the Muslims are no longer a tiny minority. They are the largest minority group within minorities. My major worry is that if marginalisation continues young Muslims will join Hizb-ut-Tahrir. I don't know who is advising the social planners up there in London, but in marginalising these minorities we shall be encouraging the extreme elements. My experience is that frustration ends in apathy or violence, there is no third outlet for it. We must not allow either.'

The Satanic Verses is still on sale. But Bradford's Muslims have notched up a significant political victory: over *halal* meat and Ray Honeyford, a Bradford headmaster who attacked the council's multi-cultural education policy and opposed the provision of *halal* meat for Muslim pupils. Honeyford went. *Halal* meat stayed on the menu. 'The *halal* campaign was a major victory. Muslims were ratepayers, tax-payers, they were entitled to some things they were not getting. They struggled for two or three years to get that right for their children. They couldn't understand why the council was not willing to provide the kind of meat that their children could eat. Any group of immigrants, such as the Jews, has to go through this struggle. Muslims are desperately trying to learn lessons from previous communities who have settled here in Britain.'

For now the buzz-words in Bradford and London, in mosques across the country, are 'British Muslims' and 'British Islam'. But Ajeeb, as always the far-sighted politician, is looking further ahead, to Europe. A common European home means one for Muslims as well, whether they are Bangladeshis in Bradford, Algerians in Amiens or Turks in Tubingen. 'The sense of being British, being English, is being eroded and once we become full members of Europe, that will become less and less significant and relevant. There will be new dimensions introduced into the concept of nationality, among those there will be Jews, Muslims, Hindus, Sikhs, so in that respect I don't think that the question of identifying truly with Britain will be inescapable,' he says.

'What we need to recognise as soon as possible, because the later we leave it the more problems we will face, is that Britain has become a multi-faith society. I use this word deliberately – it is irreversible – you cannot reverse it now. What are we going to do with these Muslims? Ethnic cleansing, like in Bosnia? We need to start from that recognition and then we can move on. That's why the Muslims are concerned. This is their country, they don't know any other country, if they want to fight for their rights they have to do it here, not in Palestine or Saudi Arabia.'

*French school students demonstrating for the right to
wear Islamic headscarves*

Chapter 6

FRANCE: THE DYSFUNCTIONAL FAMILY

'Liberté, Egalité, Fraternité' (Freedom, Equality, Brotherhood)
Slogan of the 1789 French Revolution

'France has two kinds of children, French children and Beurs [Arab] children but she doesn't want to recognise all her offspring, as though she had a bastard child.'
Nassera Sarah Oussekine, Paris-based feminist activist

Had I sat next to Mustapha Tougui on the Metro, as it snaked and rattled its way under Paris on the way to the city's main mosque, I would never have guessed that he was a lecturer there in Islamic theology. A sports teacher perhaps, or a musician, but not an expert on Islam, who has studied his faith everywhere from Saudi Arabia to Indonesia and translated the Quran. Tougui is quite pale-skinned, clean-shaven, eschewing the beard favoured by many Islamic radicals, and, indeed, looks like a slightly portly New York home-boy, with his blue baseball cap, white poloneck, furry thermal jacket and sports shoes. He is a very amiable man who smiles a lot and I imagine that he is a good teacher, for he has a pedagogue's gift for explanation. We met in the gardens of the Paris mosque, where twice a month on a Sunday morning he teaches the tenets of Islam to about 100 students, most of whom are from pure French, rather than north African, families, and who nearly all eventually convert to Islam.

A magnificent complex of mosque, school and courtyards that takes up most of a block in Paris's fifth *arrondissement*, the mosque was completed in the 1920s as a recognition of the contribution of the many Muslim, mainly north African, soldiers who fought in the French army during the First World War. It is a tranquil site, composed of several symmetrical courtyards with arched walkways that in the spring and summer are awash with verdant trees and shrubs, red and pink flowers and gently gushing fountains, a sort of mini-Alhambra. The ancient Islamic love of symmetry and geometry permeates the site, with its intricate arrangement of multi-coloured tiles that advance and retreat in patterns that are simultaneously rigid and linear, circular and flowing, symbolising and emphasising the unity of God. Just like the Alhambra, the Paris mosque complex is more ornate than the sparser mosques of the Arabian Gulf. It is a place of rest and worship, where both Muslims and those of other faiths can find a few moments' peace and tranquillity amid the bustle of modern-day Paris. Step inside the gate and you are transported to Fez or Marrakech or perhaps medieval Islamic Spain.

'All this work is by Moroccan artisans, they are specialists. If you go to Morocco it looks exactly like this,' Tougui explained as we examined the wooden cornices and inner coverings of the mosque and he pointed out the Quranic verses that have been carved into the panelling. The Paris mosque is built in the architectural tradition of Muslim north Africa, an area where several empires from Roman to Spanish have left their imprint. That mélange of cultures has produced something more intricate than the vast plains of the Arabian desert, says Tougui, with a different style of building. 'Morocco is a wet country, not a dry country like Arabia, it has water, trees and forests. The people there have a different style of life to the Bedouin people and you always behave like the place where you are. You have a look around you, at your surroundings. The mentality, the style of life, the mixture of people from the Arab world, Spain, the French, they all meet there.'

Talking to Tougui, who fluently expounds the doctrine of Islamic universalism, is an enjoyable and illuminating experience. 'The Quran is the synthesis of religion, not something new, a universal message for all people. You have absolute freedom to follow it or not. But as the Quran says, and the religions before it say, good deeds will bring their own rewards, and so will bad. Just as when you cross into a country, you have the right way and the wrong way, the long way and the short way, and you have very wide space to decide yourself which one to take,' he explained as we strolled through the gardens.

Born in Marrakech, Tougui, now 45, arrived in France over thirty years ago. Tougui is one of over four million Muslims in France, the largest Muslim minority in Europe, and the second biggest in the western world, after the United States. Unlike Germany, whose Turkish immigrants had no historical or cultural ties with their new homeland, most French Muslims were either born in France, or brought up in French colonial possessions in north and central Africa. They spoke French, understood French culture to a greater or lesser extent and felt ties of language and understanding. An Algerian who left Algiers for Paris after the war of independence in 1962, felt far more at home there than a Kurd transplanted from Diyabakir to Dortmund, or a Bengali who settled in Bradford.

In Algiers too, he could eat croissants for breakfast, read Albert Camus – himself born in Algeria – and drink *café au lait*, as well as thick Arabic coffee. France's Muslims felt an ambivalence, certainly, about the white European power that had ruled their countries, and helped itself to their riches, railroading their economies for its own benefit, but they also absorbed French ideas about liberty and social justice, the legacy of the 1789 revolution that still reverberates across the country today. But the immigrants' naive views of France were sorely tested when they arrived to work during the 1950s and 1960s. They were housed in ugly concrete developments on the edge of the great metropolises such as Paris and Marseilles, classic inner-city ghettos that soon deteriorated from neglect and isolation. The welcome that they hoped for did not materialise. Instead they found jibes and hostility, the sort of prejudice that would, in the late 1980s, boost the openly racist National Front. While Muslims in France have not suffered the physical attacks that Turks in Germany have endured, they must live in a country where the extreme right enjoys more electoral success than in any other developed European nation apart from Austria.

Tougui had been brought up a Francophile, in the tradition of that country's literature and culture, a land that claimed to be the home of human rights and human dignity. But it didn't seem that way when he arrived in 1966. 'It was the shock of my life when I came here for the first time. I was shocked at the reception. When I met French people in Morocco I received them very well, my family and my friends, like they were perfect people. When I came here they treated me like shit. It was everywhere. I can't give you an example because there are so many. They insulted you, completely insulted you. Now it's different, it's not better, I think it is worse, because they disguise it, before it was direct. They said all racist things, they call Arabs goats or rats. I was invited in by a family and the father couldn't resist from telling me that Morocco is full of rats. It meant I was one. The son, my friend, was very angry. He told me that his father was quite racist. These words give no dignity to the people who use them.'

As Tougui talked, an anger and resentment began to bubble to the surface and his voice tightened, the first manifestation of an almost-rage that I would sense or hear repeatedly as I travelled in France among its Muslims. It was the anger of a guest, in a house or a country, who is at first bemused, and then bitter that where he thought he would find a welcome, he encounters only hostility. 'I didn't come to France to get a job like a labourer. I have been to university, I can work everywhere. I chose this language from love, we came here for love. But we were very shocked when we came for the first time to see how people received us. They make a sort of advertisement in our country that Paris is the centre of the world, that French culture is most wonderful, just and perfect, democratic. But when you see the truth you are very disappointed, they talk in an opposite way on purpose about things at home. For example, about Islam, or customs in Morocco, when you come here the media turns everything upside down. In France they say when you are invited to a Moroccan family and you eat, you must burp. This is just rubbish. Or if they kill a lamb for you in your honour, they give you the eyes to eat, this is absolute rubbish, rubbish, a lot of rubbish. It is very harmful, because it's a little bit of rubbish here and a little bit there, and so it's more insidious.'

Now the media stereotypes – of bearded terrorist, or crazed fundamentalist – are more sinister than the former picture of eyeball-munching, burping Arabs, and their near-universal permeation across French society has disturbing implications for the lives of French Muslims. They affect everything from education and civil liberties to the simple freedom to build a mosque, the very idea of which drives provincial French politicians, who are happy for Muslims to carry out their town's dirty and menial jobs, into a collective frenzy. In Marseilles, for example, home to many hundreds of thousands of Muslims, there is not a single building that has been built as a mosque. Every Muslim place of worship there has been converted from a flat, shop or warehouse. Tougui, like most Muslims in France, is furious with the French media for their constant portrayal of Muslims as Islamic radicals who either wish to undermine the secular French state – that is based on the sacrosanct principle of separating church and state as a legacy of the 1789 revolution – or are planning a fresh campaign of bombings on the Paris Metro, such as the rash of attacks in autumn 1995.

That climate of hysteria, he believes, leads directly to the kind of physical attacks that several of his students have suffered. 'As you see I don't look very Arab or Muslim, so my life is not very miserable. But in the people who come to my lectures, three women have been stabbed on the Metro, just because they wear scarves, by normal people, not by thieves trying to rob them. They came with black eyes, people said to them you are Muslim and then boof! Another came with broken teeth. This is the media, the media who are responsible and the government as well. The media prints any rubbish, they say Muslims are the worst people in the world, Islam is the most horrible religion in the world, and you have stupid people with no conscience, no imagination, no instruction, no nothing and they think they are doing something good by attacking Muslims. I told them, when I saw these three women, I told them, it is the media who have stabbed you, not the others.'

At first I yawned inside when I heard this, for blaming the media for one's ills is an age-old past-time, and one that I, as a journalist, have heard many times and usually have little time for. I was told several times as I travelled in Paris and Marseilles that if I was a French journalist nobody would talk to me, particularly young people from the deprived urban satellite towns that are still home to many French Muslims of north African origin, who have suffered the brunt of misreporting. After just a few days in France I began to see why. Islam is an obsession for

France, an obsession stoked up by politicians and headline hungry reporters who feed off each other, creating a climate of intolerance and hysteria – it is no exaggeration to describe it thus – that I found nowhere else in Europe or America.

In the space of just a couple of weeks, in early 1996, I found the following special features on Islam on the newsstands. *Le Point*, a weekly news magazine, ran an eight-page story head-lined *'Islam en France, Les intégristes sapent la République'* (Islam in France, the fundamentalists are sapping the Republic), with other headlines inside such as *'L'Islam radical est une idéologie de combat'* (Radical Islam is an ideology of combat). *Courrier international*, a digest of translated articles from around the world, ran a special issue entitled *Islam, Occident: L'Affrontement* (Islam, the West, the confrontation), its cover design overlaid on a background of Arabic calligraphy. *Le Nouvel Observateur*, another news magazine, also ran an eight-page feature entitled *Ce que veulent les Musulmans* (What the Muslims want), although some of the articles were quite balanced. *Enquête sur l'histoire*, a historical magazine, had *L'Europe et L'Islam, un conflit séculaire* (Europe and Islam, a secular conflict) as its main story. And so it goes on, day after day, week after week, an extraordinary obsession with the supposed Muslim menace.

But in a strange way, the media's obsession with Islam is that religion's best recruiting agent. In France, like everywhere, people don't believe everything they read or see on television. Many of Tougui's students wonder about the truth that lies behind the headlines. 'Everybody talks about Islam, the media of course are over the top, so they want to know. This bad propaganda in some way is the best help for Islam. Of course it makes your life a bit miserable, but it helps. The people who come here are looking for truth, they are serious people. They are the sort of people who want to know what Islam is, whether it is good or bad. Nearly ninety-nine per cent convert to Islam. They say it is incredible when they learn what Islam is, they thought it was something else. The media talks about Islam like Muslims are just crazy, we are terrorists, extremists, whatever. But as Giscard d'Estaing said, if you want authenticity you have to look at the origin, the source, which for us is the Quran.'

Tougui, like many Muslims, believes that France's Islamophobia is just a more subtle form of racism. Blatant anti-Arab prejudice is no longer acceptable, so now it's masked as an analysis of Islam – with the conclusion that Muslims are a menace to France – a perspective that gives those views a spurious intellectual gloss. 'In South Africa, racism is now frowned upon, in America they try to disguise it as well, the world now doesn't accept racism because it doesn't look good. So they make the same record, they just turn it over on the other side, and when they want to say the same thing about Arabs, they use Islam. If they say Arab, it's directly racist, but if they say Islam it's something intellectual, something different, they can pretend it is some kind of analysis. But of course not everybody is the same. I still love this country, the people who made the culture here and I still have very nice and lovely friends in this country. They feel sorry about what the majority says.'

Tuogui now spends half his time in London, in Earl's Court, a lively multi-cultural area in the west of the city that is home to a myriad of different cultures and nationalities. The difference in attitude is palpable, he says, for while Muslims in Britain certainly have their problems, there is an attitude in London of live and let live. 'There is a very obvious difference between France and England, how they talk about Islam. In England, I don't care if the people look cold, but they are all right, they are not nervous, they are quite fair. They are respectful of everything. You can feel it straight away at the airport, even at British Airways, where I have my silver executive club card, I always advertise for British Airways. As you get in the airplane you can feel the different atmosphere. Then when you come to England you can see straightaway that people are very calm, fair, you respect yourself and respect others, and you can live in peace. People here are very surprised when I tell them that in Britain if you work in the post office or somewhere else you can wear a headscarf, they think it's impossible. The Sikhs have their turbans, when I saw that I said I feel very proud of Britain. Here it's like a horrible dream. France is a lovely country, with a lovely culture but the people, the media and the government make it like a hell.'

The Paris mosque is something of a family sinecure, in the

hands of the Algerian Boubakeur family since the establishment of the Muslim society in Paris in 1921 that collected subscriptions for the mosque's establishment. The mosque's first director was Si Hamza Boubakeur, the second is his son Dalil. Dr Boubakeur was formerly a medical practitioner and, sitting in his office under a large painting commemorating the mosque's establishment, he chooses a medical metaphor to describe the state of Muslim life in France. 'Islam in part of its life in France, is like a patient who has suffered and needs a convalescence, in its spiritual life, in its practice and its way of understanding with general society. The Islamic population has grown too fast in a country which was not prepared to receive such a great community in such a short time, but Islam has roots, legitimacy in France for a long time.'

Like Mustapha Tougui, Dr Boubakeur says the waves of Muslim immigrants into France, who arrived in France after Algerian independence, expected to adapt quickly to life in France. 'If an immigrant is from Sri Lanka, he does not know the mentality of French people and the way they think. But not in Algeria, so there was a natural installation. Then France saw that these populations were fixed, and needed things to live like schools and so on. So in the 1970s and 1980s a new problem arose when the immigrants became part of the French population. They are Muslims, and we have a role in their spiritual, religious and Islamic life. Their children are Muslim, they need mosques, religious leaders and spiritual guides, and that needed an attitude from the political authorities, to take a decision, to clarify its attitude towards these new problems in France.'

But French Muslims are still waiting for that decision, for a framework for them to live and organise within. The mosque is important, not just because of its location in the capital and subsequent prestige, but because it is one of the few Islamic institutions to be formally recognised by the French government. That lack of recognition has serious implications for France's Muslims as they struggle to legalise and protect their status along similar lines to the country's Jewish and Protestant minorities. Islam is now France's second religion, but there is no central Muslim organisation to run its affairs and negotiate with the government, a legacy of French officialdom's unwillingness to recognise the faith, but also of internal political and religious squabbles among French Muslims.

France's Muslims also want their religion to be officially recognised by the government with a formal concordat that would regularise its status and guarantee the civil rights of Muslims, says Dr Boubakeur. 'There are political reasons to make Islam something apart, there is a concordat with Jews and Protestants, but even now there is nothing with Islam. This mosque was built in 1922 under French law, there was a willingness then to give to Islam a structure. But that was 1922, and now it is 1996 and there has been no progress except this mosque. Many Muslims feel that Islam is considered not only the second religion, but as a secondary religion, and the authorities do not treat it equally. Take schools, there is an accord with other religions, to have schools, but with Islam there is nothing . . . In other countries in Europe, such as Britain or Germany, they have found an attitude of conviviality with Islam, with Muslims.'

But for all its pride of place as the public face of Islam in France, the Paris mosque is itself deeply controversial among France's Muslims. Many Muslims refuse to worship there because of the clashes of personality around its leadership and because of its strong north African emphasis. France's Turkish community, for example, more or less completely ignores the Paris mosque in favour of its own places of worship. Some Muslims decry Dr Boubakeur as a stooge of the French government, eager to do its bidding in return for power and prestige. Certainly he has his criticisms of the government, but he also has kind words to say about the right-wing minister of the interior, Charles Pasqua, the man whom many Muslims charge with infringing their civil rights and whipping up a nationwide anti-Muslim prejudice.

As the tempo of Algeria's civil war speeded up in 1994, and French casualties of the war lay dead next to Algerian ones, Pasqua ordered deportations, arrests and checkpoints to be set up in Muslim-dominated neighbourhoods in a police dragnet to catch suspected illegal immigrants. A whole community was labelled as potential terrorists, an image aided when French police proudly displayed a cache of arms they had discovered in a raid. Still, says Dr Boubakeur, Pasqua had an open mind

167

when it came to the problems of France's Muslims. 'He was a man open to understanding of Islamic problems. With him there was a beginning of an understanding. He accepted an accord of an Islamic organisation in France, that was the first time that a Muslim organisation came to the ministry and got official recognition. But we have now returned to ancient considerations. Perhaps it is secularism and perhaps the period of last year that changed something in the consideration of Islam in France. That was a very difficult period, and now there is a convalescence. The Muslims did not accept the situation, or violence, absolutely not. But there was a change in people's social and psychological attitude. Muslims found it more difficult to find work and extremists can have a new influence against Muslims.'

Dr Boubakeur's view of Charles Pasqua, as a friend of French Muslims, is met with hoots of derision by one north African worshipper at the mosque, so much so that he rushes to tell his friend and they laugh out loud, before making a series of claims about strange connections between the government and the mosque's administration. 'You cannot say worse rubbish than to say Pasqua is good for Muslims. He is a bully boy. If Muslims have the possibility to pray somewhere else, they don't put their foot here, because of these connections. Many people hate this place, but you live and you have to do your prayer and you have to do what you can.'

Two dates define the lives of Muslims in France: 14 July 1789 and 1 July 1962. The Bastille, the prison in the centre of Paris, was stormed on the former, arguably the start of the French Revolution, and on the latter, Algeria declared its independence. Few, if any, Muslims raced with the mob on that summer's day over 200 years ago, but its demands to be freed from royal tyranny and to separate church and state are now enshrined in the constitution, and are wheeled out in defence of the status quo whenever Muslims ask for their own civil rights, such as the legal freedom to wear headscarves at school.

For many French Muslims, the headscarf affair, as it became known, was a defining moment, confirming them as perpetual outsiders in French society and pushing them towards a more radical Islam that is less accommodating with life in the late twentieth century. The headscarf affair began in 1989 in the Paris suburb of Creil, when three Muslim girls were expelled for refusing to uncover their heads, and its repercussions still reverberate across France today. Their headmaster argued that wearing a veil contradicted the principle of separation of church and state and what began as a local row ballooned into a nationwide debate, about how France can accommodate Islam, and how Muslims can adapt to life in a secular country. In the tolerance corner were the then Socialist education minister Lionel Jospin, who argued for a dialogue with the pupils to persuade them to uncover, but said they should not be expelled for refusing to do so. 'Society has changed, today it is more pluralistic,' he said. He was supported by Danielle Mitterrand, wife of the late President, who supported the pupils, saying: 'If today the principle of secularism proved itself incapable of welcoming all religions, this would be a significant step backwards.' In the intolerant corner, were, of course, National Front leader Jean-Marie Le Pen; other socialists; and a whole slew of French intellectuals and media pontificators such as Bernard-Henri Levy, who would later enjoy much acclaim as the self-appointed voice of Bosnia's Muslims in France when the war erupted a few years later. There are, it seems, fashionable Muslim causes, in Sarajevo, and less fashionable ones, in the suburbs of Paris.

But even more than the legacy of 1789, it is France's history in north Africa that still hinders French Muslims as they struggle to get acceptance in the country they now call home. It is a history, say many Muslims, with which France has yet to come to terms. Like all the great European powers, such as Britain, Spain and Germany, France had colonies and spheres of influence abroad, hers mainly concentrated in north and central Africa and the Levant, in countries such as Lebanon and Syria. But France has yet to make a gesture of reconciliation for its annexation of a slice of north Africa, and nor is it likely to. The blow to national pride is too great, the scars too fresh.

Even so, beneath the mutual resentment between former colonial master and subject, a web of strong historical bonds links France and north Africa for ever. There are Arab restaurants on virtually every street in France, serving cous-cous and kebabs, usually to a background of Arabic music. Admittedly, eating foreign delicacies does not necessarily trigger a broader interest in its country of origin – Britain's legions of beer-swilling and vindaloo-guzzling lager louts are rarely avid readers of Hindu vedas – but for those interested in other lands, food can be a gateway into other cultures. On a more serious level, there is still a strong Arabophile streak in French intellectual life, as witnessed by the construction of the Arab World Institute in Paris. The Institute, a few minutes' walk from Notre Dame Cathedral, is, in the words of its brochure: 'A symbol of the partnership between France and twenty-one Arab countries, and aims to generate a dialogue between cultures that have been in frequent contact for centuries.' It is a remarkable building, light and spacious, whose southern façade is composed of an intricate web of steel shutters that open and close according to how brightly the sun shines, to let in and shut out light. The Institute also houses a print and video library and hosts cultural exhibitions that can draw hundreds of thousands of visitors, testament to an enduring interest in France in Arabic culture.

That tangled relationship began in earnest with Napoleon's occupation of Egypt in 1798, the start of a serious French presence in north Africa, and the first military invasion of the Middle East since the Crusades. Its repercussions are with us still. Writing in *The Arabs in History*, Professor Bernard Lewis says:

> Their rule in Egypt was of brief duration, but profound significance. It began the period of direct western intervention in the Arab world, with great economic and social consequences. By the easy victory which they won the French shattered the illusion of the unchallengeable superiority of the Islamic world to the West, thus posing a profound problem of readjustment to a new relationship. The psychological disorders thus engendered have not yet been resolved.[1]

French claims on north Africa peaked with the repeated assertion in the 1950s, which seems ridiculous now, but was then taken very seriously indeed, that, in the words of the late President Mitterrand, 'Algeria is France'. All around the world empires were dissolving and former colonies gaining independence, but not Algeria. Those three words still colour French attitudes to its Muslim community, for while Britain had its empire in India and Pakistan, it was never government policy to claim that these lands were actually part of Britain. For France though, Algeria, unlike Morocco or Tunisia, was a *département*, or rather several *départements*, of France itself. This idea, that a part of another continent was as French as Calais or Bordeaux, was fantastic in its conception – and the native Algerians took a rather different view – and perhaps it may have worked better if they had been granted full political rights. But they were not and the legacy of bitterness on both sides lives on, poisoning relations between Muslims and non-Muslims in France. Countries, like people, are traumatised by events in their lives, and many Muslims believe that French national anger at the loss of that country still determines its current attitudes to Islam and its Muslim minority.

The Algerian war of independence began in November 1954, organised in part by Muslim veterans of the French army who had fought in the Second World War. Like the conflict in Bosnia, it was a semi-civil war, between two sides who both claimed a common land, and it was a brutal affair, marked by atrocities and torture on both sides. The National Liberation Front (FLN) won, and set up an authoritarian socialist regime that was corrupt and economically inefficient. The war was a disaster for France. It divided the country politically, over whether to grant independence, it was socially divisive and it brought down the Fourth Republic, bringing to power Charles de Gaulle, who became the first president of the Fifth Republic. De Gaulle reached an accord with the FLN in spring 1962 and independence followed soon after. The *pieds-noirs*, French settlers, flooded into France, angry and bitter at their betrayal, for many had lost everything they had spent years building up in Algeria. Algeria's large Jewish community left as well, together with thousands of Muslim Algerians, who saw little future under the FLN's Marxist-orientated regime.

France's domestic politics are still shaped by events in its former possessions. Mainstream French politicians are happy to play the race card, partly to head off the challenge from the National Front, and partly because they know their constituents and which notes to play to summon up ancient communal fears of Islam, which is why Charles Pasqua, the hard-line interior minister, was put in charge of France's Algerian policy. The civil war in Algeria started in earnest in 1992, after the government cancelled the elections that the Islamic Salvation Front (FIS) was sure to win. Ever since, French governments have backed the military regime against the will of the people. The nightmare scenario in Paris is a takeover by FIS and the mass exodus of hundreds of thousands of Algerians to France. Xenophobia would rocket, as would support for the National Front. But however events play out in Algeria, its fate is locked to France's, because it has nowhere else to turn, says Serge July, editor in chief of the daily newspaper *Libération*. Writing in *Newsweek* he argued that, 'France cannot break with Algeria. Algeria cannot turn for help to any other European power. The French and Algerians are condemned to co-exist . . . France can never escape the inconvenience, the side effects, indeed the direct impact of the Algerian tragedy.'

The most direct impact of the Algerian tragedy was the wave of bombings that terrorised France in the summer and autumn of 1995. Eight people were killed and 170 hurt in the first terrorist attacks in Europe blamed on radical Islamists. The Armed Islamic Group (GIA), a split-off of the FIS, reportedly claimed responsibility for the bombings. The communiqués attributed to it demanded that President Jacques Chirac convert to Islam and then vowed to continue the campaign of attacks until 'Islam has triumphed in France', a vow accompanied by a map showing the Eiffel Tower exploding. The attacks were greeted with horror by the overwhelming majority of French Muslims, both because they utterly opposed the loss of life and because they knew that the bombings were yet another setback in their struggle for acceptance. Not all believed that the GIA was responsible. Many Muslims saw the hand of the Algerian secret services, which maintain active networks among France's north Africans, in the attacks.

As one north African told me: 'These bombs originate from the special services. They manipulate people to do it. It's quite funny, but all these bombs went off just before the Algerian presidential election, and once the dictator was confirmed in power, they stopped, just like that. Every Muslim thinks this and even some of the media have said it. They need something like these bombs to justify their war against us, that they have to fight against the "Islamic monster".'

Certainly there are strange events occurring among France's Algerian community, such as the murder in a Paris mosque of Sheikh Abdelbaki Sahraoui, the 85-year-old co-founder of the FIS. And then there was the Kelkal affair. Khaled Kelkal, a 24-year-old Algerian, was shot dead by police in a village outside Lyon after a three-day manhunt. His fingerprints had been found on an unexploded bomb on the Paris–Lyon railway line. Police claimed that he opened fire first and so was killed by them in self-defence. Perhaps he did, but the shooting was filmed by the independent French television channel M6. The end of the crew's film showed Kelkal lying wounded on the ground, while an unidentified voice shouts, 'Finish him off, finish him off!' followed by Kelkal pointing his pistol. Shots ring out and a voice says: 'OK, it's good,' and the camera shows his dead body. That last part, that to many smelled of execution rather than arrest, was edited out of the segment broadcast on the news.

For France's Muslims all roads lead to Algeria, but I could not go there, as journalists are regularly targeted for killing in that bloodied land. So I went instead to the next best place, to Marseilles. I took the TGV train as it raced down the spine of France and transported me from chic metropolitan Paris to the ocean, to a city where the spirit of north Africa, its smells, tastes and languages hang heavy in the salty sea air. Marseilles is on the other side of the Mediterranean to Algeria, but the same ocean laps at the beaches of both countries, for the city is the doorway to both France and north Africa. Here, in tiny garrets on the steep, sloping backstreets, homesick Muslim exiles listen to Algerian radio and save for satellite dishes to watch the television news from home. In the villages nearby, their Christian counterparts, the *pieds-noirs*, do the same, except their dreams are of the businesses and estates that they lost and of the homes they were forced to flee when the FLN came to power.

Like all ports Marseilles is a tough town, where life is lived a little bit harder and a little bit faster than in the sleepy villages and holiday resorts nearby. It is home to a myriad of immigrant communities, from every former French possession from the

Antilles Islands to Algeria. Step off its main streets and into the Arab quarter and you are transported out of clean, antiseptic, ordered 1990s Europe, almost straight into the Middle East. And where there are Arabs taking a coffee, there are often policemen, stiff and unsmiling in their blue uniforms, standing and watching with their pistols at their sides. Halal butchers brandish cleavers as they hack at lamb carcasses, Arab music drifts from the tiny cafés and gaggles of men sip tiny cups of thick Arabic coffee. This is not the tourist's south of France, and the price of an Orangina on the beach at Nice will here get you a blow-out meal of cous-cous and lamb washed down with a few glasses of rough *vin de table*. Plush yachts bob up and down in the docks of the old port, but it is the creaking ships that ply the route from here to Algiers that are the city's lifeblood. The boat ride to Algiers from Marseilles takes twenty-four hours, the ferries ploughing across the ocean an aquatic link in the umbilical cord that even now binds Algeria to its former master.

For Ramzi Tadros, who works at the city's foreigner reception centre, Marseilles is the bridge from France to north Africa, and neighbouring countries. 'Marseilles is the gate between north Africa and Europe. If Marseilles cut its links with north Africa it would be a dead city.' The centre, which opened in 1977, is often the first port of call for bemused north Africans when they arrive in Marseilles. It provides legal help, a library and organises cultural events.

Its work is not always welcomed and it has been bombed several times, says Tadros, although nobody was charged with the attacks. Its clients' problems have changed over the years. 'Ten years ago it was to find somewhere to live, to learn French. Now we see the problems of the children of the first generation, who have the same difficulties as every young person in this town, to find work and to find their place in society, but that is very difficult. In most [French] people's minds to be an Arab is to be a Muslim, and to be a Muslim or a fundamentalist is the same thing. Everywhere young Muslims are told that they are fundamentalists, and they see that apparently the only people that are moving, or fighting, the West or the Christians are the fundamentalists. So it becomes a self-fulfilling prophecy. The problem is all the racist propaganda that has won plenty of people in France, but especially in this region.'

One reason for the high support for the National Front is the many *pieds-noirs* who live in Provence, says Tadros. 'They have long histories in Algeria, they had difficult lives there, they lost everything, so the National Front has easy support among them. They say, "The Algerians wanted us to leave Algeria, so we did, but now they want to come here because of the problems there, so let them stay where they are." But the idea that France is white and Catholic is not only a nonsense, it is using social and economic problems for political reasons, without knowing reality. They know that in the areas where there are social and economic problems it is very easy to say that the problem comes from these foreigners, and if we eliminate these foreigners it will eliminate the problems. It is easy and they use it. But in France one quarter of the population has somebody in his family, grandparents, that is foreign, Spanish, Italian.'

As a Palestinian, Ramzi understands the reality of exile and starting anew in a different land. He is a thoughtful man, who knows well the problems of the Muslim community in Marseilles, although he himself is an atheist, born into a non-Muslim Arab family. So what, I asked him, would he say to the *pied-noir* argument that Algerians have made their bed and should lie in it? 'To that I say that France stayed for one hundred and thirty years in Algeria. There are plenty of relations with Algeria and the Algerians, the language, the history, the economy, all these years and interventions. France transformed Algeria, in every way. If you go there you see the small villages were turned into French villages, the economy was turned to serve the French economy, producing wine and things that were used for France. The whole social and cultural structure of Algeria was adapted for France, more than in Tunisia or Morocco. There was never colonisation in other countries like in Algeria. I think it was an error to think this, to try to transform the whole country into a French *département*.'

Tadros, like many Arabs living in France I spoke to, argues that the very idea of a national, homogenous France is a relatively new idea, and one belied by the regional identities of areas such as Brittany in the north, and even Provence itself in the south, both of which still boast their own dialects and different cultural traditions. So France's Muslims are merely the latest tile in the ethnic mosaic, the argument goes. 'For a country that says it is the place where human rights were first established it's time now for France to build another type of human rights. This is a multi-cultural society, not only with Muslims and Arabs, but with Bretons and Basques. This must be the place to have new ways of thinking about citizenship. We are citizens of a world that is changing. When you accept people from north Africa to come and work in your country you must also accept them with their families, with their sons and daughters, with their culture and their religion.'

Acceptance yes, but France's Muslims want more than that. The key word that I heard repeatedly was 'respect'. Respect for their culture, respect for their religion and respect for them as human beings and not to be denied jobs, a flat, even a policeman's basic civilities because of their different religion. But there is not much respect for human values in places like Bassens in Marseilles, where Malik BenMessaoud grew up. The concrete jungle of Bassens was a dumping ground for the droves of Algerian immigrants brought to France during the 1950s and 1960s. Its inhabitants, a mixture of north African families and Gypsies, struggle to keep a sense of community, but that's difficult when the shops and school have closed and the city administration ignores the quarter's requests for aid, say locals.

BenMessaoud is a quiet, gently spoken 26-year-old, a street kid turned sculptor, but his body is hard and wiry and the muscles on his back and arms flex visibly as he moves. I would not like to see him angry, for there is rage as well as art in his soul. He was working in his studio in La Friche, an old tobacco factory turned arts centre, when we met, a cavernous site home to pop groups, theatre companies and musicians. He was building a model of a Citroën DS car, part of his project called Bassens Support Cité 1, its theme partly based on the mental and physical separation between Bassens and the rest of Marseilles. The choice of the Citroën DS represents the era of the Algerian war, he says, as well as the endemic car thefts that plagued Bassens when he was growing up there. 'The others in Marseilles have no idea about our lives. Bassens too has turned in on itself and made a closed community. We are not respected but we want to be able to express ourselves and to be listened to, to understand why things have happened this way. Now I have opportunities that I didn't have before and there are a lot of people whose potential is not being realised. Everyone has it, they are enraged and they have a message to get across.'

BenMessaoud is a believing Muslim, although not a very observant one. Islam for him is a set of ethical guidelines that governs the way he lives his life, rather than a set of strict rules. His girlfriend is Jewish, for unlike in Britain close friendships, love affairs, even marriages, are commonplace in France between Jews and Muslims. The film of life in a Parisian version of Bassens, *La Haine* (hate), which won best director award at Cannes in 1995, has three multi-racial heroes: Said, an Arab, Vinz, a Jew and Hubert, an African. *La Haine*, shot in black and white, is a gripping but deeply depressing slice of life in an inner-city ghetto where racism, violence, drugs and police brutality are daily occurrences. The events that might occur over a few weeks in real life are telescoped into one night for dramatic appeal, but most French Muslims I spoke to told me that its underlying perspective of despair, alienation and *La Haine* itself was accurately portrayed. Indeed, a report compiled by police intelligence units in 1995 warned that as many as 200 inner-city neighbourhoods suffered from 'extremely high levels of insecurity'.

BenMessaoud has found himself as a sculptor. As a child he dreamt of becoming an artist but never really believed it would be possible. *La Haine is* subsiding, slowly. 'Today, through this project, I am respected. Respect is very important. If I go somewhere to ask questions, I get answers.' Islam too, he says, gives him a moral and spiritual grounding as well a framework for his art. 'There is no sexual representation in my work, or portrayals of violence. I believe that sex is very personal and not something to be spread about. My religion gives me limits, culturally and morally. It's good because I have principles to work with and a framework to work in.'

A mile or so from the paint-spattered artists of La Friche lives Kamel Khelif, a friend of BenMessaoud. He is an artist who draws graphic novels. His work is dark and shadowy, vivid and detailed, but somehow gloomy, perhaps a bit like his life itself, I imagine, with pictures of men reading letters from home with lonely faces, smoking cheap Spanish cigarettes. 'Ah, yes, Malik, he has the rage,' says Khelif, as he makes a coffee in the tiny kitchen of his top-floor flat in Marseilles' Arab quarter. His flat is a sparsely furnished attic, an artist's residence, where drafts of future strips and finished illustrations are piled up on his desk. Critical acclaim is growing for Khelif's work, especially since the publication of his graphic novel *Homicide*, and he proudly shows me a letter from a professor at Miami University who wishes to meet him.

Together with his family Khelif arrived in Marseilles thirty years ago and, like BenMessaoud, he grew up in Bassens. 'There is a lot of hate on both sides in the suburbs, this hate is what they suffer, racism, rejection. A human being cannot see himself in the mirror and like himself because he has been rejected that much, so they become aggressive and start a war.'

At school Khelif's teachers told him he would never be an artist, so he trained instead to be a mechanic, before studying industrial design. 'For my parents, for the people in Bassens, being a graphic artist means nothing,' he said. 'When I decided to draw again, I drew the boat, it's my oldest memory. I will always remember the sentence that my mother whispered to me one night, "We are going". And then the voyage, what a voyage, I especially remember the smell of the ocean and the noise of the sheep and cows. My family and other families were together with livestock.'

Khelif is now working on a new project with a writer of Algerian origin, about the civil war there, but using symbolism instead of the television images of Islamic radicals and armed soldiers. 'There are two stories, one set in Algeria in 1968 and one in Marseilles in 1995, so it will be a double story. The main character imagines that the bees are coming out of the floor, a cockroach is walking on the wall, and it walks into his mouth. It's set in 1968 but this is what is happening in Algeria now, with the bombings and the extremists, that's the cockroach. It's telling in an indirect way, I don't draw people with beards and military uniforms, but I express it in a different way. It's very important for me what happens in Algeria.'

That same anger and rage that permeates the concrete suburbs of Paris and Marseilles, Lille and Lyon festers in the bazaars and tenements of Algiers, says Khelif, and is the best recruiting agent for radical Islam. 'The FIS is a long story and very complicated. But it's not the same story as in Iran or Saudi Arabia. The FIS was extremely popular in Algeria, because the leaders are not giving lectures in universities but in the street, like the National Front here, they are the ones who have contact with people. It's not just politics, it's also about hate. In both France and in Algeria young people feel hate. In Algeria 18- to 25-year-olds represent over two thirds of the population and when they have no hope of work and nothing else to occupy them, they live in a cultural *misère* [misery]. So they dream and you need to dream, not just to go to work at a factory, because we can do other things, we have other qualities. And all of this hate is expressed politically through the FIS, because the other parties are not representative, they are only interested in the élites.'

Khelif once said that he had never been to a chic place, unlike Sadia Ayata. I met her in a café in central Paris, a typically Parisian scene as we talked in the bustle of a busy morning with shoppers and office workers popping in for a quick coffee or beer. If there is an educated Muslim élite in France, then Ayata is part of it. Born in Algeria, she is a journalist who speaks fluent French, Arabic and English. For many years she returned with her family for two or three months.

'It was something inestimable for me to go there, because I understand something of my own past. I don't feel any rupture with my history, I know exactly who I am. When people talk about integration I feel very well integrated. The problem is the French people who don't want to integrate me. When I was young and we lived in the suburbs of Paris, it was mostly French people who didn't want to speak with my mother. I am a Muslim. I don't go to the mosque, but for me Islam is not only religion, it is part of a culture, but I feel Muslim anyway, for me it is part of my heritage, of my parents' roots, of a kind of *Weltanschauung*, a world-vision. My father was not religious, although my mother prayed, but both kept Ramadan, and for a long time I kept it as well. The way I feel, the way Islam influences my vision is how tolerant I am of other people, I accept them. At home in Algeria everyone was welcome. But here I always had the feeling that French people can never forget the past. They are trying to find something to prove that you are under them, that you are an Arab, or something.'

179

As well as knowing herself, Ayata also knows her civil rights, knowledge that was to prove extremely useful when she was arrested in a case that has since turned into a Muslim *cause célèbre*. For there are two Parises in France. The first is the tourists' metropolis of Robert Doisneau posters of kissing couples, the Eiffel Tower, and the *Mona Lisa*. The other is the Paris inhabited by north African Muslims. They may be physically the same streets and squares, but they live and work in a place where harassment by police is a daily reality and where racism and Islamophobia breed hate and hostility. On a hot summer's morning in August 1994, while waiting for a bus with her sister, Sadia Ayata found herself in the second Paris.

It was the time of Pasqua's crackdown, soon after several foreigners had been murdered in Algeria. Ayata had just returned from Berlin and was shocked at the number of policemen and women on Paris's streets. A few feet away policemen were checking a north African's identity. 'I started to speak with my sister about how the controls are always on north Africans, just because they have a darker face and are recognised. The control was finished but the policeman stayed and heard what I was saying to my sister, he told me to shut up. I told him that I was not speaking to him, that we were in a democracy and I was just expressing my opinion, I was not insulting him. It doesn't interest me to insult the police. Then he got nervous, pushed me and he wanted to search me. I told him to stop and said I preferred to be searched by his colleague, who was a woman. He called the police station and they sent a car. He asked me for my papers and I gave him my identity card. He showed me a card saying that the police can take anyone who is making a disturbance on the street.'

Ayata was arrested and taken to the police station in handcuffs. Her sister started calling French human rights organisations, who in turn telephoned the police station, driving the station chief into a fury. 'He went completely crazy with anger, asking me who I thought I was, and so on, he told me he was a *pied-noir* and he said, "I will take care of you personally".' Ayata groaned inside at this news, but held her ground when she was charged with 'committing an outrage against the police'. She demanded to see a doctor and was carted off with six policemen as an escort, again in handcuffs.

When she returned to the station she was interrogated about her religious beliefs. 'They asked me if I was a Muslim, if I was a practising Muslim, if I was for or against the Islamists. When he asked me if I was a Muslim I said: "If I say to you that I am a Muslim, you will think that I am an Islamist. If I say no then you will say that I don't even respect my own religion." He asked me if I put ham in my sandwich, I told him it was not his business what I have in my sandwich. When he asked me if I was for or against the Islamists, I told him that in the place where I was, I could only say I was against them. I kept my sense of humour, it's the only weapon you can keep.'

After six hours Ayata was released in a daze, at first unable to believe what had happened to her. 'I was really shocked. I didn't know which country I was living in any more. I wondered what was happening if they arrest me and hold me for six hours for just saying that, what will they do with others, someone from the suburbs? That was my great worry. I know how to speak French, how the system works, but what about the other young people who don't know their rights, who feel alienated, who feel uncomfortable in French society? Luckily I was not hurt, I didn't slip over in the police station. A lot of things happen like that. I can understand how some people come to hate the system.'

Ayata's case came to court on 15 November 1994. She was found guilty. 'It's a small crime, but it's a way to identify people, so when they pick up someone, they put the pressure on them and they have their name in the computer. At the trial Madame Mendès-France [widow of the former French president] came as a moral witness. I was fined 4,000 Francs, I appealed immediately. In June 1995 I had the appeal. I spoke at the stand, I said that a whole community could not be charged with events happening outside France, there are other means to fight against violence. I won the appeal on the basis of freedom of speech, in the universal declaration of human rights.'

But *La France* does not take defeats from young Algerian French women so easily and the police appealed against the appeal, setting the stage for a lengthy legal battle. Should Ayata win, then it will set a legal precedent and boost citizens' rights over police powers. 'If they find me guilty, they should not be surprised at all the shit that is going to happen. People will not respect the law and the police. I am adult enough to fight this case with papers, but if I was not I would become crazy, because what else can I have, what opportunity? I know the mind of the people in the suburbs, I know who they are in their minds, I know how despairing they are.'

For Ayata, her case has disturbing historical overtones. 'Fifty years ago the identity controls on Jews started like this, and nobody said anything. I didn't compare the French police to the Nazis, I just remember the facts. Anti-Semitism is not acceptable anymore, so the Muslims are the new scapegoat. People think that because I am a Muslim I am against Jews, but I have many Jewish friends, I am always interested in discussing with them how deep must be their wounds to have been so integrated in society and then start to be exterminated. I have a very good friend, when he was twelve he was in the subway with a yellow star on his jacket and he had to hide it, to go through the police controls. So now I wonder if there is the possibility to say to the police, "you are doing something wrong", if a citizen can interfere in this, not to insult them but say, "hey, come on, what are you doing, you are obeying rules that are not good". If there had been this possibility to intervene then, probably those things could not have happened and also those things today could not have happened.'

Sadia Ayata left the police station in one piece. Nassera Sarah Oussekine's brother did not survive his encounter with the Parisian forces of law and order. Malik Oussekine was beaten to death in December 1986 by three policemen after leaving a jazz club. He was 22, couldn't speak Arabic and he hoped to be a Jesuit priest, but his last, fatal, mistake was to be on the streets while students were demonstrating, for some French policemen always enjoy the chance to crack a few Arab heads.

'The cops were supposed to follow the demonstration on their motorbikes, but they left the route just to beat up some Arabs. Two of them were sent to prison for two years,' she says. Her brother's death changed her life, and her view of France, for ever. 'Until then I lived normally, I was working, I went home, I wanted to be happy, professionally, mentally, to have any kind of happiness. That day I realised that I was living in a racist country. We always talk about integration, but we are integrated, my roots are here in France, I was born in Paris, not in Algeria, so what more do they want? But they always remind us that we are different, that we are not from here, even if we are. In France racist crime is quite frequent, when the cops kill somebody from north Africa they are not really punished for it. It legitimises racist crimes.'

I met Oussekine in a municipal youth centre in the suburb of St Denis, in north-east Paris, where on streets nearby a soup kitchen doles out free meals to the poor and Arabic is spoken as frequently as French. She is one of the leaders of Nana Beurs, a feminist organisation for women of French-Arab background. Nana is slang for women, or chick, and Beur means Arab, of the second generation, born in France, and the word is a corruption of 'Arab' said backwards. French slang is now peppered with Arabic words, especially in the suburbs – *baraka* means luck; *fatma* a girl; and *clebs* a dog. Nana Beurs was giving a party, and we munched on slices of bread and pâté, washed down with kir or white wine.

The group was founded a decade ago by women who took part in the March of the Beurs, a mass demonstration for racial equality. But the question of sexual equality in the French-north African community had somehow been ignored. Their slogan, *Nana Beurs Il Faut Pas Sharia* (Nana Beurs don't need the *Shariah*) is a pun on the French saying *Il Faut Pas Charier,* meaning let's not go over the top. 'The needs of women were not taken into account during the march. The question of auton-omy is very important for young Beur women who want to be independent. They are completely dependent on a residence card from a husband, and if a man gives it back, the woman has to as well. After the march of the Beurs, they obtained a ten-year visa and that was a relief because they can relax. Racism affects all of us, but sexism only the women, they have pressure from outside, racism, and inside the home, because of their sex. They are educated in a particular way, they are watched over constantly. This is a result of living in a patriarchal society. Islam does not have a monopoly on sexism, even Buddhism is the same.'

As she grew up Oussekine was inspired by the works of Simone de Beauvoir. 'She influenced me very much. There were many problems that I encountered in society and I didn't realise why, and then I read the *Second Sex*, but she deals with every class of women, bourgeois, workers, they all have the same problems as women. We have had hostility among the Beurs because we are secular, and we criticise religion in general and people don't like that and we push women's rights. Also we are from modest backgrounds, so of course there is always some kind of judgmental attitude. We criticise our religion and some aspects of Arab culture, not all of it, but everything in it related to women we strongly criticise. We are opposed to headscarves, because wearing one is not always a voluntary decision. The media are obsessed with this, they make it worse, they are always searching for a sensation.'

Whether they are artists or activists, journalists or teachers, France's Muslims are bringing an extra dimension to the country that they think of as home, but which has given them such a haphazard welcome, if welcome is the word. They ask to be considered humanely, as people, and for some understanding from the country that colonised Muslim lands for many decades, but now refuses even to guarantee the rights of French Muslim schoolgirls to cover their heads at school.

The headscarf affair was a turning point in the evolution of France's relationship with its Muslim minority. For many Muslims, it confirmed that they are forever destined to be *les étrangers* in French society, marginalised and discriminated against. It shook the very bedrock of French society, questioning the nature of the relationship between religion and the state, and bringing home, perhaps for the first time, the fact that France was home to several million Muslims, many of whom had different values and ideas to the Catholic majority.

The case was eventually referred to the Conseil d'Etat, France's highest court, which was asked to rule on whether the wearing of religious symbols was compatible with secularism. It fudged, saying that while 'in principle' it was not incompatible, anything which amounted to 'provocation, proselytism, or the undermining of the liberty or dignity of a pupil' could legitimately be banned. It was left to individual headmasters to decide. Finally, in the autumn of 1994, the right-wing then education minister, François Bayrou, issued a ruling that Muslims saw, quite understandably, as directly targeting them. Bayrou ruled that 'ostentatious' religious symbols were forbidden, but 'discreet' ones were permitted. Headscarves were ostentatious, crosses and skullcaps were discreet. Muslim organisations were quick to denounce the decision, and even the normally august newspaper *Le Monde* gave space to one of its columnists who asked, reasonably enough, 'Who is to decide what is discreet and what is ostentatious? What authority decides that the wearing of a cross, a *kippah* [skullcap], a Shield of David or a crescent is acceptable, but not a headscarf?'

I heard stories in the wake of the ban of north African schoolchildren refused entry to school for wearing T-shirts with the word 'Algeria' emblazoned on it in Arabic. Of course their peers, wearing clothes covered in logos proclaiming 'USA' have never had any problems. It seemed to me that if the very basis of the French republic was threatened by a few headscarfs – for only a tiny minority of schoolgirls wished to wear one anyway – then that mighty state was a very fragile edifice indeed.

Perhaps the last word should go to Ramzi Tadros, working on the front-line in Marseilles, where the two cultures meet and, sometimes, clash. I asked him if he was optimistic or pessimistic about the future of France's relationship with its Muslims. 'Like what is happening between Israel and the Palestinians, you cannot choose between optimism and pessimism. You must try and determine the outcome of things, and declare that another way can be found. We must do everything to get this good relationship, it will not be easy but we must do it. A good relationship is an equal one. Without saying that everything is wonderful, but to look at things like they are. If there is fundamentalism, there are reasons for it, let's talk to the Arabs and Muslims that are against it. Let's see what can be done, and not give lessons to other countries and people. If you want the second and third generation to respect French laws, you must show them that they are respected. This is the way to integrate. There is no other.'

Arrest of a Turkish demonstrator in Solingen, Germany

Chapter 7

GERMANY: THE RISE OF THE EURO-TURKS

'Hey ho house, we're neither liars, nor naturalised Germans, nor foreigners. We're just guest worker kids.'
Berlin Turkish rap band Islamic Force

'The Chancellor does not engage in condolence tourism.'
Helmut Kohl's spokesman, replying to calls for Kohl to visit the site of the Solingen arson attack, where five Turkish women were killed in May 1993

It was in a hot and smoky Kreuzberg bar in November 1988, a full year before the fall of the Berlin Wall, that I first heard the siren sound of pan-German nationalism. A clarion call for unity which, when it resounded across that then divided land, would have tragic consequences for Germany's Turkish community.

Now, as then, Kreuzberg, tucked away by the old border between east and west Berlin, is a bohemian mix of Istanbul and Islington, the trendy north London suburb. Veiled Turkish women queue for food next to grungy punks in the shops and small restaurants selling Turkish snacks. Smoky cafés are filled with Turkish men – there are no women inside – drinking tea and coffee and playing backgammon. The Wall is long gone and the nearby former border crossing for foreign trucks has become just another municipal crossroads, but the vibrant counter-culture that brought young rebels here from all over West Germany remains.

And from Turkey too, for as the immigrant community grew, the first political exiles arrived. Posters advertising a plethora of Turkish communist parties and leftist movements plaster Kreuzberg's walls, complete with stencilled pictures of Mao Tse-Tung or Lenin and clenched fists. Kreuzberg's Turkish communists still keep Marxist iconography alive. The two cultures – one German, western, green and tinged with anarchism; the other Muslim and mostly conservative – live tolerantly side by side, although separately. I have been to Berlin many times and have several friends in Kreuzberg, all young and liberal, but none of them ever introduced me to a Turkish speaker.

But back to that bar: we were chatting to Gerhard, a typical young left-wing Berliner, with a bottle of Beck's beer clasped in his hand, about the Wall and East Germany. Would it always be there? Suddenly his eyes opened wide and he declaimed: 'We were one country once. Just think what we could achieve if we were united again. Just think about it!' he said excitedly, waving his beer about.

I thought about it and I didn't like it. To me it sounded pretty ominous. If this was what they were dreaming of in Kreuzberg, capital of Germany's radical counterculture, then what were they hoping for in the small towns and villages of Bavaria and Saxony? A Germany free of foreigners, especially non-white or Muslim ones, it seemed over the next couple of years, as television screens filled with pictures of charred houses in Mölln and Solingen, weeping Turkish relatives of arson-attack victims, and the screaming faces, contorted with hate, of a German mob, as it attacked a foreigner's asylum in Rostock.

But for every action there is an equal and opposite reaction. The more the nationalists demanded that foreigners leave, the more young second-generation Turks said no, we are staying and we demand the same rights as you Germans. And now that's the message pounded out by Boe B, lead singer with the Berlin Turkish rap band Islamic Force. Boe B, whose real name is Bulent Ipek, says he wants to provoke people, and judging by the scars on his forehead he's succeeded several times. He's been in gang fights and had a violent tussle trading blows with the Berlin police. But Boe wants to put his sometimes violent past behind him and the only confrontation he seeks is an intellectual one, forcing Germans to accept the country's Turkish minority, almost two million strong, and grant them the same rights of citizenship and cultural freedom as their German peers.

Just as black rappers in America use pounding music as an expression of their identity, Berlin's Turkish youth have taken to the recording studio to get their message across: that, unlike their parents, they won't say 'please, sir' any more, because they are in Germany to stay. I met Boe at a party at Ypsilon Musix's recording studio in the Wedding district of West Berlin, celebrating the label's first birthday in June 1995. Back in the 1930s this workers' area was a stronghold of the Communist party, and was known as Red Wedding. But now, like much of inner-city Berlin, its dilapidated apartment blocks are home to Turks and their fellow guestworkers from a dozen countries, as well as plenty of gloomy Berliners dressed in the obligatory black.

The smell of spicy kebabs sizzling on the barbecue drifted through the studio as we spoke, and there were frequent offerings of ever more food and drink, for Turks, perhaps especially those living in Germany, are proud of their tradition of hospitality. The members of Islamic Force mix western and Turkish chords together, creating a new musical style that draws on its members' dual heritage as German-born, but of Turkish background. As an Alevi, whose version of Islam is far more relaxed than the Sunni one, Ipek seems an unlikely figurehead for a Muslim-inspired musical protest, but Islamic Force has more to do with rap music than mosques, he says. 'We are Turkish rappers, but we didn't want a name like the Turkish Posse or something like that because it sounds like a gang. Islamic Force comes from Afrika Bambaata's example, to show people where we are coming from. I'm an Alevi, I believe in Allah but I don't go to the mosque. I drink beer. The name aims to provoke people.'

Unlike many black American rappers, who extol a culture of violence and automatic weapons, Islamic Force calls for a peaceful change. 'Some other groups, they get on stage and rap in Turkish, they wear baggy trousers, but we don't live like that. They want to be black, and I don't understand why, those guys are shooting each other. They are like killers and gangsters and we are not killers or gangsters. That's what I hate. My mother listens to my music, she hears every new song that I make. I make songs that my mother can hear, I don't use words like "fuck".'

Born in Istanbul, Ipek arrived in Germany in 1979. The move from the Bosphorus, with its easy-going chaos and strong family life, to the Prussian orderliness of Berlin, and the formality of German culture, triggered a major culture shock, one that Ipek clearly has yet to come to terms with. 'It was hard coming here, because in Istanbul I had all my friends. The biggest problem was that it was a different atmosphere, the air, the people. When you are a kid in Istanbul and you come home from school and your parents aren't there, you sit on the steps of the house and the neighbours see you, they take you in, they feed you, and everything. When I was here, and I came home from school, I sat and waited and so many people passed by and nobody said anything. The Turkish neighbours were also like the Germans, because they learned it from them, to be closed. I think I will go back to Turkey. It's too cold here, not just the weather, the people, everything.'

Ipek has a son by a German woman, but says he barely gets to see him. 'I got a little kid, that's my son, but she don't want to show him to me because I was in trouble so much. That's what she can say against me, "Hey, he's a bad guy and I don't want him around my son", but that's not the real reason, the reason is she's cold, cold like the weather.'

But if Ipek wants to go home, Unal Yuksel, one of the founders of Ypsilon Musix record label, which has signed up Islamic Force, is definitely staying. For a start he was born in Berlin in 1969 and it's his hometown. Together with many young Turks, he is in the vanguard of creating something new and unique in Europe: a hybrid Turkish-German culture, a fitting evolution for a generation caught between Berlin and Istanbul, but neither wholly German nor Turkish. 'I take German culture from the street, and I take Turkish culture from the home, from my parents, so it's a mixed culture. From home I take religion, my character and my language, but character and language also from the streets, so this mix comes into the music as well, you make music that is mixed, it's music from a minority. But you need time for this, Turkish people have only been here for thirty years.'

The songs' lyrics make several simple points, says Yuksel. 'We are living here in Germany and I like Germany. My father has worked here for thirty years. My message to the Germans is that when you want to you can live with me, when you don't want to it's not my problem, it's your problem. The Turkish people have said to the Germans for thirty years: "We are also people, let us live together, please." But I don't want to say please. I am a human being here, I work here, I live here, I speak the same language. I feel something, although not the same as you [Germans] feel. I can't live in Turkey, so if I can't live in Germany, where can I live? But I don't say please. This is the message. The first generation cannot speak good German, but the second generation is more confident. They say we want this, this and this, and we don't want this. The first generation wants to make money and go back to Turkey. But that is not my problem, to make money and go back to Turkey. My problem is to stay here, make money and live here. What can I do in Turkey?'

What Yuksel can do in Berlin is run what he says is the first professional Turkish studio and record label in Germany, a venture promoting a new style of music that is getting increasing attention from major international companies such as Sony and PolyGram. 'There are differences between our music and Turkish music. The music that we make here is the music for the second generation and the problems of the second generation. The problems that we have here are not the same problems that they have in Turkey. I am twenty-five and people in Turkey who are twenty-five don't have the same problems as me. They can't understand me.'

For Yuksel, Boe B's angst reflects the alienation of many young Turks. 'He is in the second generation and he doesn't know how he wants to live, in Turkey, or Germany. He doesn't know and he is not alone, ninety per cent live like him. I think we must go on the street and say "I want to live here and I feel good here". Boe goes home and his parents say they want to go to Turkey. Then he goes back on the streets with his friends here. I have thought about this [identity] problem for a very long time and I analysed it. Now I think you have to choose to live either in Berlin, or in Turkey, but don't be in-between, because then you go crazy.'

First generation, second generation. He is from the first generation, she is from the second. These were the words that came up again and again as I travelled across Germany, speaking to

Turkish people. As with communities of immigrants everywhere, whether Turkish or Tasmanian, there are clear differences between father and son, but for young Turks especially, each of the two labels carried a distinct set of economic, cultural and political baggage. The first generation always knew they were Turkish and would never be anything else. They came to make money and then planned to go home, even though most have stayed. Their priorities were economic, rather than political. But the second has a different agenda: they are neither wholly Turkish or German, but a blend of both, with both the benefits and troubles that combination brings in its wake. The obsessions of many Germans, especially the conservatives in government – with their notions of race and blood, nation and order, punctuality and a rigid bourgeois lifestyle – mix ill with most Turks' relaxed Levantine approach to life, and that's before the issue of religion, of Islam and Christianity, is even considered.

It's hard to imagine that the German bureaucrats at the Ministry of Labour in Schleswig-Holstein had any idea what the eventual consequences of the agreement they signed in 1957 with the Turkish Ministry of Foreign Affairs would be. Almost forty years later debate rages over the very nature of German society and what it means to be German, as Germans struggle to adapt to the fact their country is now home, and will stay home, to one of Europe's largest Muslim minorities. Under the agreement's terms a dozen craftsmen arrived in Kiel, northern Germany, although there had been several private initiatives during the 1950s to bring in Turkish guestworkers. Although their Turkish qualifications were not recognised, immigration rules were relaxed then and the first wave of families began arriving. Many of the immigrants were from small villages and towns on the Anatolian plain, rather than the great metropolises of Istanbul or Ankara. Their concerns were local and parochial: their families and their work. Over the next few years the guest-workers' status became slowly regulated: government money went to start cultural associations and Turkish consulates opened in the many cities all over Germany where the Turks were settling.

But beneath the legal protection for Turkish workers, introduced under pressure from the German labour movement, there was always an assumption, whether spoken or unvoiced, that the foreign workers would not be staying. The very word itself: *gast-arbeiter,* or guestworker, said volumes more than any new piece of immigration legislation, with its message that: 'You Turks are welcome to come here and do the dirty work in reconstructing Germany, but then please go home.' This message is habitually reinforced by German politicians, such as Chancellor Helmut Kohl who repeatedly asserts that 'Germany is not an immigration country', as well as claiming that 'Germany is friendly to foreigners'. The statement, ritually invoked to reassure the *völkisch* right wing that the country of Goethe and Schiller will remain white, Christian and church-going, is clearly nonsense as a visit to any small German town will verify. But even among the first generation of Turkish immigrants, many have stayed on and are staying, such as Bilal Yuksel, father of Unal.

Formerly a builder, Yuksel senior, 51, now runs a stationery and toy shop in Kreuzberg with his wife Kevser. He came to Germany to make money and he succeeded, says his son Bilal. 'Now he has everything in Turkey, three or four homes and car. He could go back to Turkey now, but really he cannot. I am here, one of his three sons, one still goes to school. He will only return when he knows everything is OK with me and my brothers. I asked him why he doesn't go back? He said what can I do there? His mother is dead, his father is dead, he would live alone. Turkish people live with more than one person in one room, there is action everywhere. Nobody feels good alone. Nobody.'

Bilal Yuksel arrived at Munich's main station in 1966, after a two-day train ride from Istanbul. 'I have been in Germany for thirty years and that's a long time, it's a different situation for me now. I cannot go back to Turkey now, my wife has come and my sons are here. The thirty years went well, I learnt German. I have German friends, I never had any problems. We were one big family in the company, Turks, Germans and Arabs.'

At this claim Unal chips in, as we speak in the little kitchen behind the shop. 'This is the attitude of the first generation, this "please". Perhaps he had problems but he won't say. For all those years he went from home to work, from work to home. He doesn't have any conflicts, he doesn't go to the discotheque. He has his community.'

His father replies with dignity, smiling at his son: 'What is important is that every one of my sons can stay here on his own, can get money alone, can have a community. Then, when I see that everything is settled, I can go back to Turkey. I want my sons to have both cultures. I give my culture to my sons, the street and school gives the German mentality. This is something not German, not Turkish, but something new. When you want to live in another country, first you must learn the language, secondly you must integrate yourself into the culture. When you do both of these you won't have many problems. I achieved my aim, I did what I wanted to thirty years ago. These are the thoughts of a worker.'

The thoughts of the workers also exercise Safter Cinar, spokesman for the Turkish Union in Berlin. The Union's member organisations include groups for women, those promoting Turkish culture, for the elderly and even for hotel and restaurant workers. Its diverse membership is testament to an immigrant community that is now finding its voice. A youthful 49-year-old, Cinar came to Berlin to study economics over twenty years ago, stayed, and is now head of the German Trade Union Confederation's bureau that advises foreign workers. During the 1980s, when Turkey suffered a series of military coups, it was events in the homeland that exercised Turkish activists in Germany, but now community organisations are focusing on building a future in Germany, he says.

'Now we want to solve problems here in Germany, not like in the 1970s and '80s, when we made organisations to save Turkey. After the military coup in 1980 many immigrants, political ones, came to Germany. For a while everyone was only shouting about Turkey. But this produced a reaction, from the people who were born here or already living here who said we don't want people to come here from Turkey and tell us to fight for the problems in Turkey. This is a healthy and very important development.'

But the integration of the Turkish, and other minorities, must be a two-way process, says Cinar, and one that starts with German politicians recognising that their country *is* an immigration country and must adapt to the needs of its Muslim minority. 'Integration is happening, but it could be better if German politics were different. If they stopped making foreigner politics and began to make immigration politics, integration would be better and faster. The ideological position that we are not an immigration country is nonsense, every fact tells the opposite story. This is one of our problems, that politics is denying reality, with all its negative influences. If you say that seven million people here are not part of society, then you handle them as not being part of society.'

For all the politicians' rhetoric, German society is slowly changing under the influence of its immigrant communities. Germany's dull cuisine – one of the blandest in the world – is getting spiced up and evolving under Turkish and Asian influences. The country's legendary bureaucracy is even learning to bend some rules to cope with a massive influx of immigrants who don't always share Mr and Mrs Schmidt's legendary awe of authority. 'Not only the Turks but all the immigrants have had an influence here in daily life. In food, for example, the culture has changed. When I first came here in 1967, there were very few foreign restaurants, now it's hard to find a German one in Berlin. This influences what people cook at home and buy in the shops. Music has been influenced and also behaviour. This German idea of strong law and order in daily life, this is a little bit liberalised. I just read a book about hospital regulations that said in the 1960s and '70s you were only allowed to visit people two days a week, for only two hours. Now you can go every day, and the author says this is the influence of foreigners, because their families came every hour and so they changed the regulations. Such things cannot be measured, but there is a little liberalisation in daily life.'

German law is also evolving to cater for the beliefs of its Muslims, who are not just Turks, but also include north Africans, Arabs and Iranians. Judges have so far ruled that Muslim parents can refuse to allow their daughters to go swimming with boys and can wear headscarves to school. 'These court decisions also have a political aspect; they said, we are not only a Christian society now. It doesn't state that but this is the logic of it, the positive part. So to say that we are not an immigration country and we don't have to change anything is nonsense. But it is better if we have a general concept developing and we wouldn't have to keep going to court,' says Cinar.

But compared to, for example, Britain's Afro-Caribbean and

Asian communities, the Turks in Germany are substantially marginalised in public life. There are two German-Turkish MPs, one in the national parliament in Bonn and another in the Berlin state senate. But there are no Turkish news readers on German television, no senior Trade Union leaders – important in a country with a still powerful labour movement – no nationally acclaimed comedians or artists or musicians, although the German football team has one player, Mehmet Scholl, of Turkish background. The lack of a public face for Turkish people is the legacy of policies that deny Germany is an immigration country, says Cinar. 'This is because of factors such as the problem of the citizenship law, because to work in much of the official sector, you need German citizenship. But if you propagate only minority politics, that is how the majority sees you, only as a minority. For example, last year Berlin television invited us to discuss foreigners. I told them it would be good if they had a job training scheme for newcomers, and take people from ethnic minorities. Everyone said, yes that's a good idea, we could have better contacts with the Turks. I said it would be better the other way round, to take a Turkish person who has nothing to do with Turks, he specialises in traffic. They see you only as a Turk who only deals with Turks. And these are liberals.'

Not all Germans are liberals. Many are outspoken racists, such as the far-right Republikaner Party and its supporters and many more are tacitly prepared to condone, or even apparently tolerate – even exploit— racism for political advantage, such as Chancellor Kohl.

A very few Germans are killers, and the sites of their deeds, such as the city of Solingen, are seared into the consciousness of every foreigner in Germany. Durmus Genc, a Turkish immigrant, lost five members of his family – two daughters, two granddaughters and a niece – in an arson attack by neo-Nazis in May 1993. The youngest was Suyime, four years old. The Genc house at 81 Untere Wernerstrasse is no more, and the site is marked by a stone in commemoration of those who died there. A few days before the Solingen attack in May, the German parliament had passed a law limiting the right to political asylum in Germany. After the killings at Solingen, following a similar fire-bombing in Mölln in 1992 when Bahide Arslan and two young girls died, Turks invested in strong doors, dogs, alarms and security systems as they suddenly confronted the possibility of violent attacks by neo-Nazis.

The Solingen attacks also triggered four nights of riots by local young Turks and demonstrations across Germany. Chancellor Kohl's government expended much energy on denouncing the rioters, almost as much as it did condemning the firebombing. But while Kohl and his spokesmen dished out weasel words, Germany's President Richard von Weizsäcker seized the moral high ground when, speaking at a mosque in Cologne, he denounced the spreading anti-foreigner hatred. '[The attacks] spring from a climate generated by the extreme right. Even criminals alone do not emerge from nothing.' He parted company completely from Chancellor Kohl's government, though, on the question of citizenship and its refusal to amend restrictive laws that kept immigrants marginalised as permanent aliens. Many Germans, he said, 'speak too easily of "the Turks" . . . would it not be more honest and human to say "German citizens of Turkish heritage"?'

Yes, say the members of Germany's Turkish community. It would. Citizenship, more than any other issue, apart perhaps from physical safety, is the biggest concern for Germany's Turkish community. For many conservative Germans, the idea of granting German citizenship to millions of Muslim immigrants triggers a wave of horror at what they view as the inevitable subsequent pollution of the *Volk*'s blood-lines. Germany is one of the few countries whose citizenship laws are based on the idea of blood, rather than birthplace. Under the Nazis the obsession with pure blood-lines reached absurd and obscene heights as bureaucrats invented and carefully catalogued a maze of classes and sub-classes of Jews and part-Jews. The current rules, which state that citizenship is passed from parent to child, stretch back to the Imperial Naturalisation Act of 1913, and share a legacy of racism. In this case, originally, it was anti-Semitism, as the Act was passed to prevent granting citizenship to the many Polish and Jewish immigrants pouring into Germany. But now the rules are a wall against Muslims rather than Jews. Even *The Economist* described Germany's current citizenship statute as 'one of the oddest citizenship laws among large industrial countries'.

That 1913 act was inspired in part by the romantic nineteenth-century idea of Germany as a culturally uniform entity, of a *Volk* unified by blood and a common culture. That vision, still embedded deep into many Germans' psyche, does not encompass mosques or minarets. The current rise of Germany's intellectual new right, with its ideas of a homogenous German nation and the subsequent disturbing historical resonances these concepts stir up, has not helped the cause of extending German citizenship to its Muslims. The new right's buzzword is 'ethno-pluralism', which in the best Orwellian tradition may sound like a call for tolerance, but in reality is a mask for cultural apartheid. Many German intellectuals, instead of analysing how their country could integrate its Muslim minorities, are working out how to further marginalise them, drawing on the same old tired ideas of blood and race that obsessed Hitler.

For German nationalists the collapse of the Berlin Wall was a vindication of their *völkisch* ideas about the indivisibility of the German people. But for the Turkish community, indeed all non-white foreigners, unification has been a disaster in many ways, says Cinar. 'By the end of the 1980s we had reached a better acceptance of ethnic minorities. But now this problem is sidelined, because all discussions are about reunification. It cost a lot of money, and so there is less for immigrants social programmes. However, the murders in Solingen, Mölln and the riots in Rostock caused a stronger anti-racist discussion, because people who were indifferent to the problem were shocked and are getting active.'

The neo-Nazi murders have left a legacy of fear and uncertainty among all of Germany's immigrant communities. Racism, and the fear of a racist incident, from abuse to arson, is now a constant worry for foreigners, says Cinar. 'It is something there in daily life, not with something happening every minute, but there is the fear of something happening. Before the events of 1990 to 1993, if the children come home from school a bit late, the parents were just angry. Now everybody thinks maybe a racist incident has happened. This feeling is everywhere now, if you see a house burning, you think it was a racist attack. This fear is real and permanent. Factory workers say that there has been a change since the 1990s. Before, if a

Turk or non-German had a conflict with someone German, they shouted a bit and it was over. But now they say that the Germans say very quickly that you are a non-German. This is to do with the changes in the atmosphere, to be more German, more nationalistic. The skinheads are a problem because they are violent, but their numbers are small. The problem is what makes skinheads possible.'

But slowly, across the mainstream political spectrum, there is a growing realisation that the guestworkers are no longer guests, but residents. Even some on the conservative right believe that Germany's Muslims will have to be integrated into society, and that means granting full rights of citizenship. Debate continues over how to achieve this. Currently, immigrants can become German citizens if they have 10–15 years' residency and no criminal record or eight years of schooling. But, and it is a massive but, they must give up their original nationality. Many Turks, unnerved by the neo-Nazis and the opposition to granting them citizenship, understandably refuse to hand in their Turkish passports. As the wave of violence against foreigners grew in the early 1990s, many in the Turkish community began to compare themselves to the Jews in the 1930s. They had lost their German citizenship and many could find no other refuge, and died in the camps. Nobody in the Turkish community expected a second Holocaust, but many believed that what Germany gave, it could then take away. This feeling is widespread among the second generation, says Safter Cinar.

'There are two reasons for the problems over dual citizenship. First, the German policies that deny these people are part of society, which is a funny psychological position, although nobody says it outright. The second is that some [Turkish] people say, and the number is growing, "We don't know what will happen in Germany and we don't want to be in the position of the Jews in the 1930s who didn't have a country to go to." This is not yet a mainstream opinion, but if this situation of racism and violence continues to develop in Germany it could be stronger, not mainstream but it would be a big minority.'

The Turkish government has substantially changed its position on dual citizenship to help its nationals in Germany. Laws on property ownership and military service have all been altered to ease the guestworkers' position. In fact many Turks find a way around this, for they reapply for their Turkish citizenship, often even as they give it up, without telling the German authorities.

The twin devils of German society: the refusal to grant joint citizenship and the rise of neo-Nazism, are helping the rise of Islamic sentiment, especially among young Turkish people. Perpetually marginalised, subject to racism, marooned in a birth-place that rejects them, not surprisingly they are turning away from Germany, and towards Turkey and their religion instead.

Turkish Muslim groups, particularly the Islamic Welfare Party's (Refah) shadow set-up in Germany, provide a ready welcome, organisational infrastructure and perhaps most important, an immediate identity. The Islamic revival in Turkey, and growth in support there for Refah, is mirrored on the streets of Bonn and Cologne, Hamburg and Berlin. Almost everything that happens in Turkey reverberates through Germany, says Cinar, sometimes within hours. When Islamists torched a hotel in the Turkish city of Sivas, in protest at *The Satanic Verses*, there were demonstrations in Germany almost immediately afterwards.

Refah has no official presence in Berlin, but its supporters congregate at the Kreuzberg branch of National Sight, an Islamic club. A shop front, with a door onto the street, National Sight's walls are covered with posters expressing solidarity with Bosnia, the country which was once home to Nafiz Ucan's grandparents, who came originally from Tuzla. Quietly spoken and articulate, Ucan, 24, was born in Berlin and is studying law. He already delivers his opinions with a lawyer's careful use of language. 'I am a supporter of Refah, but not a member or representative. But objectively seen I will support the party's goals. I will support any decision that is rational and not violent. There is growing support for Refah among young Turkish people in Germany. People over fifty will have prejudices and heard all the propaganda that this is a radical Islamic party and is dictatorial, which it is not. Young people who objectively assess the information about Refah are very interested in it.'

Status, identity, the fundamental question of who they are, all these are driving young Turks in Germany into Refah's embrace, admits Ucan. 'The problem of identity that many young Turks have is definitely a reason why they are interested in Refah. Over the years Turks who lived here felt abandoned by their home country, there have always been many promises from Turkey, to support the community here, but none have ever been fulfilled. They feel hopeless, that they no longer have a homeland. This party has a mission and certain goals, and tells young people who live here that they will represent their interest both here in the community and in Turkey. It also offers strength among young people who live here, who want to live in peace in the community, and a philosophy to integrate and remain Turkish and Islamic.'

Refah's message to young Turks, that they can be proud of their Islamic heritage, both among Germans and among their fellow Turks, many of whom are fiercely secularist, also brings them support. 'Young people in the Turkish community don't feel recognised, they don't have an official status, they feel the pressure to assimilate but resist it, but they have nothing else to grasp at to defend their rights. Refah tells them we will support you in your attempts to form your own culture and not be assimilated. We will help you with lobbying for education, with the right to your own schools, with the right to be respected in this society. Young Turks will feel that this is very important. In Turkey French or British citizens have the right to protect their own culture, to go to school, or show films. But young Turks here don't have them, and Refah offers them the chance to keep a sense of identity and a sense of pride.'

The contrast between Islamic Force's Boe B, thumping out his rap lyrics about alienation and uncertainty, and Nafiz Ucan's fluent analysis of his situation and identity, could not be greater. It is the precepts of Islam that have brought him a peace that eludes many young Turks in Germany. 'First of all I am a Berliner, but one with a different cultural background. Berlin is a special place, I find it fascinating here that I can keep Turkish identity and still integrate in a foreign country. I can study here and be socially active, and lead the kind of life that I want. I am still attached to Turkey, but it's more cultural, whereas my attachment to Berlin is a realistic day-to-day one. This is my home city, where I feel first and foremost attached to.'

Beyond his love for Berlin, Ucan says he is both German and

Turkish simultaneously. 'I feel I have a double identity and I feel comfortable with that. I see myself as German, definitely, *and* Turkish. But beyond these questions of national belonging, there is something that comes from my religious beliefs, I feel first of all that I am a human being and must act in a humane way, and aspire to certain values, rather than a national identity. For me Islam is the idea of all people living together, to have a mixture of different cultures, religions and political tendencies. Religion is one way of attaining this, another is through my day-to-day life and how I live here in the city. That's what's so wonderful about Berlin. There is a great tolerance here, to live the life you want.'

Berlin is now home to forty mosques, and Islamisation has expanded so much that Turkish people can live an almost completely segregated Muslim lifestyle, says Safter Cinar, which, for him, is not a healthy development. 'This has been happening here, parallel to Turkey since the 1970s and '80s. They organise themselves here, not just religiously but economically, from birth to death. They have all their stores, groceries, everything you buy you can get in Islamic stores or travel agencies. Most of them are somehow connected to Refah. The main impulse comes from Turkey and other Islamic countries, the whole Islamic renaissance. They find good ground in Germany, because the people are feeling discriminated against, not accepted and Islam is something they can hold on to. I'm afraid this [parallel lifestyle] is becoming more popular.'

But why, I ask, is that a problem, for Turks to live an Islamic life?

'The problem is part of this Islamic community isolates itself from living here, it becomes more theologically undemocratic, this is the problem. This discussion will get more difficult unless Germany changes its politics and opens itself to these people. The normal German man and woman on the street see Islam as something from the last century, something undemocratic and so on. This is of course nonsense, but [this lifestyle] confirms their preconceptions.'

Several groups far more radical than Refah are active among Germany's Muslims. Rabah Kebir, the exiled leader of Algeria's Islamic Salvation Front (FIS) is under constant police surveillance at his home near Cologne. A report by the German counter-espionage service entitled 'Islamic extremism and its effects on the Federal Republic of Germany' identifies fourteen radical Muslim groups and over 22,000 active sympathisers across the country. German intelligence officers believe radical Islamists have set up a network stretching across eastern Europe and Germany to buy arms and detonators, which are then smuggled to Algeria, often via Hamburg. The reports says that: 'FIS sympathisers living in Germany have been involved in the dispatch of weapons and other technical material to Algeria.' Rabah Kebir though denies that FIS supports violence. 'We have chosen the peaceful path,' he has said.

Ismail Kosan, a Green MP in Berlin's senate, agrees that Germany's refusal to integrate Muslims into society is driving them to the mosque. Kosan, a well-groomed, paunchy and patronising radical, joined a Marxist party while at school in Turkey. His Marxism has faded away now, but he still shares the sense of self-worth and self-righteousness that is a hallmark of so many on the far left, constantly picking apart the wording of my questions. In fact he reminds me of nothing so much as the harder-line Islamic radicals I have met, who are far happier explaining what they believe is the true meaning of words such as democracy, rather than outlining the actual changes they would make in power. 'Do you know what an Alevi is?' he demands, when I mention the Muslim grouping, practising an extremely liberal form of Shiism, that forms about a third of Turkey's over 60 million population. And when I ask him if it is important for members of the Turkish community to be politically active in Germany he replies:

'It's important that all people become politically active, but what do you mean with regard to the Turks by politically active?' Oh dear. It's clear that we are not hitting it off, but I press on. As one of Germany's two elected Turkish politicians, his views carry a certain weight.

As for the Turkish community, that doesn't exist at all, he claims. At least in the sense that I use the word. 'There is no Turkish community here, but just people from Turkey. But there are people who speak Turkish but that does not necessarily make a Turkish community. When you talk about the Turkish community there are several different groups within it, Arabs,

Albanians, Kurds, Alevis. The European tendency of lumping together these different nationalities as Turks is completely false, because you cannot come to that simplistic conclusion, it's much more complex and there has never been proper research. It is not a homogenous community . . . The only thing in common they have is being a foreigner.'

Kosan's point is a fair one, although the members of all these groups have Turkish nationality, but even his allies in the Turkish community admit that his constantly hectoring tone does not make the best advertisement for his community. Whether or not it exists. He will agree though that Islamic sentiment is on the rise. 'Religious fundamentalism is becoming more popular everywhere. The Turkish-speaking community here does appear to be becoming more religious, for the simple reason that Europeans are the true fundamentalists, they are the ones who have rejected them, who pushed them out and marginalised them into having an Islamic identity. In the 1970s, very few women covered their heads and now you see them everywhere.

'This new religious identity has happened as a reaction, as a kind of self-defence, against European marginalisation, some-thing completely different to what is happening in Turkey. Turkey has sent religious teachers here to Germany, to preach Islam and keep their Islamic identity. This fits in with the policy of inte-gration which the German state has as well as the Social Democrats, that Turks should stay here and they should have a distinct Turkish and Muslim identity, when there are no distinc-tions made in terms of how heterogeneous everything really is.'

Germany's Turkish-speaking community may well be multi-ethnic, but religious Turkish Muslims are all united in their worship of Allah. At Friday afternoon prayers at the mosque in Cologne, there is the same sense of serenity and devotion that I have witnessed from Tirana to Washington DC. There is not enough room in the squat, square building for all the worship-pers, who overflow into the courtyard outside, which, as is the Muslim custom, also boasts communal buildings and a kitchen. As the Imam recites the prayer the hundreds of worshippers fall as one to their knees, prostrating themselves before their God as they intone the verses from the Quran. There is an extraordinary sense here of spirituality, unity in worship and equality, for when all Muslims are kneeling on the floor facing Mecca, all are equal in the eyes of God. Unlike the many churches and synagogue services I have attended, nobody talks here during prayers, they come just to worship, and they chat and socialise later outside. For some reason it is at this mosque, rather than the glitzy new buildings at Regent's Park, or the plush Islamic centre of New York – for Cologne's mosque is certainly one of the plainest I have ever seen – that I begin to understand the true meaning of the word Islam: submission, surrender to a power greater than all of us, as I watch the rows of worshippers on the floor and sense the inner peace their faith brings.

A faith and a power that Ankara seeks to control, even at a distance. While Germany and Turkey argue about dual citizenship, they both agree on the need to control the rising Islamic sentiment in the Turkish community. Turks in Germany, like those in the mother country, reflect the diversity of Islamic beliefs. During the 1960s and 1970s some of the most active Turkish Muslim groups in Germany were part of the radical Islamic opposition, such as the Suleymanci movement. During the 1980s allies of Necmettin Erbakan, who in the summer of 1996 became prime minister of Turkey, were active, especially in Berlin. But even they were perceived as too liberal for followers of Cemaleddin Kaplan, who split off to form his own pro-Iran movement. Kaplan, nicknamed 'the Khomeini of Cologne' and 'the Dark Voice' for his aim of turning Turkey into an Islamic state, died in exile aged 69 in Cologne in May 1995.

For the majority of Turks groups such as Kaplan's and the Suleymancis had little appeal. They wanted to practise their religion and keep their cultural identity but had not come to Germany to make an Islamic revolution, either there or in Turkey. The answer, for Bonn and Ankara, both growing increasingly concerned at the Islamic radicals' activities – spurred on by the Islamic revolution in Iran – was firstly to control the influx of Turkish Imams into Germany. Bonn and Ankara signed an agreement that the only Imams and religious teachers that would be allowed to work in Germany would be licensed by Ankara. They would then have to return home after five years. (An immediate result of this agreement was a drive by radical Muslim groups in Turkey to infiltrate the new structures and get their people posted, with official approval, to Germany.) The two governments' next move against the Islamic radicals was to take control of the growing network of mosques in Germany, through setting up *Diyanet Isleri Turk-Islam Birligi* (DITIB), a branch of the Turkish Department of Religious Affairs.

By the end of the 1980s between half and two thirds of mosques in Germany were controlled by DITIB. The organisation has also helped draw up educational syllabi for Muslim schoolchildren in Germany, the classroom being another important arena for the battle between Turkey's Kemalists and Islamists. Many secular Turks, such as Safter Cinar, oppose DITIB's role in education. 'We are against this, and not just because of the connection with Turkey. Even if we had a very democratic Turkey this would be wrong. Firstly because of the books, which should be written here because of the conditions in Germany, and the teachers as well, must also live here to understand the feelings and problems of the children. The Turkish government saw that this was an opportunity to organise the religion of the immigrants in Europe under Turkish state control, in competition with Refah.'

The DITIB office in Cologne, within the mosque complex, is the first Turkish workplace I have seen to boast both a picture of Kemal Atatürk and several verses of the Quran, inscribed in ornate calligraphy, on the wall. The usual choice of decoration – homage to the founder of the secular state, or verse from the Quran – says everything about the dichotomy now cleaving Turkey. As a virtual arm of the Turkish government, but one dealing with Islam, DITIB carries out a delicate balancing act among the Turkish immigrant community. The secretary, a jolly man who I'll call Mehmet, and I, chat for a while about why I am in Cologne, but Mehmet, 55, who arrived in Germany from Tarsus in 1964, doesn't want to discuss controversial issues like the rise of Refah or the influence of the Suleymancis. He's far happier in his role as a sort of ambassador for Islam to the many Germans who visit the mosque, curious about what it means to be a Muslim. Just as in America and Britain, a growing number of Germans are becoming Muslim.

'Sometimes a Christian man or a woman comes to us and

says, I would like to become a Muslim. We say, all right, everybody is welcome for us. We write a paper, name, surname and address saying he was here today and wanted to become a Muslim. There is a chapter in the Quran, three sentences, "I believe and bear witness that there is only one God and Muhammad is his prophet." I say it, he says it, when he is finished, I say OK, you are a Muslim and we give him the paper. They need the paper if they want to marry a Muslim, woman or man. Perhaps because of a big love. Or perhaps he really believes and wants to be a Muslim. After this a few days later he may call us and say I changed my mind, I am not a Muslim and I need a new paper. But I say to him: "In the moment that you said you are not Muslim, you are not." You don't need a piece of paper saying it, we don't have it.

'We have school groups and university students, I go with them to the mosque and I explain what it is and what we are doing there. They have some wrong ideas, I correct them and say what the newspapers and television say, it's not true, because they don't know us or our religion. For example, they say why does the woman pray behind the men, is it discrimination? I say no, for God says this is not discrimination. Our prophet says that the key to paradise lies under the feet of the mother, that means you must respect a woman or a mother. If the Muslim religion discriminates against woman, he would not say it. This is not only a sentence, it is a book. You must think about it, what does it mean.'

But, I reply, a woman can never become an Imam. 'You know how Muslims pray, a man or the woman must go with their head to the floor, imagine such a woman doing the same thing in front of a man. Is it all right, is it praying if a woman lies before you? You don't think about praying if she lies on the carpet in front of you, can you think of God? There is no man in the world that would think of God while a woman lies in front of him. A Muslim wants to be in front of God but if the woman lies ahead he can't think about Allah. He thinks about the woman. That's why the woman cannot become a priest because she cannot lie in front.' That a woman might be distracted from her worship, for whatever reason, by the sight of rows of male posteriors doesn't seem to matter.

*

207

A few miles away from DITIB's bureau in Cologne is the Bonn office of Cem Ozdemir, Germany's first ethnic Turkish MP, elected for the Greens. A youthful 30, with a pierced ear, Ozdemir, who was born in Bad Urach, is positively buzzing with enthusiasm for his work. For many young Turks in Germany, whether Sunni Muslims, Alevis or Kurds, Ozdemir's election shows that even the corridors of power are opening to the Turkish community. 'Everybody in Bad Urach knows my parents and me, and they all say "our Cem", the Germans also say that, "our Cem, he's an MP".' Now of course, Ozdemir is a local hero, but growing up in Bad Urach his family's welcome was more ambiguous. 'I remember my teacher in the first class said, when I was seven, that there was no need to send me to the next class because we would go back to Turkey. Now when I see her in the street she says, "Of course I knew that you were going to be an important person." Unbelievable.'

Ozdemir became politically active in his teens, but while many of his Turkish compatriots in the early 1980s concentrated on opposing the then military junta, he threw his energies into the burgeoning Green movement. 'After Mölln, Solingen and Rostock I realised that it was important to be in Parliament and show the second- and third-generation immigrants that it was possible to change something here, and that we are a part of this society. I am not in the governing party so it is hard to change the law with a majority. But it is possible to use the media, to help some parts of the government to talk about things. I am from a workers' family, not an academic family. My mother works at a tailor's, my father works at a fire extinguisher factory. At the beginning some people said I sold out, but at meetings I tell people, look, I am not something different. I am one of you, nothing unusual and you can do it too.'

Now, says Ozdemir, all three main sections of the Turkish community – Sunnis, Alevis and Kurds – want to claim him as their own. His own background is Sunni, but his name, Cem, is the word for an Alevi prayer meeting. 'I was in Hamburg where I made a speech, and afterwards lots of young Turks said, "I've heard you are Alevi and I am so proud of you." I said I'm not Alevi, but I don't have to be one to think like one and understand the Alevis. Another one said you must be a Kurd, because only a Kurd can understand us. I said no, because I don't have to be a Kurd to understand what the Kurds are fighting for. This is a good sign that people say you must be this or that, because I can give the image that I work for the Turks and the Kurds, for Sunnis and Alevis.'

Ozdemir shares a different vision to the observant Muslims of the National Sight office in Berlin, but he agrees that Islam is on the rise among Turkish youth. 'These people who are not really integrated into society, who are in between, they are searching for another kind of identity because Germany never made it possible for them to feel part of the society. There are two possibilities here, either to become a nationalist, a real Turk, or become religious. Now a lot of people who never went into a mosque in Turkey started to be religious. This is very interesting, it's a sign that some things are not going in a good way. It gives those people feeling that they have something. They think: I am a Muslim, I have a mosque, community, security in this foreign world, foreign country. This is more than Refah, there is also a radicalisation in the classical Muslim organisations which are not near to Refah. In Turkey education is totally under the control of Islamic fundamentalists. That definitely has influence that spills over into Germany.'

The radical Muslims' recruiting drive is also fuelled by the graves of those killed in Solingen and Mölln and the squirming response of the Kohl government as it sought to balance enough outrage to appease international opinion and the votes of German nationalists. 'Mrs Genc in Solingen, she said we have to live together and she told me about the signs of friendship she has got from lots of Germans. But she also said this: that she can never forget what Kohl said and that he didn't even call her, or send her something, even a little token. Nothing, absolutely nothing.'

More positively, MPs from Kohl's Christian Democrat Party are now consulting Ozdemir about issues to do with their Turkish constituents, he says. 'They come to me and ask, "I have a mosque in my constituency, I don't know whether I should go there or not, what do you think?" Or they have been invited to something by the Turkish community. I feel like a kind of ambassador.'

Everything that happens in Turkey, the conflicts in Turkey

between Sunni and Alevi, Kurd and Turk, all these spill over onto the streets of Bonn and Cologne, Hamburg and Berlin, splitting the Turkish community on similar lines to their compatriots in Istanbul and Ankara. After an attack by gunmen on Alevi coffee shops in Istanbul, in March 1995, Alevis took to the streets across Germany and Europe to protest, from Cologne, Frankfurt and Hanover, to Innsbruck, Zurich and Paris. Kurds also regularly march to demand an independent homeland in the eastern part of Turkey. Coming back from my interview with Cem Ozdemir, I caught the tail end of a demonstration by tens of thousands of Kurds, marching across Bonn on an otherwise sleepy Saturday afternoon. There are about 400,000 Kurds in Germany, about 20 per cent of the total Turkish-speaking population. Some demonstrators waved the flag of the Kurdistan Workers' Party, the PKK, which is illegal in Germany and Turkey, the armed wing of the separatist movement. The PKK runs a nationwide underground movement across Germany, with cells in most major cities.

For Ahmet – not his real name – a Kurd living in Berlin, who is in contact with the PKK underground, the conflict between Turks and Kurds is part of his daily life in Germany. Ahmet fled Turkey after the military coup in 1980. As a member of a left-wing Kurdish political organisation he was an obvious target for the wave of repression that followed the generals' takeover. After being told initially by the German authorities that they considered him to be a terrorist he somehow acquired a French passport. He married a German woman, they divorced and he is now legalised in Germany, where he paints and writes.

'Relations between Kurds and Turks in Berlin are very tense. The atmosphere is terrible, they used to be one community when everyone first arrived, but increasingly as the conflict has developed militarily and socially, this has had consequences for the community here. Now it's very rare to find a television or newspaper in a [Turkish] café, because people try to remove any reason to heighten that conflict. To discuss it is to light up a powder keg,' he said when we met in a Greek restaurant in Kreuzberg. Most Turkish cafés are out of bounds for Ahmet, he says, as they would recognise him as a Kurd and he is scared to enter them.

'It changed three or four years ago, when it became especially bad. It started with the Gulf War then got worse. Now I would not dare to go into a Turkish café and order a tea, because I look Kurdish and I speak Turkish with a Kurdish accent. I don't feel comfortable. It's sad but it doesn't bother me that much. The PKK has a big presence in Berlin. It's not a question of noticing it, simply that they do, I know the people involved and I know what they do.'

What do they do, I ask?

He pauses. 'They look for help in every possible area, wherever they can for their cause. It's very strictly organised.'

Turks and Kurds are involved in the drugs trade out of proportion to their numbers, say German police officers. Certainly in Kreuzberg it doesn't seem hard to find heroin. A fresh harvest of syringes is scattered around the U-Bahn station at Kottbusser Tor every morning, a few feet from the Turkish snack stands. Heroin is the main narcotics problem in Berlin, says Chief Superintendent Rudiger Engler of the Berlin State Police. Of those involved in dealing in heroin, 40 per cent are foreigners and of those 49 per cent are Turkish, according to police statistics. 'There are known spots, in Kreuzberg at Kottbusser Tor, if you go there in the evening and open your eyes you can see the problem. A lot of the active street dealers are Turkish. Their parents came here to earn money, but they are dealing in drugs. Many are Kurds, from the cities and villages around Diyabakir, in the east.'

Other, Kurdish, sources say that while the PKK does not deal directly in Germany's heroin trade, it receives a percentage from many sales. Its members are suspected of several firebombings of Turkish businesses and assassination attempts against would-be defectors.

As the Berlin correspondent of the international edition of the Turkish daily *Hurriyet*, Ali Yumusak is a long-time observer of the Turkish community in Germany. He arrived in Germany in 1970 to study engineering in Augsberg, and began sending home stories about the lives of guestworkers. He has watched spreading Islamisation, the rise of the neo-Nazis (prompting him also to invest in new locks and security doors at home) and now the emergence of a new culture – the Euro-Turks, something new and unique.

Young Turks in Germany are distancing themselves from

German culture and regrouping amongst themselves, he says. 'The new generation is more self-confident and refuses to allow itself to be oppressed or discriminated against. They have reacted to the discrimination by forming their own networks. Young Turkish men used to date German women and even marry them. But now that trend is reversing, where Turks will only date and fraternise among each other. Now there are special Turkish discos, and some of the contact between the nationalities has been severed.'

Art, music and culture are building this new identity, he says, echoing the ideas of Ypsilon Musix's Unal Yuksel. Turkish-German writers such as Renan Demirkan and Emine Sevgi Ozdamar are fusing German and Turkish culture together to much critical acclaim. In Demirkan's first book, *Schwarzer Tee mit drei Stück Zucker* (black tea with three lumps of sugar), she told the story of a young Turkish woman's childhood and family in an Anatolian village as she waited to give birth in a German hospital. Some argued that the book received such praise because it presented the kind of picture of 'exotic' Turks in staid Germany that readers expected, and Demirkan has moved away from portrayals of a remembered Turkey in her newer work such as *Die Frau mit Bart* (the woman with a moustache), the tale of two German women's lives.

The first work of Emine Sevgi Ozdamar, winner of the Ingeborg Bachmann prize, the German equivalent of the Booker Prize, in 1991, was a play in broken German, inspired by a letter she received from a fellow Turk. 'He had typed his letter without knowing how to type, painfully finding the letters, just as I had to painfully find my words in German. This man had lost much of his Turkish; his mother tongue had become entangled with his newly acquired German and now not even his wife could understand him without difficulty. But this man never spoke out against Germany. He kept repeating: home is where you have a job,' she has said.

It was her prize-winning novel *Das Leben ist eine Karawanserei hat zwei Türe aus einer kam ich rein aus der anderen ging ich raus* (life is like a caravan trail: through one door you come in, through the other you go out), that propelled her into the serious writers' league. German critics saluted her achievement but remarked that the prize had gone to a foreign writer who had chosen German as her second language. 'I was accepted, but merely as a "guest-writer",' she said. In some ways her writing is similar to that of another writer who settled in a foreign country, the late Nobel Prize for Literature Laureate Isaac Bashevis Singer. The writings of both share an emphasis on the themes of relations between men and women, sex, are tinged with magical realism and shot through with a sense of psychological dislocation and the heavy baggage of exile.

Ozdamar's work reflects the fractured nature of not just the life of an immigrant, but of Turkey itself, as it juggles its secular system of government with its Islamic heritage. She uses a language that draws from both German and Turkish: 'We have no choice but to rebuild the tongue which we have lost with the tongue that we have found,' she has said.

As one of her characters proclaims: 'I screamed out poems on the anniversaries of Atatürk's death but he should not have forbidden the Arabic writing. This ban, it's as though half my head has been cut off. All the names in my family are Arabic: Fatma, Mustafa, Ali, Samra. Thank God I still belong to a generation that grew up with a good many Arabic words.'

The record producer Unal Yuksel, his father Bilal, the trade unionist Safter Cinar, the Refah-supporting law student Nafiz Ucan, the MPs Cem Ozdemir and Ismail Kosan, the Kurdish exile Ahmet, the writers Renan Demirkan and Emine Sevgi Ozdamar, all these, by their work and by their very lives in Germany are both changing that country's society and helping spawn something new, a Euro-Turkish hybrid lifestyle, that draws on both the norms of Bavaria and the Bosphorus, enriching Europe. And that doesn't necessarily mean an overlap in style or approach with the work of the French-Algerian artists of La Friche in Marseilles, or the books and films of Hanif Kureishi in Britain. Germany, like Britain and France, is spawning its own indigenous unique Muslim-local hybrid culture, as the Muslims of each European nation blend their own heritage with Islamic culture. Certainly there are common themes between the young Muslim artists and musicians of Berlin and Marseilles for example – of identity and alienation, say – but the work of all is shaped as much by their daily environment as by Muslim culture itself.

'This new generation is culturally richer than the first generation and its German peers, because they live in a mixture between two worlds, that is how they think and how they live,' says Ali Yumusak. 'They have adopted some of the German characteristics, of a good work ethic, they are disciplined and organised. But they think very pragmatically and practically, which they learnt from their parents who had to adapt to life here and learn how to integrate. They have kept some of their Mediterranean instincts, they are more mobile, more spontaneous and they can react more quickly. They also have a vision of the future, they see themselves between two cultures and they understand that they have two home countries. They can think in those terms, beyond national borders.'

Mme Matilt Manokyan, Turkish brothel owner

Chapter 8

TURKEY: THE VEILED REVOLUTION

'Turkey is at a crossroads, either it will go on in this despotic way or they will listen to the voice of the people. There is no third way. The voice of the people is the voice of Islam, Islamic values and beliefs. The West is not the solution for Turkey, nor is the East, but Islam.'
Ahmet Hakan Coskun, news manager at the Islamic
television station, Channel 7

'The Refah [Islamic Welfare] Party says if we come to power we will bring you equality, the world and every-thing you need. But Turkish people are not inclined to ask what is inside this everything.'
Izzettin Dogan, a community leader of Turkey's
minority Alevi Muslims

The road some colleagues and I took to Istanbul followed a similar route to the one tramped along by Suleyman the Magnificent's soldiers over 400 years ago, as European city after city fell to the advancing Ottoman forces. He captured Belgrade in 1521, Rhodes in 1522 and wiped out the Magyar armies at Mohács, southern Hungary, in 1529, before taking Budapest. But while the Ottomans marched north, eventually reaching the gates of Vienna, we were headed south through the Balkans, from Budapest through Belgrade and Sofia to Istanbul, former capital of the Ottoman empire.

In the flatlands of Hungary, across much of Serbia, there are but few signs left that this whole swathe of Europe was once under Islamic rule. But while much of the Muslim contribution to the Balkans' cultural mosaic has vanished, the best traditions of Ottoman bureaucracy live on, as travellers are logged and registered. There are forms to be filled in and stamped, puddles of grubby-looking disinfectant to drive through and a succession of taxes and visa fees to be paid. As we drove across into Turkey from Bulgaria, our papers duly franked and authorised in the best traditions of Ottoman bureaucracy, a bank of duty-free shops glittered in the afternoon heat, their rows of shiny bottles stacked on the shelves. It was an unexpected welcome for an Islamic country, but one that perhaps symbolises the contradiction of a nation that forms the bridge between the Muslim Middle East and Christian Europe. Seeing the Budapest number plates on our car a shop-owner jumped forward excitedly, beckoning us over in the Magyar language, for this is a popular route for Hungarian shoppers. We asked if he had any whisky. 'Of course, of course, how many bottles do you want? Buy ten! Buy ten!' he exclaimed. One sufficed for a few nightcaps in Edirne.

The Thracian plain stretched away in front of us as we sped down the motorway towards Istanbul. Platoons of women worked in the fields by the side of the road, their heads covered, in accordance with Islamic custom, as they bent over the earth. The men, I learnt later, were busy in the coffee houses, smoking and chatting. The road was almost deserted until we approached the engaging chaos of Edirne when suddenly we were swept up in the shoals of ancient German cars which ebbed and flowed around us, while in front, high on a hill, the four minarets of the Selimiye mosque, Edirne's landmark, pointed skywards, to heaven.

Tucked away in the corner of north-west Turkey a few kilometres from the Greek and Bulgarian borders, this frontier town has been the stomping ground of a string of different empires' armies, from the Romans to the Ottomans. Murat I took the city for the Ottomans in 1361 and several decades later Mehmed the Conqueror garrisoned his forces here in preparation for the assault on Constantinople. The city was shunted back and forth over the next centuries between the Russians, Bulgaria and Greece, until Turkey regained its sovereignty in 1923 at the Treaty of Lausanne. Now Edirne is firmly Turkish, with a fine Ottoman heritage of mosques and markets. A small-scale

Istanbul, its streets are crowded with meandering pedestrians, cars hooting as they wander across roundabouts and junctions and everywhere stalls, shops and restaurants.

Towering over the city is the Selimiye mosque, whose minarets, the second tallest in the world after Mecca, are visible from kilometres away on the Thracian plain. The Selimiye mosque is the work of Mimar Sinan, court architect to three Sultans including Suleyman the Magnificent. Its dome is just a few centimetres bigger than that of the church-turned-mosque, Aya Sofya in Istanbul, a symbol in brick and mortar that the Islamic Ottoman empire would surpass its Byzantine predecessors. Centuries after the death of Sinan and the Sultans who commissioned him, Edirne is crowded with the heritage of urban Islamic architecture, for Islam at least in its Ottoman variety is an urban religion that demands schools, markets, bazaars and public kitchens as well as places of worship.

That the Ottomans could bring a rich and intricate civilisation in their wake, one that could teach medieval Europe plenty about religious tolerance and civic infrastructure, was unimaginable to Christendom's scribes. When the Ottomans captured Constantinople in 1453, for many in the West it was the darkest day in the history of the world and masses were said all over Europe. Here is the writer Kritovoulos on the capture of the city: 'This crowd made up of men from every race and nation, brought together by chance, like wild and ferocious beasts, leaped into the houses, driving them mercilessly, dragging, rending, forcing, hauling them disgracefully into the public highways and doing every evil thing.' His words sent a wave of horror across Christian Europe, just as they were intended to.

Blood ran in the gutters and a carpet of severed heads floated in the sea as the Sultan's soldiers took their three days of plunder, promised to them by their leader, Mehmed the Conqueror. Eyewitness reports from survivors describe an orgy of arson and destruction as children were raped and slaughtered while others were carted off to the slave market. Horrific, certainly, and the basis of a folk memory that still inspires fear to the cry of 'The Turks are coming', but standard practice for marauding armies, both then and now and certainly no different from the tactics of the Christian First Crusade, as they set off to rape and pillage their way across what is now Turkey.

When Pope Urban II's holy warriors set off in 1096 for Constantinople they never even reached the city, having expended most of their energy in the Rhine Valley where they set about slaughtering the region's Jews with great enthusiasm. When Constantinople was finally captured by the knights of the fourth crusade in 1204, Rome's warriors looted its Byzantine treasures in exactly the same way as the soldiers of Mehmed the Conqueror over two hundred years later. The Crusaders plundered so many valuables from Aya Sofya that they had to bring in mules to carry off their booty. For added entertainment they seated a prostitute on the Orthodox patriarch's throne.

The fall of Byzantine Constantinople on 29 May 1453 and its subsequent transformation into Muslim Istanbul was the Ottomans' greatest prize. Its importance was both strategic, for now Mehmed the Conqueror controlled the straits of the Bosphorus, gateway to both the Mediterranean and the Black Sea, and immensely symbolic, for the seat of Orthodoxy had been captured and Rome stood alone against Islam. Aya Sofya was converted into a mosque by Mehmed and stayed a house of worship until it opened as a museum in 1934.

Mehmed also built the first buildings of the Topkapi Palace, epicentre of the Ottoman empire for almost four hundred years. Now the *Bab-i Humayun* (sublime gate) is crowded with tourists and taxis, the general air of lax chaos in historical tune with its function as a space always open to the public, where citizens could petition the government. Virtually everything remains in the complex from the heyday of the Ottoman empire, including the Divan (council), from where the Sultan would listen in on its decisions, and the infamous cage, in fact a claustrophobic suite of tiny rooms. Tired of slaughtering their brothers on their ascension to the Ottoman throne the Sultans instead incarcerated them here for decades, complete with a retinue of deaf mutes and a harem. The Sultan's concubines had their ovaries removed to prevent them becoming pregnant, and giving birth to another potential rival to the throne. If they did conceive they were trussed up and drowned in the Bosphorus.

Not surprisingly most of those locked up in the cage went crazy. None more so than Deli Ibrahim (Mad Ibrahim) who emerged after twenty-two years to engage in unrivalled sexual excess. Egged on by his mother and his ministers, for the more time he spent in affairs of the bed the less he could devote to those of state, he designed his own orgy robes, lined with sable fur and studded with precious stones. His jaded tastes demanded ever fresh stimulation, and one day he decided that sexual pleasure was proportional to size. His messengers were sent out to find the fattest woman possible and located a gigantic Armenian woman who soon became his favourite. Sadly her appeal to the Sultan proved no insurance against the jealousy of her rivals, and she met the classic end of those who took a wrong turn in the intrigue-drenched corridors of the harem, and was strangled at a feast.

The institution of the harem is the source for centuries' worth of orientalist stereotypes about Turkey and 'lustful Turks', but its narrow corridors are more symbolic of a decaying empire, rotted by corruption and unable or unwilling to reform itself than any national sexual characteristics. Guarded by black eunuchs, who had suffered radical castration, the harem took its name from the Arabic word *haram*, meaning forbidden. As the Ottoman empire declined, the numbers of odalisques increased and by the reign of Sultan Abdulaziz (1861–76) they were over 800 strong. Many of the women, chosen for their beauty, were kidnapped from the outer reaches of the Ottoman empire, such as Georgia or Hungary. Only a few reached the Sultan's bed, when they would be given their own slaves. Many died of disease in the unhygienic conditions of the harem, their miserable end speeded up by boredom and homesickness.

From Topkapi Mehmed and his successors, particularly Suleyman the Magnificent, launched wars of conquest that saw large swathes of eastern and central Europe, Persia and the Arabian peninsula fall under Ottoman rule. At its furthest extent the Ottoman empire extended from the shore of north Africa, down the Saudi coastline, along the Black Sea to Daghestan in the Caucasus, north through the Crimea into Transylvania and northern Dalmatia. The international diplomatic, and sometimes military, consequences of its dissolution continues today in places as far apart as Sarajevo and Gaza.

So does the internal fall-out from the abolition of the Sultanate in 1922 and Turkey's transformation into a republic the following October. Turkey was among the losers of the First

World War, but compared to Germany or Hungary, she emerged with dignity, keeping reasonable natural borders in a state of manageable size and expelling the various foreign armies hoping for control of a slice of Turkish territory. In 1923 the capital was moved to the dreary central Anatolian town of Ankara, and Mustafa Kemal was designated head of state. The only undefeated general at the end of the war, Kemal had organised a campaign of guerrilla warfare against the plans to slice up Turkey between the victorious allies. An arch-westerniser, he was determined to drag Turkey into the twentieth century. In quick succession Kemal abolished the Caliphate, exiled the last Caliph Abdulmecid and all members of the royal house of Osman; closed the *medreses* (religious schools) and religious courts for the Jewish, Greek and Armenian minorities, and a new Ministry of Religious Affairs supervised the assets of the *vakifs* (religious endowments).

More was to come. The old lunar calendar was replaced by the Gregorian one, *seriat* (Islamic) law was abolished and a version of modern European law installed. This new corpus covered marriage and divorce which became civil matters, polygamy and the veil were outlawed and in 1930 women were given the vote. Surnames were made compulsory and Mustafa Kemal became Kemal Atatürk, meaning 'father of the Turks', for nobody could accuse him of modesty. The old Ottoman script, of Turkish words written in Arabic characters, was replaced with the Latin alphabet. Many of these measures appeared laudable decisions, by western liberal standards.

But Kemal's secularism was not of the western kind that decrees a separation of church and state and allows normal public expressions of religious belief, in communal structures or even dress. It was a planned anti-Islamism – in the sense of Islam providing the basis for a system of government – aimed at ripping out the old Ottoman society and replacing it with a secular government that drew on the 1920s ideas of nationalism and the corporate state that also inspired the early Benito Mussolini and the Soviet Communists. He tried, and succeeded, in creating a modern state out of a plethora of nationalities, for Turkey then, and now, is home to a plethora of minorities that include virtually every letter of the alphabet from Abkhazians to Turcomans, binding this ethnic mix together to form a new nation. Out in the villages in the vast stretches of Anatolia, his radical measures triggered anger and confusion. Atatürk was a great Gazi (fighter for Islam) who had liberated Turkey from the foreign infidels of the allies' armies and was revered by every Turk. But why did he change the alphabet and smash the power of the Imams in the drive for a one-party state, they asked?

Just as Stalin purged the old Bolsheviks in his drive for a completely new society, Atatürk jettisoned virtually every facet of the Ottoman empire that had centuries-old roots as he shaped his new republic with consequences that are even now sending ripples across Turkish society. By changing the alphabet, for example, he cut off many Turks from their own literary and cultural heritage. The legacy of his drastic attempts to kick-start a parochial, backward-looking Muslim country into a modern, secular state drove many Muslim clergymen underground, to form the nucleus of an Islamic opposition movement that, seventy years later, is gaining increasing political power in Turkey.

For Atatürk inflicted a trauma on the national psyche that only now is slowly surfacing, and helping build an Islamic revival, like a long-delayed case of national post-traumatic shock. By the time Atatürk took power the Ottoman turban had been replaced by the more modern Fez, but even that was not up to date enough, and that headgear was replaced by Atatürk's panama hat. A uniform western-style dress also helped bind his nation together, with its mix of national minorities. He wore his new hat for the first time in 1925 at Kastamonu, speaking in the heartlands of Islamic conservatism, records Andrew Wheatcroft, in his book *The Ottomans*, announcing that:

> A civilised international dress is worthy and appropriate for our nation and we will wear it. Boots and shoes on our feet, trousers on our legs, shirt and tie, jacket and waist-coat – and of course, to complete these, a cover with a brim on our heads. I want to make this clear. This head covering is called a HAT.[1]

Serpil Orcalan does not wear a hat. Her hair is covered instead with a shining grey, gold and green headscarf and she is dressed in a long skirt. An engaging young woman in her twenties, whose nose wrinkles when she smiles, Orcalan made history in July 1995 when she started work as a newsreader, reciting the day's events on television dressed in full Islamic garb, for the first time ever in Turkey's history.

Orcalan is a newsreader at Channel 7, a private Islamic television station set up in autumn 1994, with strong links to the Islamic Welfare Party (Refah). The station began with broadcasts to Istanbul and Ankara and plans satellite expansion to Europe, and the Turkic former Soviet republics of Azerbaijan and Turkmenistan. Refah's victory in municipal elections in 1994 gave it control of the city councils in both Istanbul and Ankara and led its supporters to proclaim that it was on the path to national political power. Its triumph was regarded with horror by Turkey's secular liberals and intellectuals, although the hysterical predictions of many that Turkey could become the next Iran are both premature and simplistic.

Like many young women who have now adopted Islamic dress, Orcalan is not from a religious background. Her family was split by her decision to cover her head, with her father unhappy and her mother supportive. 'The first time I put on the scarf I felt very happy and at peace, which I never found before in my life. I felt sheltered. I'm not from a religious background although my mother is religious. There was a lot of very powerful emotion at home about this. My father doesn't want me to wear it. He is a secularist, although now he accepts it. I was not religious when l grew up. I made a decision to dedicate myself to Islam. It was the search for truth. I was always searching for truth from childhood and what it was. When I was twenty I realised that Islam was the truth. I began to read the Quran during these years and that made me realise that Islam was the truth. I felt that God spoke to me, I felt his weight.'

For Orcalan, covering her head was more than an expression of piety. The choice, or lack of headgear, is a symbol of a desire for a whole regime: secular and democratic, as Turkey is now, or Islamic, with a form of government that would take shape only after a victory by Refah at the next general election. Donning Islamic dress is also a political and cultural statement, one that seeks to assert what observant Muslims see as traditional Turkish values and an Islamic heritage that is rapidly awakening after its eradication during the last seventy years of Kemalism, as Atatürk's doctrines are dubbed. 'I am not happy with living in a secular society. Secularism has oppressed Muslims. Secularism here is not the same as in the West, here it is a tool to oppress Muslim people. I and those like me underwent some bad experiences. Now there is a return to Islamic beliefs and values. It is a return to our origin, because Turkey has its origin in Islamic values and beliefs and now we are returning to the authentic ones.'

Like many young Turkish women who have turned to Islam Orcalan is keen to emphasise her modern credentials as an independent working woman, defying the western stereotype that Muslim women must be bound to the kitchen and the baby's bedroom. 'I am not against Muslim women working, this is a job among jobs. I am aware that there is such a wrong idea about Islam and women and Islam. I do not know the origin of this. They don't know us enough. Women are human and are equal in Islam. I've worked here for about two months. I don't have any previous experience but I always wanted to be a newsreader. Channel 7 is the only place where I can do this job without giving up my beliefs and wearing my Islamic clothes.'

Channel 7 broadcasts a varied menu of news, women's programmes, music shows and films. Some of the latter appear unexpected choices, at least to western eyes, for an Islamic channel. 'On Saturdays we broadcast classic films such as Laurel and Hardy, Tarkovsky and Charlie Chaplin. We find it normal to show these films. We don't show Sylvester Stallone films, because they are inhumane. That which is human is also Islamic. Charlie Chaplin's *Modern Times* is an Islamic film,' explains the station's news manager Ahmet Hakan Coskun, who is polite but cool towards me.

Dressed in a snappy check jacket and yellow shirt, with a neatly trimmed beard, Coskun works out of a modern house in the suburbs of Istanbul that is Channel 7's headquarters. It could be a private television station anywhere, full of state-of-the-art computers, editing equipment and shiny new desks. The only difference is that every woman in the bustling building is dressed in a long skirt and a headscarf. Channel 7's *raison d'être*, he says, is to make programmes based on genuine Turkish values, which are not those of the West.

'Our programmes at Channel 7 are liked by our grandmothers. The people themselves, our people, see themselves in Channel 7. In our news programmes we do not look at things through western glasses. For example if there is something happening in Algeria, the other channels are highly dependent on western sources in their news, but we rely on other sources. We underline the oppression of the Algerian government against Muslims. We depend on Muslim sources.'

As an Islamic television station, Channel 7 must carry out a difficult juggling act. 'If Muslims have made the discovery of television, it's because they think television as an instrument produced by man is in a sense inhumane, because it turns social life upside down and it poisons people. It is a western instrument. Being aware of all the dangers of television we try to develop a new model of television broadcasting. As far as possible we make coherent programmes. We are making a new philosophy of television. There is no propaganda for Islam in our programmes, but they support the view of Islam. When we make a programme of course we have Islamic women in it. They are there, but they don't say "women, come and be a Muslim".'

Suna Kili is a Muslim woman as well, one whose family can trace its Turkish roots back to the conquest of Constantinople in 1453, but she does not watch Channel 7 television. A loquacious professor at Bosphorus University, she worked in an office next to Tansu Ciller, formerly Turkey's prime minister, for seventeen years. Professor Kili is the author of several books on Atatürk and his legacy. But even among her students that appears to be crumbling, as more turn to Islam, to her increasing bafflement and concern. In part she blames the influence, and ready cash, of nearby Islamic states for what she sees as a retrogressive step, but like many intellectuals she also realises that a seismic change is transforming sections of Turkish society as her young charges exchange their jeans and mini-skirts for headscarves and long sleeves.

'Saudi Arabia helps them, and so does Iran. I had a student here, one who was wonderful, beautiful, could have been a model and in the middle of the term she started covering herself. She said to me, "I am the same one, I just decided to cover my head, it's a symbol."'

The move of many among Turkey's youth towards Islam is a potent symbol of a growing dichotomy about the very nature of the regime in Turkey. For those such as Professor Kili who believed that the principles of Kemalism were solid and immutable, these are troubling times. 'We have to reach a consensus on fundamentals about the nature of the regime we want to embrace. In Britain there are differences between the British Labour party and the Conservative party, on economic policies maybe, perhaps occasionally, it may be a difference of foreign policy. But you do not discuss the nature of the regime itself, in that freedoms are to be enjoyed by every party and by everybody, that the state should be secular and the way the press, the universities work, and so on, these are no longer a matter of discussion.'

Atatürk's revolutionary changes, such as the abolition of Islamic law, are protected by the constitution, but many intellectuals such as Professor Kili believe that the Islamists such as the Refah party aim to change the very nature of the regime itself. 'We have an identity crisis in Turkey. That identity crisis was solved in the Kemal era: you are a Turkish citizen and then you are a human being. Then we are back to saying you are foremost a Muslim. Turkey has become a more democratic society, but it did not become a more modern society. I don't think of modernity in terms of the number of factories or hotels, but in people's pattern of behaviour, if they are [Islamic] fatalists or not, but how society and the state function. From that point of view there is regression, and now the religious elements are contesting whether the nation-state was a good idea. The process of statehood has been gone through, but they want to change it.'

But Atatürk, argues Kili, did not move too fast. His radical changes were the only way of modernising the new Turkish republic. 'I am not someone who says draft the laws according to existing society. We couldn't move an inch. In a country like ours there should be an impetus. Aren't the Turkish people worthy of a twentieth-century government? Worthy of twentieth-century legislation? In the nineteenth century, the Young Turks aimed to establish constitutional government. We had a century and a half of concerted effort to political democracy. I can tell you unequivocally, it is not going to be possible in

227

Turkey to turn the clock backward, to establish a dictatorship of any kind, whether Marxist or a religious state like Khomeini.'

Istanbul is already a city of two parallel universes and the twain are meeting less and less as support for an Islamic revival grows. With its rolling landscaped gardens and view of the sea, Kili's Bosphorus University is like a Mediterranean version of Berkeley in California. Students who would look quite at home at Oxford or the Sorbonne loll about on the grass planning the evening's partying, while rock music carries over the verges. Student societies offer their wares, as well as a holiday company selling beach vacations. This is Turkey with its face turned firmly to the West. Downtown in bustling Taksim, shops offer western designer clothes and Swiss watches. REM blares from the bars, and the cafés are crowded with stylish young Turks sipping a beer or a coffee, the women in miniskirts, the men in sharp business suits.

But the snaking back-alleys of Fatih in central Istanbul are another world, where peddlers offer Islamic books and green banners among the dilapidated wooden houses and winding streets, the heartland of the Welfare Party's support. Women keep their heads covered and the otherwise ubiquitous portraits of Atatürk have been replaced with Arabic inscriptions and illustrations of Mecca and the Haj, the pilgrimage that every observant Muslim must make at least once. The cry of the muezzin calling the faithful to prayer drifts over the backstreets of Fatih. Observant Muslims gather outside the Suleymaniye mosque, masterpiece of Suleyman the Magnificent, and carefully perform their ablutions before praying.

For Welfare Party (Refah) activists such as writer Mehmet Metiner, now an adviser to Istanbul's Refah mayor Recep Tayyib Erdogan, the future of Turkey is already decided. 'The old systems are finished, all over the world and in Turkey. Kemalism is finished. In the hearts of the people the Kemalist system was finished when it was born. The public wants a system that fits with its religious beliefs. The public wants the state and the government to be like itself. The Welfare Party tries to give an answer to these demands of the public.'

In fact many attribute Refah's success more to political and economic factors than a genuine upsurge in enthusiasm for Islam *per se*. The city's population is growing by several hundred thousand every year as economic migrants pour in from Turkey's rural heartlands. Even university graduates struggle to find a job, so the waves of peasant arrivals fight to scrape a living as prices climb relentlessly. Neglected by the established parties, the rural influx into Istanbul and Ankara provides a steady source of recruits for the Welfare Party. 'The countryside people have flocked to the cities, now Istanbul has become a large shanty town. People are poor and they see all this ostentatious living and life is very hard. So religious people are really using that. This is very important. The fundamentalist leaders play on the fact that people are living in poverty, but they had to disclose their money, and Mr Erbakan, the head of the welfare party, is one of Turkey's wealthiest politicians,' says Professor Kili.

At the same time there is a growing malaise in the Turkish body politic. A feeling among many that the Kemalist project has run its course, the secular parties have run out of ideas, and now it is time for the country to return to its roots in Islam and the East. Writing in the English-language *Turkish Daily News*, Dr Nilufer Narli, author and sociologist, described 'a crisis of identity, a belief that we are in a state of moral decadence and political decline in a non-Islamic system, and the feeling of being lost'. Turkey's Islamic movement is a response to the anxiety of modernity, she writes. 'It has found fertile ground because of the shared belief that Turkey is in a state of decline – its cause, its departure from Islamic path; its cure, a return to Islam in private and public life to restore its Islamic identity and values.' This return, to the values of the Quran instead of Kemalism, would, Islamists believe, see Turkey return to the golden era of the Ottoman empire and take its rightful place as a world power.

Europe's at best guarded welcome for Turkey is boosting this Ottoman-nostalgia and Islamicism. With their country already a member of NATO, and a bulwark against the former Soviet Union during the Cold War, many Turks feel betrayed that Ankara is being fobbed off with plans for a customs union when they seek full EU membership. Turkey has joined the Organisation for Economic Cooperation and Development, the Council of Europe, the Organisation on Security and Co-operation in Europe and the Western European Union (as an

associate member). Turkey has been an associate member of
the EU for over thirty years. If there is a western international
club, Turkey is in it. Ankara has also signed numerous international conventions in its drive to convince the world of its
modern democratic credentials.

But deeds must follow words and serious question marks
remain over Turkey's human rights record and its willingness to
conform to European norms. Human rights activists say
Ankara is in clear violation of the human rights conventions
which it has signed. In 1993 the United Nations Committee
Against Torture said that the 'existence of systematic torture in
Turkey cannot be denied'. Gross human rights violations are
being inflicted on civilians in the south-east of the country, says
an Amnesty International Report released in February 1995.
Much of these extra-judicial killings and torture take place in
the ongoing war against the Kurdish separatists, but the situation is also deteriorating in the rest of the country. In the first
ten months of 1994 there were fifty reported 'disappearances',
nearly double that of 1993, with security forces blamed for the
deaths and beatings.

Amnesty's report is a depressing and often grisly catalogue of
torture, beatings, sexual assaults and apparent executions.
Human rights activists and journalists have all been jailed for
activities that would go unpunished in mainland Europe. In
January 1996, Turkish journalist Metin Goktepe was found
dead in Istanbul after witnesses said he was detained by police.
He died from a brain hemorrhage brought on by beatings to the
head, according to the official autopsy report.

But, and it's a big but, compared to its neighbours such as
Syria and Iraq, Turkey, with its parliamentary democracy, reasonably free press and independent judiciary, is a beacon of
light and progress. European concern at human rights issues in
Turkey is seen as hypocritical by many Turks, who point to the
West's inaction over the slaughter of Muslims in Bosnia and
Chechnya. Disillusionment with the western values is growing, a
process not confined to the slums and alleys of the bazaars and
shanty-towns.

Here is Demir Inal, a manager at an Islamic bank, with a
degree from a Canadian university, the sort of sophisticated
figure who would be at home in a boardroom anywhere from

Zurich to New York. 'When Slovenia was attacked Germany came in and said "I don't want this" and the fighting was stopped in a week. But the same Germany does not do anything for Bosnia, or Chechnya. Things like this affect people's way of thinking. They keep seeing double standards. I would hope that the West does not think Muslim life is cheaper than Christian life, but it does sometimes seem like that. Look at Bosnia, 250,000 people dead and still dying. Look what America did to Libya when they killed two Americans. Imagine what they would do if it was an Iraqi or an Iranian who put the bomb in Oklahoma City, imagine what they would do to Iran or Iraq.'

The prospects of a Welfare Party government in a NATO member state, or a coalition with a powerful Welfare presence, has also caused nervous tremors in the West's corridors of power. Party officials, though, are careful to emphasise their commitment to democracy and their rejection of the Iranian and Saudi Arabian models of government. The *Refah Party and Truths*, the party's official publication, says: 'The allegation that the Welfare Party will develop policies based on enmity towards the West is not true because both East and West belong to Allah.' A statement whose intent can be interpreted in any number of ways, rather like the Refah Party itself.

The Refah Party has its roots in the National Order Party under the leadership of Necmettin Erbakan, founded in 1970. Declared illegal after the 1971 military coup it was reborn the following year as the National Salvation Party. Over the next twenty years its activists devoted themselves to increasing Islamic consciousness, especially among young Turks. Their target was not so much command of the state itself, but the building of an alternative Muslim vision of Turkey's future. Teachers, both in the state schools, where Sunni Muslim education is compulsory, and in private religious colleges, built up a solid bedrock for Refah's future Islamic edifice. In 1970 there were 72 *imam-hatip* private colleges, by 1992 their numbers had grown to 467.

Refah won 158 seats in Turkey's 450-member parliament after the December 1995 general election. By the following summer Necmettin Erbakan was prime minister of Turkey, after signing a coalition agreement with Tansu Ciller's True Path party. The agreement gave Turkey its first Islamist-majority government since Kemal Atatürk declared the country a secular republic in 1923. It made Erbakan prime minister for two years, after which he must hand over office to Mrs Ciller. There was much hysteria, both in Turkey and abroad about the victory of supposed 'Islamic fundmentalism', thanks in part to Erbakan's fiery Islamic rhetoric which included an array of unlikely and more or less unachievable promises. For example: 'We will set up an Islamic Common Market, an Islamic UN, a World Islamic Union and introduce an Islamic dinar . . . the Turkish lira is dead. Those who vote for us are good Muslims. Those who vote against us are unbelievers and atheists.' In fact only about 21 per cent of the electorate voted for Refah, and the vagaries of Turkish politics brought him to power, rather than any nation-wide lurch to radical Islam.

Erbakan's promises were enough to keep anyone busy for a while, but once again *realpolitik* triumphed over rhetoric and the reality of power proved radically different. As soon as his feet were under the Prime Minister's desk – and the Turkish financial markets began a depressed slide in anticipation of his rule – he immediately backtracked and promised to respect all international agreements, and seek close ties with the West. Even the military defence agreements with Israel, the subject of much harsh criticism among Refah's supporters, have survived. Instead Erbakan planned a visit to Iran, a smart move to keep the grassroots happy, while keeping steering the ship of Turkish foreign policy on a steady course. Why did he backtrack so rapidly? The answer is simple: had Erbakan attempted to change the fundamental nature of the Kemalist secular state the army would have almost certainly launched a military coup, leading to the nightmare 'Algerian' scenario. In one notable development Refah did open discussions with Kurdish leaders, and took a more conciliatory line towards that minority's aspirations.

Like any major political party, Refah is home to several factions and currents. It has its share of wild-eyed extremists who would force women back under the veil and introduce public amputations for theft, on the Saudi model. But these are a minority, and politicians such as its leader Erbakan who have swam in the dangerous straits of Turkish politics for decades are wily operators. He has survived the 'Bosniagate' scandal, when a parliamentary commission confirmed irregularities in the collection of millions of Deutschmarks from Turks in Germany by the Refah party. He was also little dented by revelations that he is the equivalent of a dollar millionaire in cash and property. In the autumn of 1994 he even visited the USA, reportedly to meet with think-tank analysts and intelligence officials.

But for all its anti-western election rhetoric, Refah's uniqueness is its remarkable and unprecedented synthesis of Islamic rhetoric and policies with political techniques of canvassing and recruitment that would be instantly recognisable by any Washington lobbyists. Recep Tayyib Erdogan and Melih Gokcek, the new young mayors of Istanbul and Ankara, wear suits, not turbans and robes, and appear little different from any western municipal leader. Refah party activists go door to door among the slums and alleys of Istanbul's shanty towns, offering help and a listening ear to the millions of Turks living in poverty.

Refah even formed its own tea-party brigades of female volunteers, from its women's wing, which claims almost one million members and whose activities were crucial to Refah's victory in Istanbul. Women Refah supporters were told to hold a small tea party and invite friends and relatives. Once the initial chat and courtesy greetings had been dispensed with, they moved onto politics. Videos of speeches by Erbakan were shown and calendars or perfumed handkerchiefs were handed out. It worked beautifully. No other party had bothered to court the hordes of bewildered female Anatolian immigrants who had poured into the big cities, to be completely bemused at the licentious ways of Istanbul and Ankara. Nobody ever asked them what they thought, except about the dinner they cooked every night for their husbands and families. When visitors came, who spoke their language, understood their concerns and gave them tea and attention, they were quickly converted to Refah's cause.

Battle has now commenced for the soul of Istanbul's shanty towns. Lined up against Refah's tea-party brigades are the secularist cadres composed of women such as Emine Sezer, who travel the slums for twelve hours a day and organise trips and summer schools for the children of the slums, as they seek to counteract what they see as Refah's brainwashing.

'Refah is putting pressure on, they give them money, they give them presents, and brainwash them, especially with the youngsters, and with Quran courses. About ninety per cent go on Quran courses and then they came to our summer school, so they saw the difference and they have to decide for themselves. I want to live integrated into western Europe, not into the Arabic countries. We tell this argument and they listen, because Refah hasn't told them this side of things. Refah is to denigrate western ideas and the western way of living. We tell them about the other story, the Arabic lifestyle, which is not something to admire, in my point of view. We are trying to show them two separate sorts of lives and they have to choose. I cannot dictate to people, you have to choose this sort of life or this sort of life, but if we educate them well enough they will be able to choose.'

For Sezer, part of Turkey's educated western élite, her work in the shanty towns has been a revelation. Her group should have started work there a decade ago, she says. 'Over the last few years there has been a gradual Islamisation of Turkish society and we were blind to it. That's the only way I can describe it, we talked, we had everything, we went on living grandly, and nobody ever thought of the poor. That was our biggest mistake. So we should be blamed, what we are trying to do now, we should have started ten years ago and fundamentalism would not have taken root in this country.

'But even if there isn't any danger of fundamentalism, I'd work like this. I have seen those people, they have nothing, absolutely nothing in their houses, in the way they live. Some of them have already been brainwashed, but they are open to you, they listen to you. But if I tell them don't cover yourself they will shut me out completely, they won't even listen to you, because they think it is their right to cover up themselves, so I have to respect them and I have to teach them to respect me. I keep telling them, don't give up, if you work hard and if your children are educated you can have a certain standard of living. You have to do something about it. We brought them birth control, they don't know anything about it, they have six or seven kids, they have no money, they were quite open to it. Now they keep asking us, what shall I do, please tell me, try to help me, and I am happy to see that.'

But while Erbakan, like every politician, is a prisoner of the global political and economic system on foreign policy issues, his victory has undoubtedly aided the cause of Islamicising Turkish society. Urban myth-style stories are already doing the rounds among the Istanbul intelligentsia, of armed gunmen threatening male and female swimmers for being 'unIslamic' by bathing together. Having Erbakan in the prime minister's office can only aid the cause of those who wish to steadily erode the Kemalist project. 'Refah members would like to introduce fundamentalism in Turkey. I'm scared of their group psychology. If one man says "attack the women whose heads are uncovered" the others will do it. I'm not so scared of Turkey becoming like Iran, as like Algeria,' says Sezer.

That seems unlikely at Istanbul's Refah-controlled municipal offices, where the hallways are crowded with bright multi-lingual young women, their heads covered and dressed in Islamic clothes, wielding mobile telephones. Here too, just as at Channel 7, the cliché of the cloistered Muslim female, condemned to a life of babies and cooking, has been proved wrong. 'In our country there is an idea that when you are living in an Islamic way, you must not be intelligent, you must be a fool. Our people always see us like this, as fools. I don't know why, they see the Islamic clothes as not modern,' said Isil Bulduk, an economics graduate from Istanbul University now working as secretary to the mayor. 'That view is wrong,' she says. 'I do everything the others do. I go to the cinema, theatres, I swim. There are places for us, of course, separately from men.' For many in Refah though, women have a strictly defined role. When Sibel Eraslan, Refah's women's leader in Istanbul, who many saw as a key to the party's victory for her organisational skills, demanded higher positions for women, she was sacked.

An intelligent woman in her twenties, who speaks English and German, Ms Bulduk said that other potential employers had rejected her on sight as soon as they saw her Islamic clothes. 'The others that finished the same school as me are working in very big companies. But when I went to business talks with them, with the head of the company, he looked at me, and said, "No, I don't need you." I said, "I know English, I know German, I finished university." But he said, "That doesn't matter, because your head is covered." I told him that the first thing is my job, if I do the job correctly, OK, if I make a mistake you can say everything to me.'

Bulduk became an object of media fascination after she started work as the mayor's secretary last year, to her conster-nation. 'They made a very big fuss when I got my job. They said, "How will you work in these clothes?" I wanted to tell them that I will answer the telephones and do all the other things that the mayor wants and I can do that with these clothes on. Before us in the past management, the secretaries working there only finished primary school. I said that I worked for four years and I am a university graduate and I have much more education. I said that they never took the others' photos but they took mine only because of my clothes. I felt very bad when this happened of course. But I got angry with them and I worked very well. Perhaps you won't believe me, but when I went to the toilet from my room, all the cameras were following me. I was like an animal in a zoo.' The unwillingness of many secularists to see the person beneath the scarf is substantially contributing to the growing polarisation of Turkish society as each reinforces the other's stereotype.

Married to an observant Muslim, Bulduk has found domes-tic happiness and career success. But she has lost many of her friends, who cut relations when she turned to Islam. 'My friends in university now don't talk with me. And they didn't come to my wedding ceremony. Of course I was upset, but I think why didn't they? I believe that they are not real friends. For example my old boyfriend from college came to me when I put these clothes on. He came to me and said: "I heard that you put your head under the cloth. I want to see you." He hugged me and he said, "You are very nice like that." That was a friendship, a real friendship.

'He said to me perhaps you won't be able to come to the bars with us, and you won't be able to drink alcoholic drinks with us, but I know your mind, and for me your mind is as important as your views. My college friends all supported me, but my friends in university, I don't know why, perhaps I didn't choose them very well, never accepted this. They thought that my husband made me so. He didn't, because putting these clothes on your head is a very difficult thing, because you give up things. I want to tell them that nobody can do this just because her husband wants it. And it is not a period for one or two years, it will continue for all your life.'

Modern Muslims such as Ms Bulduk reject the restrictions of regimes such as Saudi Arabia. They say they stand for a modern Islam, one that gives full rights to women. Turkey, they say, and on this many liberals agree with them, is a special case with its own history of tolerance and traditions. But it's hard to imagine a Welfare Party government ever joining – or being allowed to join – the European Union.

'Our face is turned to the East. Turkey has an Ottoman heritage. Our first target is to make good relations in politics, military and trade, with the countries that were once in the Ottoman empire. But that doesn't mean we are the enemy of the West, because we are not. We support political, military and trade relations with the West, but they must be just,' said Mehmet Metiner.

Other policy proposals may be less easy to implement. A system of differing religious courts for each faith, as existed under the Ottoman empire, will be introduced for each community, said Metiner. 'Everyone can live according to his laws. Christians and Jews have different legal systems. We don't want the government to insist on one legal system for all people, it is not democratic. That system [of different courts] worked very successfully in the Ottoman empire. We won't take that system into today's world but we will take it as a reference, and we will get some basic ideas from it and apply it to this world's concrete needs.'

Sorting out the more abstract needs of young Turkish women is the job of Leyla Melek, editor of Turkish *Cosmopolitan*. A softly spoken woman aged twenty-eight, Melek works out of the glass and steel extravaganza of the Sabah publishing house that also publishes several daily newspapers as well as *Penthouse* and *Playboy*. Like all of its international counterparts, Turkish *Cosmo* serves up a cocktail of sex, fashion and relationship advice, leavened with social and political features.

But there are limits to Turkish government tolerance. 'There are things we cannot print. We cannot show penises for example, if we do it will be censored. We do print explicit sex articles and we didn't have any problems until recently. We published a sex supplement, like all the women's magazines have done for the past year. Our March supplement was censored, but everything is so slow in Turkey so it was censored in April. I think they just had to pay a fine. The censorship is after it comes out. They inform us [if there is a problem] but usually that issue is already sold out and finished, so that nothing really happens. It was a very explicit educational book that we put out. *Penthouse* and *Playboy* don't seem to have many problems.'

Even here, in the heart of trendy medialand, Islam is making inroads, she says. 'I started working in this building in 1992, now it's 1995. Three years ago I would say maybe a third or a quarter of the 1,500 people working here used to fast during Ramadan, and this year it was more than half. Suddenly a lot of people started fasting. You think there's nothing wrong with that and nobody tried to beat me up or say something bad, but when people start staring at you if you are drinking a cup of coffee or some water it starts to become disturbing. It's not knowing what is going to happen in a few years that is disturbing. I'm trying not to think that it could be another Algeria.'

Islamic activists are focusing attention on young women, says Melek, and those who worked in western-oriented fields such as fashion are particularly prized. 'The Islamic section is very organised, probably the most organised in Turkey, where everything is very disorganised. In the high schools outsiders come to talk to the girls and try to convert them to Islam. It was effective over the years.

'Now they are converting models, because when someone who models clothes, or lingerie or swimwear, suddenly starts converting to Islam, covering their head, it's a very good image. westerners think it is disturbing, but a lot of Turkish people still believe that it's not disturbing and nothing will happen to the secular Turkish state. There is always the comparison with Algeria. I'm trying to be secular, everybody is free to believe in what they want. On the other hand I do believe that it is frightening and bad things may happen. I don't know yet, I haven't decided.'

For Matilt Manokyan, Turkey's richest woman, Refah's electoral triumph is bad news. Mrs Manokyan, an elderly Christian lady of Armenian origin in her late seventies, has built her multi-million-pound business empire on real estate and hotels, but she is best known for the string of legal brothels, somewhere between three and thirty-two, depending whom you believe, that she owns. Brothels are legal in Turkey, and her 'houses' as she calls them are supervised by doctors. Her palatial flats on the top floor of a block in downtown Istanbul are the most extraordinary residences I have ever seen. Lavish shrines to the cult of her personality, they are bedecked in portraits of Manokyan as a young girl, staring into the glorious future in classic socialist realist style. Every inch is taken up with press clippings, pictures, photographs and framed letters of thanks for the massive donations she makes to charity every year, including commendations from President Suleiman Demirel and Tansu Ciller. A battalion of servants bring a never-ending stream of tea and sweets and packets of opened cigarettes lay in ornate glass dishes all over the table. One of her officials cannot contain her excitement as we speak, and keeps jumping forward, proffering another letter of thanks from a charity to better illustrate the full extent of Manokyan's munificence.

Manokyan started in the sex business when she was working as a fashion designer and a client could not pay the bill. The client offered her a brothel instead and Madam Manokyan was born. 'The houses play an important role, they are necessary. In Europe relations between men and women are comfortable, if you like a girl you can go with her. But in Turkey it's not like that. We need these houses, because here a man cannot go out with a girl and just take her for a drink or something like that. I don't care if people criticise me for running the houses, everyone is free to speak in the way they want.' Such is her devotion to Kemal Atatürk that she has even written a poem in his memory, praising his merits as the founder of modern Turkey. 'Suleyman Demirel, Suleyman Demirel,' her assistant suddenly yells excitedly at the mention of Atatürk.

As we spoke, various men in suits, bodyguards and other functionaries, appeared and disappeared. Manokyan's wealth has earned her many enemies, and for all her charity work, not everyone wishes her well. In September 1995 her bodyguard and driver were killed in an explosion as she was getting out of her car in front of her apartment, and she was hospitalised with a broken leg.

*

But the question of a Muslim revival and its implications for Turkey and the West are more complicated than a simple dichotomy between the Sunni-Muslim-led Refah party and the pro-Atatürk secularists. There is a third force in Turkish society, firmly Muslim in its identity, but strongly aligned with Kemalism. These are the Alevi Muslims, about 20 million strong, including many Kurds, and they are now starting to flex their political muscle.

The Alevis have their own distinct version of Islam, one heavily influenced by the shamanistic roots of Turkic culture as it travelled to Anatolia from Central Asia. It is far more liberal, in western terms, than the majority orthodox Sunni Muslim faith. Like Sunnis, Alevis believe in Allah and his prophet Muhammad. However, they also follow Ali, one of the four Caliph, or successors, to the Prophet, after his death in AD 632, from whom they take their name, as do Iranian Shiites. But Turkish Alevis take a radically different approach to their religion than the Ayatollahs of Tehran. They pray together with women, include music and dance in their rituals and may drink alcohol. Alevis have a strong allegiance to the secularist ideology of the Turkish state, seeing it as a bulwark against a rising tide of Sunni Islam. This is not fully reciprocated: while Sunni Islam receives generous funding from the state, Alevis must finance their own religious and cultural activities. At the same time, religious education is compulsory in school, but the syllabus follows Sunni Islam, although community leaders believe this will soon change to include Alevi Islam as well.

That Alevis receive no financial help from the Ministry of Religious Affairs is in the tradition of the discrimination they have suffered for centuries from the Sunni majority, says Izzettin Dogan, an Alevi community leader and professor of international law. 'With the creation of the new republic [in 1923] Alevis found some kind of freedom to exercise their beliefs as they wish. But unfortunately this was special to the time when Atatürk was alive, and after his death the Alevis began to have difficulties. The Ministry for Religious Affairs is occupied only with the Sunnis and not with the Alevis.

'They have been pushed in a sense out of the social order of Turkey. They have to do something for the integration of this part of the Turkish community. The first step is to put in the

programmes of education, beginning from next year, information about Alevi beliefs of Islam. If you are more than 20
million people you can influence the structure of your democracy. If they continue to ignore the Alevis it can cause some
problems.' Sitting in his office in Taksim, Professor Dogan is
clearly a major player in the Alevi community. A stream of visitors pours into his office to pay their respects and discuss the
issues of the day, each greeting, and being greeted with, kisses
on the cheek. In the background his black mini-dress-clad secretary bustles back and forth with trays of tea and coffee.

With the increasing support for Refah, which does not accept
the legitimacy of the Kemalist project, Turkey's mainstream
parties, and moderate Islamic groups, now see the Alevis as a
useful ally in the struggle for the country's soul. 'They think
they could bring the necessary freedoms to Alevis plus the other
Sunni parties who believe the Atatürk model is still valid, and by
the combination of these two parties they can overcome in a
democratic way the danger of the Islamic parties coming to
power. I don't believe that Refah is a danger to Turkey. But it
can come to power. When Refah says "If we come to power we
will bring you equality and the world and everything you need",
Turkish people are not inclined to ask what is inside this everything. It creates, like Marxism or other ideologies, a kind of
hope that a human being is intended to believe without analysing what is inside this ideology.'

While leaders of Refah are careful to cultivate good relations
with the Alevis, both for reasons of PR and political expediency,
both sides know that their visions of Turkey's future are radically different. Alevis will never transfer their allegiance to
Refah, both because of politics and theology. 'The Alevi
approach to Islam is quite different from the Sunni approach. It
is that reason must reign in the state's affairs and not religious
principles. Much of the Alevi way of life spread into the
Ottoman empire in its first two hundred years, such as the tolerance of minorities, when the Ottoman empire accepted the
refugees from Spain in 1492. But what is important to us is not
to violate the rights of another, to respect everyone and not to
injure them. We believe that all of us are very little pieces of
God, the same God. So to injure a man, a human being, is the
equivalent of injuring God himself. So you mustn't harm people,

241

especially not to violate another's right. The rest of what we believe is not very important at all. This is something concerning man and God himself and not society.'

The differences between Sunni and Alevi Islam are also cultural, thanks to Alevi Islam's shamanistic and nomadic roots, which reject the rigid formalism of the Bedouin and Arabic lifestyle in favour of a relaxed humanistic vision. 'Sunni Muslims are based much more on the Arabic approach, which means what is important is the formalities of Islam, like the mosque, the way of prayer, fasting at Ramadan. This is very important for the Arab and the Arabic approach to Islam. We believe in the Quran and the Quran is the holy book of Islam and we are very attached to it. But we do not interpret it as the Arabs do. The Turkish approach is not the Arab approach. The Turks of central Asia did not accept Islam very easily. There were many wars between them and the Arabs before they accepted it. They did not cut their ties with their traditions and their past. They accepted Islam by making a mixture of Islam with their traditions with their Shamanistic traditions.'

As you might expect from a professor of international law Izzettin Dogan has a ready and fluent explanation as to why Alevis are permitted to drink wine. 'Alevis drink alcohol and they are very happy when they take it. It is not true that it says in the Quran that you must not drink alcohol. It is true that it says in the Quran that wine is not good to drink but we have translated that in another way. We believe that for the people who are going to be drunk if they drink then it is not good. But you know what Omar Khayyam says to God: "My God, if you have really forbidden to drink wine then why did you create grapes." For the people that are going to be drunk when they drink, then it is *haram* [forbidden]. But if not there is no problem and you can have it.'

Not surprisingly, for many hard-line orthodox Sunni Muslims, the Alevi approach is anathema. They consider the Alevis little more than heretics, who flout the five pillars of Islam. In March 1995 two radical Sunni Muslim groups claimed responsibility for an attack by gunmen on a coffee shop that killed three people in the Gaziosmanpasa district of Istanbul, home to many Alevis. Those deaths triggered mass riots by Alevi and between fifteen and thirty people were killed in the fighting against police and security forces that followed. It was an ominous sign of the tension that lies under the surface of Turkish society, provoking memories of the street-fighting that raged across Istanbul during the 1970s, when different groups controlled their own suburbs, turning some into no-go areas for the security forces, until the military coup of 1980.

The coffee shop attack was the second fatal assault on the Alevi community since 1993. In July of that year thirty-seven people died when a hotel in the city of Sivas, where a group of writers, poets and singers were celebrating an Alevi festival, was set on fire. Last year tension flared again when Istanbul's Refah party mayor Recep Erdogan tried to demolish Alevi mosques, used also as charity houses, triggering weeks of vigils in their defence, until he backed down. For Dogan, the violence is further proof that society must be based on modern democratic lines and not ruled by theology.

'It is true that if you like you can organise a society according to the Quran's principles. But it is not an obligation, the obligation that the Quran brings is the organisation of your entire life and your inner life, but other people's lives are not included. But there is another principle and many people don't give the right translation for this Sura: the Quran says that before everything I gave you reason. That means in all your approaches you have to ask your reason and if you put your reason before everything, before all your actions, then you can see that a state organisation must be based on rational principles and not religious ones. That's why I don't see any contradiction with a secular system. The source of a secular state system is also based in the Quran and in this Sura of the Quran . . . That's why I think the regimes that conform with the Quran are the democratic and secular systems, like in the West.'

From the activists of Refah, through the merchants in the bazaars, the generals who organised a string of coups, the tired politicians in the squabbling centrist parties and the nervous secularists, everyone agrees on one thing: after seventy years of Kemalism, an island of democracy in a sea of Islam, Turkey is at a crossroads.

Held at arm's length by Europe, nervous over increasing Russian influence in the Balkans, part of its former empire, and building pan-Turkic links with the former Soviet states of Central Asia, Turkey is searching for its place and role in the world. But wild predictions that as Refah's influence grows Turkey could turn into another Iran or Saudi Arabia are unlikely to come true, for the simple reason that Istanbul is not Tehran and Ankara is not Jeddah. Time and again Turks, of whatever political and religious hue, will proclaim exasperatedly that Turks are not Arabs or Iranians, but their own nation. And ultimately, the large population of educated women, the sizeable Alevi minority and, perhaps most of all, the guns of the strongly secularist army, will prevent a Turkish Islamic theocracy, where *Shariah* law rules. Turkey also has its own distinct Islamic Ottoman heritage, with a tradition of religious tolerance of Jews and Christians quite at odds with the present-day Muslim regimes of the Middle East.

Perhaps more likely is that Turkey could be the cradle for a new modern form of Islam that seeks to reconcile the dictates of the Quran with the twentieth century, where working Islamic women hold mobile telephones to their headscarves as they help run city governments, or edit the night's news on a computer screen. Refah itself is divided over the country's future and its proposed model of government, between the hardline Islamists and the pragamatists, who realise that even an Islamic Refah government cannot turn away from the modern world.

For Suna Kili, Turkish women could be the engine for this evolution. There is already a political battle inside Refah between its 60,000 women activists and the conservative old guard, who did not field a single woman candidate in the 1995 election. 'I am not expecting this reform from the men, I am expecting it from the women. I am expecting something to come out of all this religiosity in Turkey, from the educated Muslim women,' she says. Over seventy years of Kemalist modernism have left their mark on young Islamic women, such as the technicians and newsreaders of Channel 7, and they will not surrender so easily. Time, and the increasing age of their opponents within Refah are on their side, if nothing else.

'They are educated and they will not accept being thought of as second-class people. Today in my class on Bentham, the best interpretation was given by the girl who covered her head, in impeccable English. So what do you expect, they are driving cars, they speak languages, they own small businesses, they are running newspapers. I don't think religion in itself is that dogmatic. We wouldn't have so many sects if it were. If Islam is going to get a new liberal interpretation, it will come from Turkey, precisely because we have a different background, and it will come from Islamic women.'

The Nation of Islam's million-man march,
Washington DC, 16 October 1995

Chapter 9

THE UNITED STATES

'We Muslims will be the new communists. This country has always needed a bogeyman, we had the red threat and now it's the Islamic one . . . I'm a Muslim fundamentalist. That doesn't mean I'm ready to blow up a bridge. It means I strive to practise my religion in pristine purity.'
Abdel Hakim Mustapha, African-American Muslim, author and activist

'In many ways you are freer to be a Muslim in America than in many Muslim countries. I've lived and travelled in Muslim countries. You can't write a letter to the editor there, you can't hold a protest sign in front of an embassy, you can't do anything that is at variance with whatever government or dictator happens to be in power there.'
Ibrahim Hooper, of the Council on American–Islamic Relations

It is a busy winter morning at the Phoenician Art Gallery on 2580 Broadway and owner Hani Adawi, a Lebanese Palestinian, is juggling the demands of a stream of customers while explaining how he came to New York from the port city of Sidon, and has made a new life here for himself and his family. The snow lies thick on the ground outside and a bitter freezing wind is blowing up West 97th Street from the Hudson river, just a few blocks away. Framed prints and photographs line the walls as the prospective buyers wander in, steam floating above the ubiquitous cups of weak coffee that Americans seem to thrive on. Adawi's gallery is located on the Upper West Side, whose elegant brownstone buildings are home to an eclectic New York mix of Jewish professionals, students at nearby Columbia University and young singles who crowd onto the express subway every night to hit the bars and clubs in downtown Greenwich Village.

Adawi arrived in the United States in December 1982, the winter of the year that Israel invaded Lebanon, triggering a storm of international condemnation and a fresh flow of refugees from that battered country. 'I came here because of the war in Lebanon, and because of the lack of educational opportunities. I wanted to go to college but it wasn't safe, because of all the checkpoints. I still remember what happened, you can't forget these things, what the town and families went through. What the Israelis went through with the Nazis, they practised on us. Not everything. They didn't burn us, it wasn't that extreme, but it was psychological warfare, big time.'

He made it through the front-lines to Beirut to the American embassy, where he filled out the necessary forms, and, to his slight amazement, was quickly granted a student visa. He left soon after, to a country that seemed like another universe, free of checkpoints, warring militias and invading armies, although admittedly some of New York is considerably more dangerous than present-day Beirut. For the young Lebanese student America seemed like the promised land. 'It was a completely different world, like a paradise. In Lebanon it was like being in the darkness all the time. Here there were lights, traffic and buildings, everything was so quiet and peaceful.' Now married to Fatima, an Afghan woman from Kabul, Adawi studied in Oklahoma before starting work as a salesman for seven years. Then, like almost every other immigrant to the land of the free, he decided to go it alone and opened the gallery in the autumn of 1995. 'I decided to try the American dream and have my own business, and I opened it with my brother. We set it up with our own money.'

Like millions of immigrants before him, Adawi found that the United States, where almost everyone is descended from foreigners, whether recent arrivals or generations-old families, is still the land of opportunities. Unlike in Germany, the six million or so – nobody knows the exact numbers – Muslims in the United States are not perpetual outsiders, legally marginalised because of their skin colour and foreign culture or deprived of citizenship on racial grounds. Over half were born in the United States and for the immigrants there are no requirements to have the right pure blood-lines for gaining citizenship. Adawi plans to stay and become an American citizen. 'Eventually I will be like an Irish American, an Italian American, or an African American, but I'll be a Palestinian American. It means that I'll be an American citizen from Palestine, with my ancestors, my parents from Palestine. My parents come and visit me often. They are very happy that I'm living in America,' says Adawi. America is still the promised land across the Muslim world, even for many of the extreme Islamic radicals in the Middle East, who denounce the 'Great Satan' while wondering how to get a tourist visa or Green Card residence permit for the country they claim to see as a den of vice and debauchery.

Muslims are a comparatively new minority in the United States in this century, their numbers growing rapidly during the 1970s and 1980s as war and strife spread across Turkey, Afghanistan, the Levant and the Indian sub-continent and a major influx of immigrants arrived. Over half of American Muslims, 56 per cent, are immigrants, with the remainder born there. It's easy to meet Muslim immigrants – just hail a Yellow Cab. For just as the archetypal London cabbie is a Jewish man called Morrie, the New York version is a Muslim called Mustapha. Take a taxi there and it's odds-on that your driver will be Islamic, probably Arab or Pakistani, although not all immigrants from the Middle East worship at a mosque. I took a ride with a Coptic Christian from Egypt, who said he left Alexandria because of pressure from Islamic radicals, who were making life difficult for Christians. 'These Muslims, they want to ban everything, nothing is allowed, no dancing, no singing, no music, no drinking,' he exclaimed as we roared up the Hudson river embankment. 'All they know is Allah, Allah, Allah. That's OK, have God in your soul, all right, but not all day, every day,' which was as good a description I have ever heard of the puritanical, repressive streak that runs through one variety of Arab Islam.

But Islam is no stranger to America, as many of the millions of African slaves uprooted from West Africa and brought to America were Muslims. Yarrow Mamout, an African Muslim slave set free in 1807, may have lived to be over 128 years old, according to a pamphlet published by the American Muslim Council, and later became one of the first shareholders in America's second chartered bank, the Columbia Bank. His portrait now hangs at the Georgetown Public Library, Washington DC. Half a century later the United States cavalry hired his co-religionist Hajji Ali to raise camels in Arizona. In 1865, at the end of the Civil War, librarians at the University of Alabama saved one book from the advancing Yankee troops who would destroy the library. It was a translated copy of the Quran.

Islam is now America's fastest-growing religion, say Muslim organisations, and contrary to popular belief, only a small minority of American Muslims are Arabs. In fact most of America's Arab population of about 2.5 million are Christians. By far the largest group, over 40 per cent of American Muslims, are African-Americans, according to the American Muslim Council. Many are converts, descendants of those same slaves, who have turned to Islam as much for political reasons as religious ones, as a statement to express their separation from, and dissatisfaction with, the Anglo-Saxon Christianity of America's ruling élite. The next largest group, about 25 per cent, hails from the Indian sub-continent. Arabs such as Hani Adawi comprise about 12 per cent of America's Muslim population. But while Muslims can settle down and build up their communities, from California to Chicago, from Texas to Tennessee, they must battle against a tide of ignorance about their lives and beliefs, especially outside the major conurbations such as New York or Los Angeles, where Muslim immigrants tend to congregate.

Of all the western countries to host a substantial Muslim minority, it is the United States that offers the greatest challenge to those Muslims wishing to live fully as Americans, but maintain and cherish their Islamic heritage. Not because of any institutionalised anti-Islamism, but because the values and mores of much of contemporary America – widespread use of recreational drugs, alcohol, promiscuity, homosexuality, teenage dating, gun ownership, values that are ubiquitous across the media – clash completely with the demands of Islamic morality. As a parent of a two-year-old son, Abed al-Rahman, Adawi knows he will have to maintain a difficult juggling act to raise his children according to the values of Islam, while living in a consumer society that sells and markets sex, which for Muslims is a sanctification of marriage, as just another commodity. 'I believe all I can do is guide my kids the right way. There is a big difference between the Islamic way of living and the American way. Homosexuality, dating, you don't have to do this stuff to realise it is bad. Dating we believe is sinful.'

How do you know it is sinful, I ask?

'Because God said it's sinful, because it can lead to a lot of problems, sexual diseases, minor things to major things. If you don't have sex before marriage it rules out a lot of these things. It causes psychological problems too. There is too much freedom for teenagers. Eighteen-year-old kids live on their own and their own parents can't do anything. For us the family is extremely important. My brothers and I support our family. My father is retired, we support him. But we still listen to him, he can't stop us doing anything, he can't stop our money, because we support him, but we listen to him and we respect him. I don't think Americans have that much respect for their parents. They want to be independent, live on their own without family support. Young girls get pregnant and they don't know what to do. One girl I read about recently beat her kid, nearly killed it because it was crying and she didn't know what to do. There was no aunt to come round and chat, no mother to guide her. They want to be independent but there is a price for that.'

But these things could happen to Muslims, as well, I reply.

'But not as much. In Lebanon my neighbours are like my brothers and sisters. I lived in my apartment for three years and all I say is good morning to my neighbour. I don't even know her name. Most Americans are cold, everything is business, even friends are friends to a certain limit. You cannot say this is my best friend, I can rely on him. When I went back to Lebanon my friends were there, if I needed help I ask them and it is done. Here they say, "Well, I don't know. If it is convenient, OK." They put themselves first.' Hearing Adawi's description of America's lack of neighbourliness reminded me of an interview I once read with a Bosnian Muslim refugee who had gone to live in England and was amazed that even after months in his new flat, nobody had invited him in for coffee, that great lubricant of Muslim social life.

251

Adawi says that living in New York provides him with a challenge to live as a Muslim, one that brings its own rewards. He tries to observe the precepts of Islam, both religious and social, but to live as a Muslim in New York, without the support of family – for Islam is an intensely social and communal faith – is more difficult than in Sidon, although it's definitely easier in America's most cosmopolitan city than in Arkansas or Alabama. Adawi says he has encountered sporadic hostility, but that was probably based more on racism than any specific hatred of Muslims. More endemic, and sometimes more tiresome to deal with, is the inability of many Americans to understand why, for example, he doesn't drink alcohol, a refusal that is often met with baffled incomprehension. 'I don't drink and it is difficult when everyone around is drinking. They say, "Come on, have a drink, just a vodka, I'll mix it with orange juice." They don't understand. But I don't drink, I don't eat pork, I do my reading of the Quran, I say my prayers, I try to be a good person, to be good to my neighbours. I keep Ramadan, which is difficult to do here. Here there is no support like there is at home. You can look at it in a negative way and say how hard it is to do it here. But you can also look at it in a positive way and say to yourself: "I'm different. I am a Muslim but I can do it." Not because someone is telling me to, but because I want to do it. I'm doing it for myself.'

For Adawi, like many religious people, Muslim, Jewish or Christian or of whatever faith, there is a spiritual vacuum at the heart of the United States. The classified pages of newspapers such as the *Village Voice*, New York's weekly listings magazine, support his claim. They are filled with rows of advertisements promising instant fulfillment through everything from encounter therapy and self-exploration to Buddhism and even Sufi (Islamic mystic) dancing. Spirituality, like sex, is for sale to anyone with enough dollars, but that's only one half of the equation, for the peace that Islam or any of the great faiths brings their adherents comes at a price, of following a set of rules and requirements that do not always marry well with life in 1990s America. But in a society where more or less anything goes, many still yearn for some structure to their lives and a set of rules to live by, just as in western Europe an increasing number of Christian Americans are converting to Islam, finding in that faith the means to fill the spiritual vacuum in their lives. When I interviewed spokesmen and women in Washington for the American Muslim Council (AMC) and the Council on American–Islamic Relations (CAIR), both were white converts, who clearly found in Islam a faith and a cause around which to build their lives. But none of this is news to Muslims such as Adawi. He tells the story of one of his customers who brought him a picture of an Indian lady to be framed. 'I asked her, is it a relative? She said, "No, it is my mother, my spiritual mother, she's my healer, she gives me strength." I asked her what she meant. She said "She gives me an energy by her presence."'

He looks both incredulous and sympathetic as he talks. 'This woman, she's educated, beautiful, well dressed, not stupid. She asked me if I wanted to go and visit her spiritual mother with her. I said, no thanks. They are like a sponge, empty. They want something to fill them up, fill the emptiness. They absorb it all, there's nothing there so they need something. They want to belong, and when somebody talks to them sweetly they fall for it. They'll believe in anything. It's the way they are raised. They are empty. When I sat down and talked about religion at college they know only the basics. But they don't really know anything. When it is time to learn they are busy with girlfriends, sports, superficial things. But Islam answers my questions and satisfies my spiritual needs.'

Adawi prays at the Islamic Centre, on the other side of Central Park, a plush building financed by money from the Gulf states, popular with Muslim diplomats at the United Nations as well as local Muslims. On a quiet weekday afternoon a few dozen worshippers are gathered there for afternoon prayers, among them Abdel Hakim Mustapha, an African-American originally born Cedric McClester in Boston fifty years ago. Like many black Americans he has converted, or reverted – a term many Muslims prefer – to Islam.

Mustapha is keen to talk and so we retire to a nearby café where he tells his story over coffee and bagels. Born a Christian, he found it difficult to grasp the theological complications of a faith based on a trinity, rather than the unity of God. And like many African-Americans he has found an identity and a cause in Islam, with its message of universal brotherhood, where skin colour is irrelevant, that eluded him in white America. 'We see Christianity as something used to enslave us. Christianity said our pie would come from the sky, but Islam deals with the here and now. It challenges you, it's the perfect religion, always trying to improve you. Muslims are always reading, stressing education, constantly seeking knowledge. I was brought up a Seventh-Day Adventist, I always had a deep spiritual side. I challenged things at Sunday school, they couldn't describe the Holy Ghost or explain why prayers end in Jesus's name, not God's. I respected Jesus and I believed at one time that he was the son of God, but the son, not God. Islam is a thinking person's religion.'

Mustapha became a Muslim in 1983, after suffering a personal crisis involving drugs and some unpleasant people who were pursuing him, he says. A big man, he outlines his progress to Islam with an easy confidence, but like many black Americans, indeed a substantial number of Muslims all over the world, his views are tainted with anti-Semitism, seeing if not exactly a Jewish conspiracy, then at least a disproportionate Jewish influence in opinion-forming parts of society. 'The educators are Jewish, the media is prominently controlled by the Jews, but they have been made scapegoats and people play on that fact and it becomes a crutch. Yes, the Jews had some complicity with slavery, but where next, who do we hate next? It's more important what we do for ourselves, recognise the historical facts and then move on. We are in a corrupt environment, but I am one hundred per cent American, I love America and I don't want to live in any other country. They tell us money is the panacea for everything, but everyone is seeking answers because of corruption and moral decay. But Islam offers a moral compass, we understand there is another life when rewards and punishments will be handed out.'

The virtual collapse of communal life in part of the African-American community is also bringing many to the mosque. About one in four black men between 20 and 29 is either in prison, on parole or charged with a criminal offence and awaiting trial. As their society and values crumple under a hail of gunfire in the inner-city ghettos, many American blacks seek answers in religion. But which one?

Christianity is seen by many as the faith of the racists and enslavers, imposed on American blacks, and Judaism they view as the religion of the landlords and exploiters. So that leaves Islam, with its message of self-improvement and brotherhood. That many white Americans have a visceral distrust of Islam and Muslims only increases its appeal for many African-Americans.

'More people are turning to Islam because of the devastation in the black community. They see discipline, structure and a moral grounding that is now missing but once existed in the black community. Black rage is real. Even the most assimilated milk-toast black person has some seething rage. It comes from the little indignities, from white supremacy, whether it's subtle or blatant racism, people moving aside when you get into an elevator, or following you around in a store when you are shopping. I'm not a kid, I don't need an escort, I'm a middle-aged man. That's the appeal of the Nation of Islam, because we were subjected to the worst form of slavery.'

The idea that Jews controlled the slave trade is widespread among many African-Americans, whether Muslim or Christian. It shapes the black perception of a community that should be a common ally on which it shares many common values, and is a root cause of widespread anti-Semitism among many black Americans, despite the role that liberal Jews played in helping to organise and bankroll the civil rights movements of the 1960s. Their reward was a book published by the Nation of Islam, the fringe quasi-Islamic, but extremely influential, grouping led by Louis Farrakhan, in 1991, entitled *The Secret Relationship Between Blacks and Jews*, which accused Jews of being 'key operatives' in the slave trade. Although it was denounced and deconstructed across America by a legion of academics, the damage was done, and even mainstream orthodox African-American Muslims such as Abdel Hakim Mustapha have absorbed its ideas, helping sour black–Jewish relations for years, perhaps irrevocably. The book had over one thousand footnotes, but its basic premise is wrong on several counts. Firstly, there were no Jewish communities of note on the African coast where the slave trade was concentrated. Secondly, slavery was widespread in the Middle East before the advent of Islam, and Arabs, both pre-Muslim and Muslim, played a major role in transporting humans for sale. The Quran does not outlaw slavery, although it encourages slave owners to treat their human chattels fairly and, preferably, to set them free.

For most Americans, orthodox Islam, whether Shiah or Sunni, is synonymous – wrongly – with the Nation of Islam. The Nation was founded in July 1930 by Wallace Dodd Ford, who claimed to be descended from the prophet Muhammad. His assistant Robert J. Poole later took over, and changed his name to Elijah Muhammad, claiming that he was divinely inspired by Allah. In his book *Message to the Blackman in America* he set out the sect's core beliefs, which include a claim that white people were devils created in an experiment by a wizard called Yakub 6,000 years ago. The Nation's bizarre creed, combined with its message of communal and economic self-help, brought it growing support among African-Americans. It came to national prominence in the 1960s, through the voice of its then spokesman Malcolm X. But Malcolm X broke with the Nation after completing the *Haj*, the pilgrimage to Mecca that is one of the five pillars of Islam. That was his epiphany, where he saw that racism against whites was both un-Islamic and unproductive. This is part of a letter he wrote to his assistants in Harlem from Saudi Arabia:

> There were tens of thousands of pilgrims, from all over the world. They were of all colors, from blue-eyed blonds to black-skinned Africans. But we were all participating in the same ritual, displaying a spirit of unity and brotherhood that my experiences in America had led me to believe could never exist between the white and non-white.
>
> America needs to understand Islam, because this is the one religion that erases from its society the race problem . . . I have never before seen sincere and true brotherhood practiced by all colors together irrespective of their color.

It was a moving personal testimony, but was greeted with fury by the radical separatists around Elijah Muhammad, including Louis Farrakhan. It was also, perhaps, his death warrant. Malcolm X was shot and killed while speaking at a rally in Harlem in February 1965. After a series of disputes that saw many of the Nation's followers adopt orthodox Islam, Farrakhan refounded the Nation of Islam in all its hard-line bigotry. Here he is, tape-recorded in a Chicago mosque, outlining his views on the Holocaust:

> Little Jews died while big Jews made money. Little Jews being turned into soap while big Jews washed themselves with it. Jews, playing violin, Jews playing music, while other Jews [were] marching into the gas chambers. We wasn't there. We had nothing to do with it. But why all of a sudden am I anti-Semitic? Tell me!

Farrakhan's most recent triumph was the 'million march', when hundreds of thousands of American males took to the streets of Washington DC. His ideology of racial separation – apartheid by any other name – is increasingly influential among mainstream black organisations. Despite his record of virulent racism, anti-Semitism and sexism – for women are often banned from his meetings – his is the loudest and most-listened to voice in black America, and he uses Islam as a platform to proclaim his beliefs, to the anger of many mainstream orthodox Muslims. In fact, by even the most heterodox standards, members of the Nation of Islam – whose members number about 10,000, less than 0.2 per cent of America's Muslims – do not qualify as mainstream Muslims. For starters, the belief of the Nation's second leader, Elijah Muhammad, that he was divinely inspired by Allah, marks him as a major heretic. The essence of Islam is the *shahadah*, the belief that 'there is no God but Allah and Muhammad is his prophet', and this definitely does not include the claims of Elijah Muhammad that he was Allah's messenger, or his 'discovery' that white people were created by Yakub 6,000 years ago. The nation's creed also diverts from orthodox Islam on several other important counts. Nation of Islam members are not required to go on the *Haj*, and fasting from dawn to dusk during the month of Ramadan is not compulsory. Instead they fast in December, when the days are shorter.

Although Farrakhan's beliefs exclude him from mainstream Islam, he found a ready welcome among the leaders of Islamic countries such as Iran, Libya and Sudan when he toured the Middle East in early 1996. Even Necmettin Erbakan, leader of

Turkey's Islamic Welfare Party, found time to meet Farrakhan and eat *iftar*, the fast-breaking meal at the end of Ramadan, with him. Compare the warm welcome extended to Farrakhan in the Islamic Republic of Iran, with the treatment of Iranian Bahais there. Both are heretics by orthodox Muslim standards. Like Farrakhan, Bahais claim that another prophet followed Muhammad, in their case Bahuallah, a nineteenth-century Persian. Hundreds of Bahais have been executed or imprisoned for their beliefs. Nobody in Tehran threatened to charge Farrakhan with heresy. But then even in an Islamic theocracy politics can still triumph over theology.

For all its small numbers, the Nation of Islam also exercises considerable influence over mainstream orthodox African-American Muslims, many of whom, like Abdel Hakim Mustapha, are sympathetic to at least parts of its message. 'The Nation of Islam was the first to introduce us to the concept of Islam, because we had lost a lot of that through the Christian heritage. They stopped us from eating pork, they stopped us from smoking, they stopped us from fornicating. They reconstructed lives, and made many of us ready for Allah. Many of the Black Muslims, followers of Elijah Muhammad, are orthodox Muslims, and they are orthodox Muslims because they are exposed to a concept of Islam. If we were to judge him on orthodox Islamic standards we would find a lot lacking, however, if we judge the work of the man there must have been some divine inspiration there for him to put us on the path.'

Thankfully though, the Nation's creed of hate, racism and separatism still puts it beyond the Islamic pale for Mustapha. 'I had contact most of my life with Black Muslims. I debated with them, my problem with them was racism, this talk of the blue-eyed devil I couldn't accept. I'm not prepared to hate, it doesn't do anything for my creed. I'm not prepared to use racism as a crutch, because that's just emotional masturbation. I'm more results oriented. We don't make nationalistic separations in Islam, we are all one nation, whether white or black, that's why the term Black Muslim is anathema to Islam.'

Play the game of word association with most white Americans, saying the terms 'Muslim' or 'Islam' and their immediate reaction will probably be 'terrorist' or 'Oil Sheikh', says James

Zogby of the Arab American Institute in Washington DC. 'I have taken cartoons from Nazi Germany and Tsarist Russia about Jews and compared them with American cartoons about Arabs at that time. You could see a definite similarity, about "the alien in the midst and beyond who threatens us". Both Muslims and Jews were feared because they were perceived as threatening the values of various states and their peoples. The way both the Jew and the Arab were presented was they lusted after women, their wealth was illicit by definition. This was still going on in the '70s and '80s, this idea that, "they have our oil" or were involved in terrorism.' The AAI even puts out a leaflet outlining the contribution Arab-Americans have made to politics, business, arts and culture. It is a proud little document, yet I found it somehow sad that such a pamphlet needs to be published at all.

But the stereotypes about oil money are wrong, as only a small percentage of American Muslims are Arabs, and most of those hail from the Levant – Syria, Lebanon, Palestine and Egypt – rather than the Gulf. As for terrorism, the vast majority of American Muslims are law-abiding, peaceful citizens. Muslims have been involved in or carried out two acts of terrorism on American soil in recent years: the murder in 1990 of the extreme right-wing Rabbi Meir Kahane in New York, and the bombing of the New York World Trade Center in February 1993. El Sayyid A. Nosair was jailed on gun charges for the death of Rabbi Kahane, although he was acquitted of murder. To put this in perspective, James Zogby rapidly quotes FBI statistics that there were over sixty-five terrorist acts on US soil between 1981 to 1992, of which just two were carried out by Arabs and Muslims.

The World Trade Center bombing, in which six people died and hundreds were injured, was an unmitigated disaster for Muslims living in the United States as well as the families of those killed or injured. The actions of a tiny clutch of fanatics, based around the radical Egyptian Sheikh Omar Abdul-Rahman, now imprisoned on conspiracy charges, tarred a whole community with the terrorist's bloody brush. When the bomb went off Hani Adawi was working for a company which had an office in the World Trade Center. His colleagues reacted, not so much with hostility, as sudden interest in his Palestinian heritage, assuming that he would be privy to all sorts of inside information about the attack. 'If you tell them you are a Palestinian, a Muslim, they think you are a terrorist and you know about hijackings and stuff like that. They asked me what's going to happen next. They ask stupid questions as if I'm the expert or I am one of them. I don't know. I'm not an expert. I may understand why it happens. But not the details. When the World Trade Center bomb happened we had an office in there. People at work started asking me about it, an army reservist asked me what kind of bomb did I think it was, he said, "All Palestinians are terrorists, they have experience." At first I got upset, then I got used to it. But I realised that they know nothing about us.'

At the other end of Manhattan to Adawi's gallery is the office of Daniel Felber, former defence lawyer for Siddig Ibrahim Siddig Ali, one of the defendants in the New York conspiracy bombing trial. Felber works out of Wall Street in the heart of New York's financial district, encased in a glass-fronted office, twenty-one floors up in one of the skyscrapers that soar up dizzily from the sidewalks. There were two trials in the aftermath of the bombing. The first was over the bombing itself, the second, in which Felber acted, over a conspiracy to organise a campaign of urban terrorism across New York. The conspiracy trial defendants, almost all of whom were Arab Muslims represented by Jewish lawyers, were accused of planning what would have been one of the deadliest campaigns of urban terrorism in modern times, that, if carried out, would have resulted in hundreds of deaths and many thousands of injuries.

Not to mention a massive national backlash against their Muslim co-religionists across the United States, that judging from the aftermath of the Oklahoma bombing – for which no Muslims were charged – would have triggered a wave of assaults and attacks on Muslim community centres and mosques. (A report issued by the Council on American–Islamic Relations on the aftermath of the Oklahoma bomb catalogues a nationwide series of arson attacks, fake bomb threats, death threats and various forms of harassment and intimidation against American Muslims.) New York prosecutors said the conspirators' planned attacks included: bombing the United Nations building in New York; bombing a string of bridges and tunnels that connect Manhattan with the rest of New York and New Jersey; planning to assassinate Egyptian president Hosni Mubarak and, for good measure, organising the murder of Rabbi Kahane.

At the centre of the plot was the frail figure of the blind Egyptian radical Islamist Sheikh Omar Abdul-Rahman, who was accused of being the plotters' spiritual leader and guiding spirit. Muslim and Arab leaders are now quick to marginalise Sheikh Abdul-Rahman, claiming that he was way out on the extreme fringe, but his bloodthirsty sermons at the mosques where he preached were always crowd pullers. Abdel Hakim Mustapha listened to the Sheikh speak several times and did not always like what he heard. 'He was a fire and brimstone speaker, not the jolliest fellow you could hope to meet. I heard him five times in Brooklyn and Manhattan. I didn't like his anti-West bent. I have difficulty with people who come here to tell me about the Great Satan, and who left a Muslim country to do it. If they were in heaven then why did they come to hell? I also prayed with Siddig Siddig Ali. I would have thought he was the most religious person in the world. If he truly believed that he was acting in the name of Islam his faith must have been weak.'

Felber's office is lined with hundreds of hours of transcripts of FBI wiretaps, taped conversations of the conspirators' telephone recordings and secret video-recordings of the house in Queens, New York city, where the operations were planned. The conspirators also practised shooting and combat at a firing range, provided to them occasionally by a sympathiser. Although Abdul-Rahman was found guilty of the charges, there are no tapes of him ordering the attacks against the target list. Much of the prosecution's case rested on testimony from Emad Salem, a former Egyptian army officer who was an FBI agent and had infiltrated the group, and who received more than $1 million for his evidence, according to Reuters. Defence lawyers built some of their argument on the claim that Salem was not so much an agent as an *agent provocateur*.

The transcripts of the secret FBI video, telephone and wiretaps on the conspirators make truly bizarre reading, a lengthy and perverse mix of domestic banality as the group has lunch at McDonald's (that ultimate symbol of the America they plan to strike so many blows against) and then plans to obliterate hundreds of innocent bystanders and passers-by in the name of their version of Islam. The conspirators had their own code language in a failed attempt to evade detection: salt = fertiliser; food oil = diesel; balls, small balls = hand grenades; chicks from the eggs = grenade detonators; groceries = bomb supplies; box = timer and toy, or children's toy = machine gun. Certainly Emad Salem seems more together than the rest of the group, whose members sometimes appear extremely amateurish in their organisation. Here is an extract of Videotape V18, recorded in the Queens safehouse on the evening of 29 May 1993, just under a month before a posse of FBI agents burst in on 24 June. Salem is Emad Salem, and Siddig is Siddig Ibrahim Siddig Ali, Daniel Felber's former client. The Sheikh is Sheikh Abdul-Rahman. Amir is Amir Abdelgani, another in the group. The comments in brackets appear as they did in the full transcripts. This tape is written up in the third person, rather than as a direct transcript.

. . . Salem then says the Sheikh is very enthusiastic about night missions and that he wants to see strikes against the American army.

Siddig then asks why (or how) did Salem talk to the Sheikh in this way. Salem explains that he whispered in the Sheikh's ear.

Salem picks up his secret identity disguise wig from the table.

After a while the discussion turns to the need for a camera, or video-camera to plan one of the attacks.

Siddig says he doesn't know how to use a camera. Salem says this is not a problem, he will teach him. He promises to obtain a very sophisticated camcorder and states that 'we are now in the training stage' of the mission.

Salem takes a small white plastic unit out of his briefcase (probably one of the timers) and places it on the bench.

He then places his wig inside the briefcase and shuts it. He places the timer on the far, right-hand corner of the bench.

Amir places plastic wrap over the cake on the table in order to keep it fresh.

Even would-be bombers don't like stale cakes. By the evening of

23 June the plans had advanced considerably and work on making the bombs had started, with Salem again playing a major role, especially on the more technical matters. The mixing of the chemicals is underway, as this extract from tape V5-V8 shows, again recorded at the safehouse. Emad Salem is giving directions to someone to get to the house, although he's not sure of the way.

> Salem: . . . nitrogen can be dissolved completely. (Amir is still mixing. Salem's beeper went off, he made a phone call.) May peace be upon you yes, (beeper noise) uh huh, did you page me twice, okay, uh huh, hello, yes, yes, okay, yes, eh? No problem, listen take the PATH train, yeah we are spending the whole night here, we have a lot of work, you know what I mean, yeah, yes, please, because we have a lot of, because there is new stuff come over. Thank you, brother, I don't know, wait one second (asking Amir). Do you know how you get here from New Jersey? Which train to come?

The discussion moves on to plans for an attack, involving stalled cars that will be left in place while another picks up the would-be bombers. And so it goes on, for page after page, tape after tape. It is depressing but fascinating reading, providing an illuminating and detailed insight into the day-to-day workings of a would-be terrorist group, for the FBI's cameras and tape-recorders have captured everything, from the most banal domesticity to the conspirators' mocking each other's accents to their plans to turn downtown New York into a killing field. Everything, that is, except a direct order from the Sheikh to carry out the group's planned attacks. Many Muslims believe that he was imprisoned because he knew too much about American operations in Afghanistan and needed to be removed from the public eye, and public access.

Certainly his conviction highlighted the American government's murky relationship with Islamic radicals, who are prepared to use violence to achieve their goals. That the American intelligence services armed, funded and helped train radical Muslim fighters in Afghanistan to help drive out the Soviets has been well documented. The Sheikh himself had reportedly been involved in the United States' secret *jihad* in Afghanistan. He had been charged, but acquitted, of involvement in the 1981 assassination of then Egyptian president Anwar Sadat, the first Arab leader to sign a peace treaty with Israel. In his interrogation statement to the Egyptian police he said that the killers had twice asked him to be the *emir*, or leader of the group, but he had refused. A few years later the Sheikh and his followers might have accepted help from the Great Satan in Afghanistan, but they had their own agenda. Like Dr Frankenstein before them, the CIA found that the monster they had created – in this case to kill Russians – cut loose from its masters' plans and soon span out of control.

The Sheikh's conviction on conspiracy charges raised several questions about the links between the CIA and Islamic radicals. He preached in mosques across New York and in New Jersey, fiery, inflammatory sermons that seemed to if not advocate violence, then at least condone it. These sermons, indeed probably his every waking and sleeping moment, were watched with interest by the FBI, the law enforcement office combating terrorism on US soil, but many agents asked how he had got into the country in the first place, his entry suggesting some degree of government collusion in his activities. The Sheikh's name was on the State Department's list of possible terrorists for some time, but he still managed to obtain an American visa in Sudan in 1990, although he was later charged with falsifying his application form. Even so, as any visitor arriving at New York's JFK airport, or any other international American airport, can testify, immigration officers run every new arrival's name through a computer before allowing them in. It's impossible to believe that those machines do not contain the State Department's list of suspected terrorists. The Sheikh freely entered and left the United States several times. The State Department reportedly said there had been a computer error about his status, a true 1990s catch-all evasion.

For Daniel Felber, the trial raised serious and worrying questions about the murky web of links between the American government's intelligence services, their operations in Afghanistan and its support for extreme Islamic radicals. 'This is my pet peeve. Our foreign relations are often wrong-headed and hypocritical. There is no question in my mind that when the Sheikh's followers were fighting the communists in Afghanistan we put money, personnel, armaments, you name it behind those Muslims. What we did in the process in order to fight the red enemy was arm and validate, comfort and give courage to a fanatical sect of Muslims. When the communists fell and the cold war was no longer a war we had to contend with them because they now became a threat to our national security all over the world.'

Felber met Sheikh Abdul-Rahman several times, both at the trial and in prison. He appeared sick and devout, says Felber. 'He was not well. He is diabetic and blind. He is a very pious and devout man. I have listened to many of his lectures and speeches as government evidence. He represents a sect of Muslims that are not opposed to using violence to achieve their aims.'

What, I ask, are their aims?

'There are short-term ends and long-term ends. I don't want to speculate on what the longest-term end could be, but in the short term they would like to have the ability to eradicate prejudice against Muslims, and to kill their sworn enemies, anyone who doesn't believe in their beliefs.'

Did he sense at the trial the involvement of American intelligence operatives, or feel that undercurrents of collusion were flowing through the courtroom?

'The court itself was an armed camp. It reminded me of the Eichmann trial in Jerusalem, because there was a glass booth, and it was that kind of spectacle. There was a ceremonial courtroom with a fifty-foot vaulted ceiling, there were marshals ringing the courtroom, and there were people with walkie-talkies and earpieces all over the place. The security was as tight as I imagine it is in Belfast. So who was there it was impossible to tell. You have to also understand that defence attorneys are treated by the government just one notch higher than the persons accused of the crimes. We are not given any confidences so I don't have any information about that.'

The conspiracy trial started in January 1995. On February 6 Siddig Ibrahim Siddig Ali entered a guilty plea and Felber's involvement ended. But that move raised more questions than it answered. Siddig has not been sentenced, even though, by his own admission, he helped plan a series of terrorist attacks across New York. Many believe that he turned state's evidence in exchange for, what? A shorter sentence, followed by a new life somewhere perhaps, under the witness protection scheme. Felber, I am sure, knows more than he can or will say about this strange case, for he is still bound by the laws of client confidentiality. But he is an engaging and helpful man, so I tried my own attempt at courtroom-style questioning, in the case of the Pushy Journalist *v.* the Not Necessarily Unforthcoming Lawyer.

'Where is Siddig at the moment?' I ask.

'Unknown.'

'This is a bit strange, isn't it?'

'You know, I can't speculate as to what is going on and what is not going on because I no longer represent him. For security reasons or whatever reasons, I'm not made privy to his whereabouts. I imagine that he is incarcerated somewhere, but I have no way of knowing where he is.'

'He's not freely wandering the streets?'

'I don't think so.'

'So he entered a guilty plea but hasn't been sentenced yet?'

'That's right.'

'Was he the one that turned state's evidence?'

'I can't speculate. I don't know.'

'But he was the one that was suspected to have?'

'I believe that he was.'

'What kind of man was he?'

'He was an intelligent man, a handsome man. He was tall with a certain muscular build. He was a weight-lifter. He had olive skin, black hair and brown eyes. He spoke English fluently. He was from the Sudan.'

'Did he seem like someone who was working on a fundamentally rational level or did he seem like a fanatic?'

'He certainly harboured at certain times in his life fanatical beliefs about fundamental Islam . . . I've listened to hours and hours of taped conversations both surreptitiously taken from his telephone and secretly recorded by a government informant. And in those conversations he says things that are very fanatical.'

'Can you remember any of those things?'

'There were certain instances when he advocates violence on American soil for its policies of supporting Zionist policies. He volunteered to fight in Bosnia on behalf of the Muslims in the Balkans. Certainly there is videotape and audiotape of him in possession of weapons. There were training camps in Pennsylvania and Long Island where they trained in armed warfare, so I would categorise him at certain times in his life as having those fanatical beliefs.'

'Why did he plead guilty?'

'He is a former client now, but even so I cannot reveal confidences. I can't talk about what he said to me and what his confidences are. I can only speculate that he believed that he could do better for himself by admitting his guilt, showing his remorse, and not making the government prove his guilt.'

For many observers, especially outside the United States, the news that radical Muslims were planning a series of bombings was perhaps less surprising than the revelation that the conspirators were free to practise shooting and engage in target practice whenever they felt like popping off a few rounds. The firing ranges were under FBI observation, but apparently were not in themselves illegal. Videotape V18 records how one day Siddig was unable to work as Sheikh Abdul-Rahman's interpreter as he was going to the Pennsylvania camp instead. The Sheikh was scheduled for an immigration hearing to legalise his status – more grist to the conspiracy theorists' mill – but Siddig could not accompany him. This is an extract from the tape, a conversation between Siddig and Emad Salem:

> Siddig says he did not tell the Sheikh that the reason he was unavailable was because he was going for training in Pennsylvania. Siddig is emphatic with Salem that the training at this camp was all legal, but nonetheless the FBI seems to be shadowing the group. Siddig then says that the fact that their training was legal won't prevent the FBI from arresting them.

As indeed it didn't, eventually. It's hard for a British person, indeed any European, to understand the depth of feeling in America about the constitutional right to bear arms. Even foreign Islamic radicals can practise their version of the *jihad* out in the forests and parks of Pennsylvania, or anyone else, as long as they have the permits. I asked Felber how it was possible that the

conspirators could have such easy access to weapons.
'Americans, as you know, have an obsession with weapons. I'm
sure that there are militias training with arms as we speak. It's
not an unusual thing to have shooting ranges and that type of
thing. They are all around the States, and providing that the
weapons are licensed and not concealable, which as rifles they
are usually not, and providing that the land is not being tres-
passed upon and providing that they carry out the other
regulations you need to comply with, then there's no harm in
arming and training.'

Felber, like many involved in the two bombing trials, does not
believe that the threat of further terrorist attacks has ended with
the imprisonment of the conspirators. 'I don't think it's been
rolled up. But I do think that our country is very vigilant in
connection with trying to observe, and surveille and infiltrate
Muslims of fanatical persuasion because they have egg on their
face allowing the World Trade Center to explode like that. And
there is the knowledge that we have now, that they had various
hints in advance and did nothing to prevent it . . . There is a
videotape that totally appalled me at the time, because I was
defending my clients.'

The videotape that so appalled Daniel Felber, indeed almost
anyone who saw it, was *Jihad in America*, reported by journalist
Steve Emerson. Emerson was kind enough to send me a copy of
his film, which was aired across the United States on the PBS
network in November 1994. The programme is extremely disturbing viewing. It purports to show the existence of a
nationwide network of armed Muslim terrorists across the
United States, who are prepared to kill their enemies, especially
Jews and supporters of Israel. Emerson summed up his claims
in an article published in *New Republic* in June 1995:

> The investigation . . . revealed that these groups have estab-
> lished elaborate political, financial and, in some cases,
> operational infrastructures in the United States. Because of
> the scope of this movement (it ranges from New York to
> Oklahoma to California), its bellicose rhetoric (it calls for
> a holy war or 'jihad' against the US and other govern-
> ments) and its advocacy of terror to achieve its ends (it

trains recruits in the use of car bombs), it's no wonder the FBI has made this network a top priority.

Although there is no evidence that these myriad Islamist groups are centrally coordinated, it does appear that they collaborate and cross-fertilise . . . In addition, Sheikh Omar Abdul-Rahman . . . had been hosted or sponsored in the US by at least half a dozen mosques and innocent-sounding Islamist 'charitable' and 'religious' organisations.

Coming in the wake of the World Trade Center bombing, the video drove Muslim and Arab-American organisations into – it is no exaggeration to describe it thus – a frenzy of denials and accusations. I have a thick file of cuttings, of claim and counter-claim from both sides about the programme. Emerson's film, which is based in part on information received from Israeli intelligence, was a watershed in American Muslim history. It played a major role in shaping many Americans' perception of the growing Muslim community. It sharpened divisions on both sides; between the Muslims who believe that prejudice against Islam is widespread and unalterable and there is a Jewish/Israeli conspiracy to smear Muslims and Islam; and among those many non-Muslims who see a potential terrorist behind every Islamic name. Time after time, when speaking to Muslim groups and individuals, Emerson's name came up, accompanied by angry denunciations. The Council on American–Islamic Relations, singled out by Emerson in the above article as promoting 'the interests of militant Islam in the US', issued a twelve-page rebuttal of the film's claims.

For me, *Jihad in America* included some valuable material. It showed that in a small section of the Arab Muslim community in the United States there is considerable loathing of Israel, Jews and the West in general, and that a few Imams in American mosques often resort to the rhetoric of hatred – fuelling what the *New Republic* has called 'a culture of incitement' to violence. However, the film's essential premise, that there is a widespread Islamic terrorist network operating in the United States, failed to convince me. As a journalist I know how easy it is to shape an argument in any direction one chooses, using original source material, of which Emerson had plenty. But if there is a nationwide network of Islamic terrorists, then what are they doing all day? Apart from the World Trade Center bombing, there haven't been any other terrorist attacks carried out by Muslims. Instead there have been a stream of hate-crimes against Muslims, ranging from abuse and violence to daubings of obscene graffiti.

What there does seem to be, says Daniel Felber, is a network of fundraising organisations that raise money for charitable causes in the Middle East, some of which could be diverted to land in the bank accounts of organisations like Hamas, which is responsible for several terrorist outrages in Israel. In January 1993 two Arab Americans were arrested in Israel and accused of transporting funds there for Hamas. Israeli officials went into full information offensive mode about the pair, pouring out streams of reports and press releases about what they claimed was an international Islamic terrorist network. Three years later President Clinton signed an executive order that bans fundraising for twelve organisations opposed to the Middle East peace process, including Hamas, Abu Nidal Organisation, two factions of the Popular Front for the Liberation of Palestine and two extreme Jewish groups, Kach and Kahane Chai (Kahane Lives). American Arab and Muslim organisations, who strongly deny that cash raised in mosques goes to fund bombers, now fear that this order will be used indiscriminately against their charitable and fundraising work in the Middle East.

'If Emerson's film is to be believed, and it is a very frightening tape, there is a very organised network of groups that solicit large sums of money for educational purposes and then this money ends up in the hands of terrorists bent on destruction,' says Felber. 'But is there an organised terror network? I don't think so. Is there an organised network of Muslim groups, some of which do good things like creating schools and help? Yes, I believe that is true. And I believe that there is probably a portion of that money that goes back to fund fundamentalism. The problem is with the Muslims that don't believe it. You listen to some of the speeches when they talk about death to blank, death to blank. There were videotapes taken that were used at the trial, where there were these individuals that had their faces masked by headdresses and who were shooting automatic weapons in the air. That kind of thing does give you pause.'

*

I took a pause then, to travel to Washington DC and meet the Muslim lobbyists at the Council on American–Islamic Relations, whom Steve Emerson accused of keeping such dubious company. If New York is where America goes to party, then Washington DC is where it does its politicking. Washington DC is not so much a city as a collection of government offices and museums, surrounded by some of the most dangerous inner-city ghettos to be found anywhere in America. The switch from one to the other is quick and total, and if you take a wrong turn at the traffic lights you could be looking down the barrel of a gun. Washington DC, like New York, also has a luxurious Islamic Center, derided by many Muslims as the 'Ambassador's Mosque'.

At lunchtime prayers on a Friday the worshippers spilled out onto the streets, under the wary eye of an armed policeman. They were a cosmopolitan group, including Arabs, Africans, African-Americans, South-east Asians and Turks. After prayers the worshippers were served a free meal of spicy lamb, rice and salad, cooked in the adjoining kitchen. It was good food, also much enjoyed by the several homeless people who wandered in for a serving before dozing off in the library. Just as in New York this Islamic Center is often the first point of call for curious non-Muslims. Americans interested in Islam telephone or write with queries or may attend one of the tours of the mosque. A minority eventually convert, and their names – overwhelmingly of European origin – are listed outside on the wall.

Visitors to the Council on American–Islamic Relations in downtown Washington are greeted with tea or coffee and a choice of bagels, that Jewish snack, ubiquitous across America, that Muslims also enjoy. CAIR is, in the true sense of the phrase, a public relations organisation.

Ibrahim Hooper, a white convert, or revert, as he prefers to be called – because Muslims believe everyone is born into their faith, only moving away as they grow up – greeted me. 'For me the explicit appeal of Islam was the anti-racism, the egalitarianism, there's no priest, no ministers. Just you and God,' he says.

With a Master's degree in television journalism, Hooper was a natural choice for the job of National Communications Director at CAIR. 'Our mission statement is that we are dedicated to presenting an Islamic perspective on issues of importance to the American public. Our main goal is to have the Muslim community in a principled engagement with the larger society. We don't want assimilation and we don't want isolation. We want Muslim school board members, city council members, Muslim mayors, Muslim views taken into account, whenever large decisions are taken in society, that they are seen as a constituency that must be served,' he explained.

And while radical Muslims in the Middle East denounce America as a den of iniquity and fornication, Hooper says it's easier to live as a Muslim in the United States than in Turkey or Algeria. 'In many ways you are freer to be a Muslim in America than in many Muslim countries. I've lived and travelled in them and you can't write a letter to the editor, you can't hold a protest sign in front of an embassy, you can't do anything that is at variance with whatever government or dictator happens to be in power there.'

CAIR is one of several Muslim lobbying and communal organisations that have started work in the last few years, many of which are based in Washington DC, because that is where America's decision-makers live and work. As well as CAIR there is the American Muslim Council, an umbrella grouping for a range of communal organisations and the Arab American Institute. In its information pack the AMC includes leaflets entitled: *Making Our Voice Heard, Educating the Media*; *Islam and Muslims: An American Stylebooklet*; *Islamic Vision on Moral Issues* and *Political Empowerment for the Muslim Community*. All these organisations have drawn heavily on the experience of the Jewish community which runs a powerful and effective political lobby, influencing American policy on Israel as well as domestic issues. Their existence is testimony to a minority that is growing in confidence as it finds and articulates a voice in America's ethnic and religious mosaic. The long-term goal of many Muslim activists is to turn the United States into a society where an Islamic perspective and the desires and needs of the Muslim community are automatically considered on issues as diverse as policy towards Bosnia and anti hate-crimes legislation.

Hooper puts a tape in the VCR, CAIR's go-getting video promotional film. When the need arises, a voice explains, for Muslims to take action, CAIR is there. 'Within the hour an emergency call to action is faxed to everyone of the 1,500

Muslim community centres and mosques in the US, uniting them into a formidable community.' CAIR also leads the charge for Muslims to reach out and be an active part of their communities, sponsoring workshops nationwide on dealing with the media and publishes a guide showing mosques and community centres how to become an indispensable part of their neighbourhood.

'Even though the Muslim community is growing by leaps and bounds it has not been able to impact the system like other minority groups have, so there is a real need for organisations like ours, to be a facilitator for political and social activism,' says Hooper. 'Probably our biggest achievement is to give Muslims a new attitude on what they approach and show that they can be successful. For example a Muslim woman will be fired because she wants to wear a *hejab* [headscarf], and she will take it and say, "Oh well, there's not much I can do, I am in this society, it is not a Muslim society, that's life." Now they are discovering through our campaigns that there are things that can be done and be done quite effectively.'

CAIR's newsletter is full of its successes in combating ignorance about, and prejudice against, Islam. Hooper is proud of how quickly the sports shoe manufacturer Nike took down a billboard in Los Angeles, after its intervention. The billboard, captioned 'They called him Allah' was intended to celebrate a local basketball hero. A local Muslim e-mailed CAIR to alert them. 'Many of our achievements take place within hours: someone called us, says there is a billboard up in LA comparing Nike to Allah, within hours Nike is saying we will take it down. We got some e-mail setting out the details, I contacted Nike headquarters, I said, "Here's the situation, here's why we think it is offensive," and they said, "We agree."'

CAIR also had an advertisement for Budweiser which featured a scantily clad model with an Islamic phrase across her T-shirt taken off air, and a greeting card removed from sale. The card, which featured a veiled Muslim woman on the cover, read inside: 'So you're feeling like Shiite. Don't Mecca a big deal out of it.' Both were offensive certainly to Muslims, particularly the juxtaposition of words from the Quran and beer, which is forbidden to Muslims. But aren't these advertisements an integral part of the freedoms that allow Hooper to live an Islamic lifestyle in peace and freedom? Isn't CAIR restricting free speech, I ask him?

'We never say to restrict free speech. When we did our campaign against *Jihad in America*, we never said take it off the air, we said PBS should follow its own guidelines, on objectivity, accuracy and fairness,' he exclaims.

Ah yes, *Jihad in America*. 'It constantly pops up, in the editorials, in the writings of those who are against Islamic activism. It's a horrible, horrible film, it was biased, inaccurate . . . If they came to us and said there is some Muslim underground terrorist network in America, and it were true, we would say go and get them. But it's not true, aside from the World Trade Center.'

So, I ask, is money being raised for Hamas through mosques here?

'Most mosques can barely support themselves, let alone send massive amounts of money overseas. They raise money to build the mosque, first of all, to build schools, to build all the things that any other community does. Believe me, I wish we had all this money that Mr Emerson was claiming, we would be a lot better off.'

Where does CAIR get its money from?

'From its members. Sometimes ten dollars, sometimes a thousand.'

Does CAIR raise money for Hamas?

'No, absolutely not.'

Either way, of all the countries I visited while researching this book on the lives of Muslims in the West, America was definitely one of the most complex and fascinating. A superpower in a state of flux, often uncertain about its own identity, it is now, perhaps slightly to its own surprise, home to the biggest Muslim minority in the western world. Four strands emerged on my travels there that define the Muslim community: the immigrant experience; the way that black Americans are turning to Islam as a revolutionary anti-white statement; the furious controversy about terrorism and some American Muslims' alleged links to terrorists; and, finally, perhaps most significantly, the slow emergence of an American Islamic lobby in Washington DC's corridors of power.

Instead of always reacting to their host society, American

Muslims have decided to try to change it to suit them. In a country based on immigration and the rights of free speech and assembly – and even with the widespread ignorance about, and prejudice against, Muslims and Islam – they have a fair chance of succeeding in some of their aims. Their ultimate strategy is to turn the United States into a society based on Judeo-Christian-Islamic values. But that will be a long struggle, and as the voice of American Muslims becomes louder, more effective and articulate, it will produce a counterweight to argue against their aims. Many Americans will already see, for example, CAIR's successes in getting advertisements that offend Muslims withdrawn, as conflicting with free speech, enshrined in the constitution. But it is in the offices of groups like CAIR and the AMC, as well as the network of mosques and community centres across the fifty states, that the debate over Muslims in America, and the sometimes uneasy marriage of Islamic and American values, is being shaped. It is a new chapter in American history, one of which only the first few pages have been written.

(Andrew Ward)

Brick Lane, London, 1996

Chapter 10

THE FUTURE

'To Allah belongeth the East and the West; whither-soever Ye Turn, there is Allah's Face. For Allah is All-Embracing, All-Knowing.'
The Quran, Surah 2: verse 115

'There is an Islamic storm blowing. It is an Islamic wind which is blowing around everything in the world.'
Izzettin Dogan, a community leader of Turkey's minority Alevi Muslims

Think of Islam not as a rock, rigid and unyielding, but as an ocean. As a vast expanse of water flowing this way and that, whose many currents, cultural, political and theological, swirl and eddy through history and across the globe. Its tides have advanced and retreated through the centuries, as the great Muslim empires, ruled from Baghdad and Granada, Cairo and Istanbul, Isfahan and Delhi, rose and fell. Each one absorbed local culture and traditions on the way, whether Jewish, Hindu or Shamanistic, for like every religion, Islam evolves in the environment in which it exists.

Medieval Muslim Spain, for example, was the zenith of Islamic history in the western hemisphere, but some *Shariah* laws were often breached as much as observed. It was an intricate and sophisticated civilisation, whose great cities were home to great libraries and universities, fabulous architecture, public parks and baths, a thriving culture of study and literature, all ruled over by a spirit of intellectual inquiry and religious tolerance for Jews and Christians. Quite an apt model in fact for a united Europe in the 1990s as it struggles to find a framework for minority rights. In Granada and Cordoba an educated

Muslim élite led a life of opulence and hedonism, and their poets often praised the joys of wine-drinking, strictly forbidden for Muslims. Other poets, such as Ibn Arabi, Spain's most famous Sufi mystic, used the imagery of Judaism and Christianity, even polytheism – the ultimate abomination for Muslims – to express Islam's universalism:

My heart has adopted every shape; it has become a pasture
    for gazelles and a convent for Christian monks,
A temple for idols and a pilgrim's Kabah, the tables of a
    Torah and the pages of a Quran.
I follow the religion of Love; wherever Love's camels turn,
    there Love is my religion and my faith.[1]

Muslim Spanish poets also celebrated the joys of sensual love and erotic passion, a literature firmly in the traditions of Islam, which enjoins both husband and wife to sexually satisfy each other. There is no monasticism in Islam, said Muhammad. Even now in some Islamic countries a woman can initiate divorce if her husband fails to have sex with her at least once in four months. 'Almighty God created sexual desire in ten parts; then he gave nine parts to women and one to men,' said Ali, husband of Muhammad's daughter Fatima, and the founder of Shiah Islam, faith of the Iranian revolution. Islam is not a puritanical faith and sex – within marriage – is something to be enjoyed and treasured. *The Tales from the Thousand and One Nights*, the famed collection of bawdy popular Arabic folk stories, are crowded with a cast of fornicating characters, or more often would-be fornicators, tales as entertaining now as they were in ninth-century Baghdad and Basra.

Take just one issue in Islam – women and sex – and you will find a myriad of opinions, each densely supported by quotations from the Quran and the *hadith*. If *The Tales from the One Thousand and One Nights* represent one extreme, of vibrant sexuality, female circumcision is its other. Many Muslim women are for ever denied the full pleasures of the marital bed, as their genitals are mutilated, usually with some form of partial or total clitorodectomy. One in five Muslim girls lives today in a community that sanction some type of genital mutilation, writes Geraldine Brooks in her book *Nine Parts of Desire*. The practice probably began in Africa, before spreading into Egypt and then moving across the Islamic world, probably as a means of defending male family honour by preventing daughters and sisters from having sex before marriage. There is absolutely no Islamic justification for mutilating a woman's genitals, and the practice is nowhere advocated in the Quran. In fact self-mutilation is not approved of in Islam, as this *hadith* shows:

> A man once said to Muhammad, 'O Messenger of God, permit me to become a Eunuch.' He said, 'That person is not of me who maketh another a eunuch, or becometh so himself; because the manner in which my followers become eunuchs is by fasting and abstinence.' The man said, 'Permit me to retire from society, and to abandon the delights of the world.' He said, 'The retirement that becometh my followers is to live in the world and yet to sit in the corner of a mosque in expectation of prayers.'[2]

Many Muslims are well aware that there is no Islamic justification for female circumcision, but few speak out against it and many Islamic leaders still advocate the practice. A clitorodectomy is a barbaric and terrible operation, often performed without anaesthetic, but most girls survive it.

The Pakistani village women set on fire by their husbands in 'honour killings' often do not. In Pakistan, still a traditional, patriarchal society, Islam has been influenced in several ways by Hinduism, some theological, others deeply misogynistic. Hindu traditions of polytheism have helped shape the South Asian Barelvi Muslim view of Muhammad as someone super-human whose presence is ubiquitous, not flesh, but light itself. Until it was abolished in 1829 by the British, Hinduism also had a history of *suttee*. The word *suttee* comes from the Sanskrit *sati*, faithful wife, and a faithful Hindu widow was one who immolated herself on her husband's funeral pyre, ostensibly to join her beloved husband in the afterlife, but in reality to prevent her having a share of his property. This traditional Hindu view of wives, as people not worthy of living after the death of their husband, has helped shape some South Asian Muslims' perception of women. Even now some Pakistani hospital doctors must treat the wives of Muslim villagers who have been set on fire by their husbands, for some or other imagined transgression of male honour, suffering horrific burns which many do not survive.

In Africa women have their genitals mutilated in the name of Islam. In Pakistan they can be immolated, although both these practices are nothing to do with genuine Islam. But in Pakistan and Turkey women can also rise to the office of Prime Minister, like Benazir Bhutto and Tansu Ciller. There seem to be major contradictions here. No issue causes as much misunderstanding in the West as the position of women under Islam, and few questions exercise contemporary Muslim scholars more than the interpretation of women's rights. It is also a vital question for western Muslim women. Will they rally to the western feminist standard and fight for equal rights, or meekly submit to a life of domesticity? The latter seems unlikely. Muslim women in Europe and America have been raised in an environment of equal rights in the workplace and public life. Those victories, won after long struggles, are totally compatible with a modern European or American Islam, say western Muslim women.

The Quranic view of women's rights was centuries ahead of Europe and the rest of the world. Muslim women can own property and are entitled to their own share of inheritance. They can get a divorce, are entitled to sexual satisfaction in marriage, can conduct business and study. Muhammad's wives and daughters played vital roles in establishing the new faith. They were pillars of the new Muslim community. And what westerners see as restrictions, such as headscarves, many Muslim women see as protection from prying, lustful eyes. Women must dress modestly, but so must men. What is modest to one Muslim, though, is still licentious to another. Many modern young Muslim women, in Turkey for example, wear a brightly coloured *hijab* (headscarf) and cover their arms and legs with fashionable blouses and long skirts. Arab women in the Gulf states often dress in the *chador*, the shapeless black garment that covers them from head to toe. Many Muslim women though argue that this drab dress stems not from Islamic civilisation, but Christian and pre-Islamic Iranian traditions. What is Islamic is in the eye of the beholder, or rather in the avoiding eye of the non-beholder.

Either way it is a fact that the Quran enshrines certain rights for women. In a seventh-century tribal society these were truly revolutionary concepts. They must be considered in the context in which they appeared, say modern Muslims, and not judged by the standards of 1990s Europe. It was only in 1870, after all, that the British law that put a woman's wealth under her husband's control on marriage was abolished. But the scales are still tipped towards Muslim men. A man may take several wives, but only if he is able to support them (and this provision was partly a way of allowing widows to re-enter society and be provided for). A woman can only have one husband. A woman cannot lead the prayers in a mosque, for fear of distracting male worshippers. A woman's testimony in court is worth half that of a man. Even so, the Quran provides the basis for women's participation in society. The problem for Muslim women who seek a wider role are the rulings of the male scholars of the four main schools of *Shariah* law, who interpret the Quran and the *hadith* and until now have decided how, in practical terms, Islamic law is to be implemented.

For Kareema Altamore, a former activist in the American trade union and women's movement, wearing a *hijab* is a means of defining her own role in the world, and setting out her space within it.

I met Altamore at her workplace at the American Muslim Council in Washington where she works on legal issues. She makes a forceful case in favour of the *hijab*. 'I really wanted to try another way of life, and this is part of the Muslim way of life. It has become very enjoyable. In this society, which is predominantly secular and very permissive, it allows me to make a statement, that some people choose to live their life in a religious framework. It identifies me as someone who has made that choice, which I'm proud and happy to. In a society which has blended the public and the private, it allows me to say I have decided what is private, my hair is private, this is for in my house and for my husband. I can decide that and maintain that. Our dress is very modest because we have that line. It's very healthy. I enjoy demonstrating that it is possible to draw this line.'

Like many American Muslim activists Altamore is a convert, who became a Muslim six years ago after long study, finding in the faith the concern for social justice that drew her to progressive causes. For her there is no conflict between Islam and feminism. At the same time Islam is a religion that sanctifies sexuality. 'I studied the basis of Islam, the Quran, and the principles of Islamic jurisprudence. I made a decision based on that study, it was conversion by conviction, that I was convinced that this is a balanced, just system . . . Islam celebrates sexuality, in marriage, very much so and it is very beautiful, and again very balanced. Sexuality is also for bonding and for affection, both the male and female have the right to be sexually satisfied so to me it is like a natural order.'

I asked her what brought her to Islam. 'That's always a complicated question, because usually it's a path that you have been on for a long time without being aware that you were on it. It culminates with the conscious choice to become a Muslim. My work in the women's movement gives me an interesting perspective, because I see things that were taken to extremes, and perhaps backfired and were detrimental. That gives me a special value for the balancing aspects of Islam. I see Islam as a way of life, not only worship, importance of balance and justice. I was a grandmother before I was a Muslim, so that gives me an idea of the importance of balance, of growth of justice. Islam highly emphasises the importance of justice, based on the idea that if Moses brought the law, Jesus brought compassion, then Islam is the balance between law and compassion.'

The concept of balance, of giving importance to *dunya*, matters of the world, as well as *din*, matters of religion, is a vital part of Islam. Islam does not reject the world, in fact it is incumbent on a Muslim to try to propagate the values of Islam. But when it comes to practically implementing Islamic laws, many Muslims cannot agree what form they should take.

In many ways Iran, site of the 1979 Islamic Revolution, is the best example of the clash over women's rights under Islam. For many in the West the triumph of the Ayatollahs was the ultimate victory of an alien and obscurantist faith, that sought to force women off the streets and back to the kitchen. Certainly there were plenty among the Shiah clergy who would have women swathed in black and kept in the house by their husbands. But the pictures of the *chador*-clad Islamic women revolutionaries marching and shouting down the boulevards of Tehran belied the western myth that Iranian women would lose all the rights they had gained under the deposed Pahlavi dynasty. Not just Ayatollahs, but women too tasted political power in the street battles of the revolution.

A defender of women's rights emerged in the – to western eyes – unlikely form of the leader of the revolution, the Ayatollah Khomeini. Where it said in the Quran that the prophet's wives were to remain in their houses, the conservative clergy extrapolated that to mean that all women should do so. Khomeini, the stern-eyed puritanical cleric, disagreed. He read the verse literally, and encouraged women Islamic revolutionaries to fight side by side with the men. After the revolution the imposition of Islamic law meant that unmarried men and women could not be allowed to be alone together, touch each other unless in a medical situation and women had to cover themselves in a *hijab*, or headscarf. The sexes were separated, to the dismay of many Iranians and the incomprehension of many westerners. But at the same time those new laws suddenly opened a myriad of new work opportunities for women: as television journalists covering women's sports events; as driving instructors, gym instructors and hairdressers. Even so, the new jobs did not compensate for the way fervent young revolutionary guards harassed women for wearing make-up or leaving their heads uncovered.

I did not travel to Iran, as this book's concern is the lives of Muslims in Europe, but I still wanted to ask some questions about the way that country juggles the demands of statehood and *Shariah*. In both Bosnia and Britain, Iran competes with Saudi Arabia for influence. The way Islam develops in the Muslim academies of the Shiah holy city of Qum eventually reverberates across Bradford and Birmingham. In London the voice of Tehran could often be heard behind the pronouncements of the late Kalim Siddiqui, leader of the self-proclaimed Muslim Parliament. Siddiqui was a frequent visitor to Tehran, although most mainstream Muslims dismiss him as an unrepresentative figure whose only strategy for British Muslim advancement was to call for the implementation of the *fatwa* on Salman Rushdie, about which he reportedly advised the Ayatollah Khomeini.

In London I met an Iranian government official, tieless of

course, because for many Muslims neckties are a symbol of western imperialism. He was a liberal and sophisticated man, keen to show that Iran too is evolving to find a balance between the demands of its interpretation of Islam and those of the international community. Even so, he wouldn't let me use his name in print, or tape-record our interview. 'That way I can deny what I told you,' he laughed.

Iran was born in revolution and street battles but by now the logic of statehood has imposed itself. In Iran, just like Moscow in the early 1920s, revolutionary rhetoric has been muted to meet the demands of diplomatic reality, but juggling the demands of diplomacy and the ideologues at home is a difficult balancing act. For example, Iranian officials have said that while the *fatwa* of death on Salman Rushdie cannot be withdrawn, as it was a religious rather than governmental edict, the country will not send assassins to seek the author out and kill him. The Islamic Republic seeks to take its place in the international community, although American and Israeli officials repeatedly accuse Iran of sponsoring international terrorism, which it denies. Most analysts believe that some elements of the hard-line Islamic clergy though are involved in supplying funds and manpower to extremist groups in the Middle East. At the same time hundreds of anti-government Iranian exiles have been killed or wounded since the Islamic Revolution. In March 1996 Belgian customs officials found a mortar-launcher and shells hidden in food containers on board the Iranian freighter *Kohladooz* in Antwerp. Officials in the Paris-based Iranian opposition group, the National Council of Resistance, believed their headquarters was a likely target for a mortar attack.

In London though, my Iranian friend is presenting a more conciliatory line. 'Like all revolutions, the Iranian one has had to adapt to the world outside and the international community. The revolutionary rhetoric has been toned down, we have com-promised,' he explains over tea and biscuits. Iranian thinking is evolving not just on foreign policy, but also on domestic ques-tions, such as weddings and the amount of celebration and ostentation that is advisable, he says. 'People used to get married in very simple circumstances in small mosques, without a big feast, and without spending a lot of money, or showing off, because that was the correct interpretation at the start of the revolution. But recently you can see the same families who had those simple weddings spending a lot of money on celebrating, because we only get married once. Now they are saying that Islam is not against people enjoying themselves. Things are changing.'

Satellite dishes are illegal in Iran, to protect its Muslim population from what the Ayatollahs believe are the corrupting influences of western culture. The ban is not very strictly enforced, though, says the official. 'People use them. Sky News came to Iran and broadcast a film of an Armenian Christian wedding, with wine, drinking and dancing, as Christians can drink alcohol. We had complaints from non-Iranian Muslims, asking how we can allow this, when we are supposed to be a Muslim state? I have met Muslims in the West who don't think we are good Muslims, who think we have forgotten Muslim principles.'

The role of women too, is changing, and they are playing a greater part in public life. 'We have women MPs, a woman minister in the Health Ministry, women working in the judicial system, and we are passing new laws to give them a more important role,' he says, beckoning me over to the television in the corner.

We tune in to Iranian morning television, and watch a few minutes of an Iranian soap opera, with a group of middle-aged women, their heads all covered. That women even appear on television angers the conservative clergy, he says, gesturing at the television. 'Ayatollah Khomeini was in favour of increasing the role of women, but the conservatives are against women on television, or women newsreaders. Some of the Ayatollahs don't like to see ladies laughing or entertaining themselves on television, they want women to be covered from head to toe in a black *chador*. We have women producers and directors who have won international awards, but they say this is un-Islamic.'

The western media tends to categorise any Muslim who stands up for his or her rights as a 'fundamentalist'. I have generally avoided using this term for two reasons. Firstly because several Muslims, mainstream ones, such as Abdel Hakim Mustapha in New York, told me that they were fundamentalists, in that they were believers in the fundamentals of Islam, as any Muslim must be, which does not imply a radical anti-western agenda, let alone support for violence or terrorism. Muslims also object to the word, not just because of its sub-text of violence and hostility, but because it was, they say, originally coined to deal with Christian fundamentalism. More to the point, terms such as 'fundamentalist', even 'moderate' are often meaningless labels, loaded with value judgments.

A more useful distinction is between those who seek to impose Islam, radical Islamists, and those mainstream Muslims who merely seek provision for the needs of Europe's Muslim minorities, and even between these two poles there is a sliding scale of opinion. Hizb-ut-Tahrir for example, are radical Islamists, in that the party is working to topple established regimes in the Middle East and impose a new *Khilafah*, a pan-Islamic state. At the other end of the scale is Dr Zaki Badawi, principal of the Muslim College in west London, who is working to develop a modern Islamic theology for life in 1990s Europe. But this process of recognising the world as it is, and dealing with reality instead of a demonised opponent, must also extend to the Muslim world. When thousands of demonstrating Iranians yell 'Death to America, death to Israel' it serves no purpose except to rally support for an uncertain regime that is riven by factional infighting over its future direction. America will not die, and neither will Israel, especially not through death by shouting.

This realisation, that the West, like the Muslim world, is a complicated mosaic that needs to be analysed and understood, not rejected outright, is slowly permeating through to Islamic leaders in the Middle East. For Raschid al-Ghannouchi, leader of the Tunisian An-Nahda (Renaissance) movement, currently living in exile in Britain, part of the blame for Islam's negative image lies with Muslims themselves. 'We ourselves are partly responsible for this. Even today, much of what passes for Islamic thought is very reactionary,' he said in an interview with the British Muslim magazine *Trends*. 'We have given ammunition to the opponents of Islam through our own actions, hijacking, hostage taking et cetera. We must change all this image. Islam is a call to all mankind. It calls for *ukhuwwah* [brotherhood], *'adl* [justice], *hubb* [love], *wahdat insanniyah* [unity of mankind], *huquq insan* [human rights]. We want to help mankind, not to hurt mankind.' That said, members of An-Nahda have been blamed for a terrorist attack in Tunisia in which a young girl was injured.

Muslims should not engage in blanket condemnation of the West, he said. 'Some Muslim groups have been telling the Muslims that the entire western civilisation is *kufr* [land of disbelief]. Was this the methodology of the Blessed Prophet Muhammad? No! The prophet did not set out to destroy all the values of the pagan Arabs . . . He said, "The best of you in *jahiliyah* [ignorance/pre-Islamic] will also be the best in Islam." So how can we just say "forget everything"?'

At the Muslim College in west London Dr Zaki Badawi is honing Islamic theology to grapple with the moral and theological dilemmas sparked by the scientific advances of the 1990s. Scholars such as Dr Badawi are developing a new European Islam. Part of that process is returning to the spirit of Islam, and stripping away all the cultural accretions that have coated and distorted the lives of Muslim believers. 'There is a great failure on the part of a large number of Muslims to understand the spirit of Islam altogether. What happens is that certain cultural traditions were drafted over Islam and given justification in terms of Islam. Like almost every society it tries to justify itself in terms of the overall embracing doctrines. If you are working in a communist society then you justify your actions in terms of communism. In a Christian society in terms of Christianity. In a nationalist society in terms of nationalism. So in Islam it's the same thing.'

I ask Dr Badawi which sort of customs he is referring to.

'For example the habits and customs regarding outsiders. Christians, Jews, Buddhists, Hindus, depending on the circumstances. The attitude towards women. Some want to make them invisible altogether, while others say that they've got to participate. It depends on your cultural heritage. Islam can be used by any culture. Islam has a system of law with which you can justify virtually anything. And because it is a universal religion it has readily been adapted by various countries. That is why I coin the phrase that we are developing a British Islam. That is quite legitimate in my view. If you want to compare societies in Muslim countries and you go from Indonesia to Nigeria across the whole sub-continent of India through Iran, Afghanistan, Iraq and the Arab world, passing the Balkans into north Africa, then going down to Nigeria, every time you cross the border there is a different culture but they are still Muslims.'

Developing a modern Islam – the religious principles of which can be relevant for all Muslims in the West – demands a theology of the minority. In most Muslim countries Muslims are either in the majority or are substantial minorities. But not in Britain and Europe, and so Islam must evolve according to its new circumstances, says Dr Badawi. 'It has to adapt and accept the new conditions and consequences. Most of our laws, like the Jewish ones, were written in the middle ages. But Islamic law had a particular characteristic. It is the law or theology of the majority. Very seldom do you find the theoreticians writing about the law of the minority, and how to operate as a minority. The Jews adapted to this because they were a minority for so many centuries. We are still grappling with how to live as minorities, develop a theology of the minority.'

The family is the cornerstone of Muslim life, but Muslim families too break up in acrimony. Divorce is allowed in Islam, but is not encouraged. The thing which is lawful, but disliked by God, is divorce, as one of Muhammad's *hadith* says. The problem in Britain for Muslim women is when their former husbands refuse to grant them a religious divorce after the civil one. There are parallels here with the situation of orthodox Jewish women, who cannot remarry in synagogue, says Dr Badawi. 'When a woman seeks and obtains a divorce in the civil court, she remains married according to Muslim law. So when she wants to re-marry there can be a problem for her if she goes to the husband and asks for a divorce but he refuses. Sometimes the woman can have an agreement before the marriage to have the right to divorce herself,' he says.

Now the Muslim Law Council, which Dr Badawi helped found, has formed a court of Islamic law to arbitrate in bitter divorce cases. It has also developed a standard marriage contract, to be developed to all mosques in Britain. It may not be accepted by every Muslim, but it is a step forward in dealing with conflicts between Muslim and British civil law, says Dr Badawi. 'If the husband will not give her a divorce, she can be blackmailed. So we decided to act as a Muslim court when there is such a case. We write to the husband and ask if he can give a good reason why there should be no divorce. If he doesn't give sensible reasons then we consider that he is acting against her interests just to spite her. Then the law of Islam permits us under these circumstances to declare a separation between them. In other words to cancel the marriage. This solved a huge problem, and now we have created a marriage contract in which the woman herself has the right to divorce.'

Three Muslim lawyers also sit on the council, to ensure that its deliberations conform with British law. 'This is part of the whole development of having a law for the minority because the people also ask us about *fatwas* [Islamic legal judgments] for various issues and we give them *fatwas*. The latest *fatwa* that has made some headlines was the one about organ transplants, which we have discussed and debated for eighteen months. We brought all the schools of *Shariah* law together and we arrived at the answer that this would be permissible. We have dialogue with everybody because you cannot live in isolation.'

It's not just community leaders such as Dr Badawi who are juggling the demands of Islam and life in a modern secular society. Every fortnight Dr Syed Mutawalli ad-Darsh has a page in the weekly Muslim newspaper *Q News*, in which he answers queries from readers. Some – usually about finance, as it is generally forbidden for Muslims to pay or receive interest – necessitate complicated responses. A whole industry of Islamic banking has developed in Muslim countries to cope with the difficulties of trading and financing without interest. Others are more straightforward. One, presumably from a woman reader, asks, in a household where both man and woman are working, shouldn't a man do his share of the housework? Yes, he should, says the paper's columnist. If housework was good enough for Muhammad, who shared domestic duties, it is good enough for every Muslim male. 'It is the husband's duty to care for his family and home, not just sit in front of the television for hours, while his wife does the cooking and looks after the children. This is simply unfair,' writes Dr Mutawalli ad-Darsh.

These are the thinkers revitalising Islam, developing the theology of the minority for the needs of Muslims in the West. But how is the interplay between science, modernism and Islam developing in the Middle East? For any new theological ideas born there will soon spread to Berlin and Bradford. I decided to ask Dr Muhammad al-Mass'ari, who is part of a trend of modern and modernising Islamists engaged on an *Ijtihad*, or intellectual struggle, honing their version of Islam as a faith for the 1990s.

A discussion with such an eminent scholar seems an excellent opportunity to raise many of my own questions about Islam, specifically on the compatibility of Islam with pluralism and the separation of religion and state that is a key element of western parliamentary democracy; the rights of women and minorities under Islam. But first, the *Ijtihad*, or *jihad* of the brain, that al-Mass'ari hopes will revitalise Islam. 'Any new *Ijtihad* will bring many buried jewels, such as questions of the rights of women, on the millet system [of rights for religious minorities], on the authority of the nation, on political power that everyone is equal. If you jump over the sectarian and party divides, you will find something which is very solid and could establish a stable society quite reasonably,' he says.

Dr al-Mass'ari, he says, wants to see an 'Islamic democracy' in Saudi Arabia. What exactly is one of those, I ask? 'I use it in the procedural sense, that all powers will emerge from the nation, the *ummah*, which everyone, man and woman has exactly the same stake, all those regulations and acts must be decided by the appropriate state authorities as decided in the constitution, such as a National Assembly, or president or a combination or both. This means that the clergy do not have any more say than anyone else. This is different from the Iranian model. . . . Generally my feeling is that the American model would be more tasty, or something with a President and prime minister. The President could choose to head the meetings of the council of ministers, or could leave it to the prime minister, head the National Security Council or give it to the prime minister. The word Islamic means that the people and the assembly will go back to the Quran as the source of Islam to produce laws. So if someone elects a communist or someone who is opposed to Islam, fine, there is no more Islamic state, then it will be a secular democratic state.'

This would be unlikely though, as secular parties will be outlawed, their members and supporters arrested. 'The state, as long as it is Islamic, will throw non-Islamic parties in front of the court, like the German model of dealing with non-democratic parties, which was applied to the communists in the 1950s. The only way to change will be to have a revolution, which is possible if the people decide.'

However much he talks about democracy, it would be a serious error of judgment to see Dr al-Mass'ari as a sort of Muslim Tony Blair, propagating a 'New Islam', with all the contentious – for non-Muslim westerners – parts excised. He may be opposed to the Saudi royal family, and planning to abolish the repressive religious police that enforce the demands of *Shariah*, but the CDLR's vision of Saudi Arabia as an Islamic democracy does not mean that the desert kingdom will be transformed into a Gulf version of Germany. The massive, perhaps unbridgeable gulf between the western liberal pluralistic agenda and the Islamist one, will remain. There will be a universal franchise yes, and women will be given the vote, but only Islamic parties will be able to stand for parliament. All others will be banned. Public beheadings and lashings will remain.

Our discussion moves on to the West's favourite *bête noire* in Saudi Arabia, the weekly public executions and floggings of those who transgress various part of the *Shariah*. In 1994, according to Amnesty International, at least 53 people were executed in Saudi Arabia, many publicly beheaded. These customs, barbaric to us, but rational to many Muslims, will remain, says Dr al-Mass'ari. 'If we abolish all penalties we will not be able to control criminality. Human beings need to be terrified and deterred by certain punishments. In Islamic history we have a great aversion against prisons, more than against lashes. We feel that if you insult someone, calling a woman an adulteress for example, a nice beating of eighty lashes is very painful, and very disgraceful. But after a few weeks he is over it, his life can go forward, and when he remembers it, it was very painful and he can learn from it. There is also a spiritual part, that if you accept the punishment and you are sorry, it leaves you free from all sins. Calling a woman an adulteress is a major crime in Islam, like murder. So if I put you in jail for this how long will it be? Six months will not be long enough. Five years? Five years, for heaven's sake, it is very demoralising and character changing and you have the problem of supporting the family.'

There are prisoners in Saudi jails, who endure a living hell, sentenced to hundreds, or even thousands of lashes, which are administered in batches over a period of weeks or months. Each time their bruises fade, and their scars begin to heal, they are taken out and flogged again. It is un-Islamic to administer more than a hundred lashes, says Dr al-Mass'ari. 'I have the feeling that lashes, purely rationally because this is not coming from a revelation, are not as bad a punishment as jail. One hundred lashes is the most you can get in Islam. If someone cannot take it it will be administered in parts, or even symbolically. One hundred lashes can be given to a sick man, who is found guilty of adultery, he gets one hit with a bundle of one hundred sticks. There is a lot of possibility for mercy.'

And so to executions, and the various methods thereof. 'Execution is a deterrent, I think it works. There are three points, the principle, the method of execution and the publicity. It seems to me, and God knows best, because nobody came back to tell us how painful it is, that cutting off the head is the fastest way of despatching a human. It is not very nice to imagine, but it is definitely superior to the electric chair. With beheading you cut the spinal cord, the blood pressure drops to zero in a few seconds and the brain itself doesn't feel pain. And the cut part, the lower part, does not feel pain anymore, because it is not connected to the brain.'

Executions are carried out in public in Saudi Arabia, usually on a Friday. Crowds are encouraged, foreigners pushed up to the front to witness Islamic justice. For most of us it is an abhorrent spectacle, although considering the overwhelming popular support for capital punishment among the British public, similar spectacles in London would probably be just as crowded. 'The publicity, it is the most terrifying, because of the blood and everything. So it combines two positive aspects – we have assumed its deterrent value. Once we decided that he does not deserve to live, we do it in the most gentle and clean way. We have to be rational, if you kill then kill in the most beautiful way. But I am inclined to think that if some people see the execution they will tell the others and it will be a deterrent.'

As for the other great bone of contention, women's rights under Islam, here Dr al-Mass'ari takes a fairly liberal position, at least when speaking to foreign journalists, arguing, as always on the basis of his interpretation of the Quran and *hadith*, particularly the later ones. Saudi women should be able to both drive and vote, he says. I ask his view of the legal situation in Pakistan, for example, where a woman's testimony in court is worth only half that of a man's. 'There are various schools on this, some say it is universal for every female witness, some say only when dealing with a written document dealing with debts and indebtedness, and some argue that later *hadith* which call for witnesses do not mention males or females and so abrogate the previous answer, and this is my point of view. Before Islam a woman could not be accepted as a witness, the first step was to abrogate that and make it half, the second was to abolish it altogether. But a woman being a scholar of Islam, that is well established, the wives of the prophets were major scholars, responsible for many *fatwas* and judgments.'

All religious minorities will have full rights, he says. 'My point of view, for which I have solid evidence in the Quran and is a point of view which will defeat any other – the reason it was not the most popular in the past is that most points of view emerged early in Islamic history before all the *hadith* were collected and the scholars were just working with the materials they had – later on, after a lot of scrutiny and weeding out, the evidence is very clear. All minorities have the same rights – the only specialisation with Christians and Jews is that there are regulations about intermarriage. All minorities will have full rights, there has been a very good model developed by the Ottomans, of the millet system, which gave the minorities very wide rights, which is a good system for other minorities.'

Dr al-Mass'ari though is a man of many voices, and the article in his newsletter *Al-Huquq* that called for the 'elimination of the Jews' – whether only in Israel or across the world – leaves room for much doubt about his real vision of a multi-faith society.

That the Muslim world can embrace so many differing perspectives shows how simplistic is the view of the supposed inevitable clash between Islam and the West. This view, popular among former Cold War warriors looking for a new enemy to justify their huge budgets and military-industrial empires, has acquired a spurious academic gloss with the publication of lengthy articles in specialist academic publications, such as Samuel

Huntingdon's influential piece in *Foreign Affairs*, published in 1993. Huntingdon argued that the next global conflict will be between western nations and peoples who do not share their values such as Islamic and Confucian civilisations. 'The clash of civilisations will dominate global politics. The fault lines between civilisations will be the battle lines of the future,' he wrote. 'This centuries-old military interaction between the West and Islam is unlikely to decline. It could become more virulent,' he cheerfully adds later.

Admittedly this view does strike an atavistic chord across Christian Europe, stirring up ancient memories of Muslim hordes besieging Vienna, and Islamic armies advancing up southern Italy towards the final prize: Rome. Muslims counter that argument with the Crusades, and the western domination of Muslim lands for centuries, a process culminating in the Gulf War. But many non-Muslim long-term observers of the Islamic world strongly disagree with the Huntingdon thesis. 'There is too much emphasis placed on this aspect of a clash of civilisations, that there is a Muslim enemy out there. We are used to dealing with enemies, so now Communism is dead, we need a new "ism" to deal with, even if there isn't one, otherwise why do we have such massive defence establishments?' argues one Washington-based analyst with long experience of the Muslim world.

And just as Islam is not a monolithic bloc, neither is the West. American experts take a different perspective on the implications of large Muslim minorities now living in the West to their European counterparts. This analyst believes that European governments are using the idea of the supposed 'Muslim menace' as a means of compensating for their own uncertainties about their continent's future. 'The European Union, which is looking for a way to define itself, could find this idea attractive. Human identity celebrates not just what you are, but also what you are not. This is ingrained into the European psyche, the Ottoman hordes at the gates of Vienna, the crusades, the old concept of Christendom against Islam, people have inherited all of these.

'The future though depends on the way Muslims integrate. Here the Muslim immigrants are not drawn from the lumpen, they are doctors and lawyers, integrating into American life.

But in Germany whole Turkish villages have moved across, from the blacksmith to the village idiot. Muslims in America are not directly associated with unemployment, they are not people on the street. In Europe a lot of Muslim immigrants have nothing to offer a modern economy, so there you have two problems in one: immigration together with a great religious antipathy.'

New thinking is needed to deal with a new situation, he argues, and old stereotypes must be jettisoned. 'There is a danger of overplaying Islam. Everybody focuses on the "danger" of Islam, as though there was a masterplan to get back at the West. This theory is falling on post-Cold War ears, of people who are used to a world of grand alliances. But you need to put this in perspective and look at the history of Christian Europe. Everybody fighting each other in the Second World War was a Christian. They have been killing each other since the Middle Ages. All the idea of Christendom means is that Christians killed Muslims instead. The Thirty Years War was a conflict between Christians, and nationalism and other factors were much more important.'

There is a rage, fueled by hatred, against the West among many Muslims. It is the anger of the slums of Algiers, of the refugee camps of Gaza and the West Bank, of the back streets of Karachi and the remains of Kabul. It is the fury of the poor, living in countries that have for decades seen their resources diverted to the West, while their own poverty increases. It is the anger of those living under corrupt and despotic regimes such as the Algerian military junta, that would have been voted out of existence had elections not been cancelled, and is propped up by western aid. It lives too, in a muted form, in the terraced houses of Bradford and Besançon, wherever Muslims live, and struggle to find work and build their lives.

Islam's message of social justice, and its holistic unity that combines religious belief with the necessity for action is rattling the old regimes, says Izzettin Dogan, a leader of Turkey's Alevi community. Like many Alevis, moderate and liberal Muslims who wish to keep Atatürk's legacy of state secularism in Turkey, Dogan is worried about the future. Islam has replaced Marxism as the ideology of the dispossessed and unless the West remedies global economic injustices, the rage will spread, he argues.

'There is a gap between the north and the south of this world. After seventy years of the practice of Marxism we saw that Marxism hasn't given any response to the problems of poor people. Islam could have this possibility, have these principles by saying that all human beings have to share their wealth and it is happening even in Turkey. All the people that were voting for the socialist parties now vote for the Islamic party, Refah, this is very typical. The western powers have to do something. They cannot continue to be selfish and if they do they will only reign by power and force because they have superiority of technology and weapons. But this will not bring peace to the world. They have to divide their revenues and bring some hope so there will be a more peaceful Islam in the world.'

Bosnia, Palestine, Chechnya, Kashmir, this is the roll call of Muslim grievances. Muslims believe that the life of their co-religionists is cheap for the West, contrasting the response to the invasion of Kuwait to the late and tawdry action to stop the war in Bosnia. They have a point. The war in Christian Croatia, the result of the same supposedly endemic ancient Balkan hatreds that prevented intervention in Bosnia, was stopped after just a few months. The war in Bosnia lasted over three years. 'Many Turks are disappointed with the West and that is normal,' says Dogan. 'I myself am very disappointed to see the weaknesses at that point of the West, their failure to bring international order and justice. They say that all that they do is on behalf of justice and human rights, as they have done in Kuwait, intervention against Saddam. But what we saw in Bosnia was a double standard and nobody can be convinced that western people do something just for humanity and justice, for the sake of humanity. Nobody believes that, because the only power that can bring order, justice and peace is the West.'

Far away from Dogan's office in downtown Istanbul, Bradford community leader Mohammad Ajeeb echoes his arguments. The Islamic resurgence is triggered by global economics, he says. 'The Islamic resurgence, the revival of fundamentalism, I think, is simply a reaction, to the western domination of the Third World, including the Islamic countries. They have no power to decide about their economies, about their future. People in the Islamic world are saying we are a billion people and still we have no power. Our fate and our destiny is being decided by Washington, London and Paris. In that type of situation you use religion as a defence mechanism. When the western forces attacked Iraq, Saddam Hussein, who was closely allied with the Soviet Union, and belonged to a party which claimed to be socialist, suddenly he says "*jihad* is the only way". He knew that was the last weapon he could use politically, to unite and boost his people's morale.'

Islam gives a voice to the streets and the bazaars, not the politicians and the diplomats, he says. 'It's the masses who are questioning why they have no control of their resources, not the rulers. They are saying to the West, "You haven't given us anything, you have taken away everything." Islam is making them realise who they are, it's a revival of identity, they think they have been cheated for too long. People there are suffering from a multiplicity of grievances, social, economic and political. Many of them regard Islam as a panacea for all their grievances. But I think it is going to be hard to find all answers in Islam in the modern age. If you want to adopt Islam, you have to do it according to today's requirements.'

Both the Muslim world – and the western countries that are now home to millions of Muslims – must realise that their fates are locked together, I believe. A mosque now stands on the global village's high street, as well as a church, a synagogue and a Hindu temple, and nearly all of their worshippers can receive CNN.

The days of countries, or even empires, as fortresses, closed bastions against the 'other', whatever that might be, Marxist or Muslim, are finished, thanks in part to satellite television. And religious and ideological questions aside, such states do not work economically. Albania and Romania under their warped version of one-nation communism were economic disaster areas. Even Iran, one of the last countries in the world to proclaim foreign and domestic policies driven by ideological concerns – in its case Shiah Islam – needs foreign trade and to be part of the international community. Islam and the West must co-exist, even coalesce, because there is no other option. I believe that Europe must jettison the tired old stereotypes about Muslims, and begin to meet their justifiable needs, within the framework of a democratic pluralistic society. The earth will not spin backwards on its axis and the French Republic collapse if a Muslim schoolgirl wears a headscarf to school. In Britain there will still be crumpets for tea if the Race Relations Act is amended to include outlawing discrimination against Muslims.

'Many of the traditional concepts that have held for a century or two are now being challenged or disintegrating, such as the notion of the nation-state, or the Cold War,' says Professor Akbar Ahmed. 'That is plunging many Muslim societies into a completely new era. The most important part of this for Muslims is the emergence and power of the global media. The global media – meaning the western media – is so dominant and so intrusive, that for the first time in history the Muslim household is no longer safe from the world media. I mean safe in a traditional sense, that a Muslim felt he was lord and master of his house, however small and humble. But now however remote a Muslim is, if he has a television, he has access to the images shown in any part of the world.

'I don't want to trivialise this as something in the West versus the East. This is a problem for traditional societies, not as a challenge between Islam and the West. This is global. The question is how traditional societies can maintain their sense of identity, even integrity, in the face of this emerging global culture. What this means for Islam is that because Islam emphasises these values so much, the sense of family, with a structure of defined roles, of a cosmological order, with man as God's finest creation, when the base of Islam is being affected, something is going terribly wrong. That is the core of the problem, this lack of balance.'

There is a whole industry in London and Washington of think-tanks and research centres, staffed by full-time professionals and experts whose job it is to ponder weighty issues such as the future of relations between Islam and the West, and the implication for Europe of its new Muslim minorities.

My reporting was almost over and now it was time to draw some conclusions, so I went to Chatham House, also known as the Royal Institute of International Affairs, to meet Dr Rosemary Hollis, head of the Middle East Programme. For Dr Hollis, the Huntingdon thesis of the inevitable clash of civilisations is too crude a mechanism with which to analyse the relationship between Islam and the West. The multi-cultural society is already a reality. 'There is an element of truth in it [Huntingdon's argument], in that when we are in a state of crisis, which we have every reason to be, in materialist and resource terms, these things will come to the fore, as justification for a scrap. There is a sense that there is not enough to go around and we have to have what we have at the expense of the others. But one of its biggest flaws is that it ignores the fact that we have now got mixed cultures all around the Mediterranean and Indian Ocean. The Muslims already live in western Europe, and they are already part of western European culture.'

This process, she argues, works both ways, and western culture and political ideas are spreading among educated Muslims, many of whom went to university in the West. 'The influence of western culture has permeated the élites across the board in Muslim countries. For example, I see an attitude towards religion that it should be the responsibility of the individual, and let's have a society in which the majority of people are Muslims, but the way they practise their religion doesn't infringe on those who don't wish to practise it to the same extent. I realise that is part of the problem because westernisation is identified with collusion with the West, but I don't think you can draw a neat split between what is a Muslim society and what is a Christian society.'

At the same time the struggle between Saudi Arabia and Iran for global influence, and ultimately, leadership of the Muslim world means that there is no unified Muslim enemy. 'Saudi Arabia is in competition with Iran to be the better Muslim. If you look at Central Asia, Afghanistan, Bosnia, it's almost as if as soon as you tell the Saudis the Iranians are spending money there, they must as well. That's another reason why it doesn't make sense to say they are the enemies of the West, because they are so busy competing with each other.'

For Dr Hollis, the focus on the supposed Islamic threat has exposed the spiritual vacuum at the heart of capitalism and modern industrial society. 'The timing is right for a focus on religious differences, because of this search for identity which has come in the wake of the collapse of the Cold War. It shows that capitalism is hardly something to live by, all by itself. It doesn't actually provide a sense of identity whatsoever, so there is a quest for identity, with religion right back in there at the centre. Some of the kinds of stereotypes that Muslims in developing countries have of the West are valid, in the sense that morality has gone to pot there. There is no regard for the extended family, there is no support for the elderly, sex and drugs are freely available.'

Life in a global village means that Europe must concern itself with events in north Africa. 'We in western Europe, including Britain, have to care about what happens in north Africa, and the viability of the systems and the economies there,' she says. The rebound effect is not confined to the Muslim communities, but has implications for the whole of the host society. Emigrants leave north Africa to find work in Europe because of political instability, and their presence here is exploited by right-wing extremists. The far-right sets a political agenda, to which the mainstream parties must respond if they are to keep up their electoral support. Which usually means police harassment of immigrants or their children, which leads to riots, which leads to increased support for the extreme-right, and so the depressing circle goes on.

'The mood has turned in western Europe against immigration, there is this association between foreign immigrants and scarce jobs, even though the reality is that the vast majority of the unemployed in France are of north African origin. Things turn ugly in Europe, right-wing racist elements in France know they can stir up trouble by aggravating the immigrant community, the majority of which would prefer to keep a low profile.'

More than that, there are implications for the very nature of civil society in late 1990s Europe. Sadia Ayata, the young French-Algerian woman I met in Paris who was arrested for criticising police identity checks on north Africans, knows all about that. 'This kind of friction could lead to a change in the nature of European society and the nature of civil rights if it boils up, with more draconian police powers, powers of arrest and search. We saw some of this when the French launched a clamp-down. It changes the nature of civil society inside Europe itself. But the connection is already there, it is not a question of kicking something out, we are already interconnected,' says Dr Hollis.

*

Indeed, we are all connected, not just by television, but by new global media channels such as computer modems. Like many Islamists, Dr al-Mass'ari spreads his message through cyberspace, using e-mail and a page of the World Wide Web, part of the Internet that globally links millions of computers. Muslims are great exponents of cyberspace, the term for the electronic media that communicate by telephones and modems, for two reasons. Computer technology is firmly in the spirit of Islamic scientific discovery, part of a chain of historical development that stretches back to ninth-century Baghdad and the academies of Caliph al-Ma'mun. More importantly, for the first time since the death of the Ottoman empire, Muslims can consider themselves part of a re-born *ummah*, or Islamic brotherhood that spans the globe, even if it only exists in cyberspace. It's hard for a non-Muslim to understand the depth of feeling that believing Muslims have for their co-religionists around the world, especially in places such as Bosnia and Chechnya, but for them the concept of the *ummah*, that all Muslims are linked in one community of faith and belief is an integral part of Islam.

The Internet is crowded with discussion and news groups about Islam, and some of the finest sites on the World Wide Web, which combine graphics, words, pictures and downloadable sound clips, are Islamic. Using my laptop computer I can take a trip through cyberspace across the world, to visit a mosque in Kazan for example, where I can examine its architecture in detail, or step back and see its whole glory. If I am feeling a little mystical perhaps, I can discuss Sufism with Muslims in Paris or Berlin. I can download verses of the Quran, soundclips that my computer will play. I can visit the Cyber Muslim Information Collective or the Azhar Mosque of the Internet. I can even download the whole Quran and keep it on my hard drive. 'Everyone is into cyberspace now and that is another aspect of the democratic debate that is happening in the Middle East,' says Dr Ahmad Khalidi, London-based advisor to the PLO leadership. 'Not that all these people are democrats, but there is an open debate.'

For repressive regimes like the Saudi one, the Internet is bad news. It cannot be fully controlled, either domestically or internationally, and the House of Saud expends much time and money on controlling information about the Middle East and its own activities. 'They want control and they won't allow, as far as they can, criticism of their own regime to go beyond a certain limit,' says Dr Khalidi. The Internet though, cannot be bought, or realistically controlled. 'There are a few outfits, but not many, which can resist this. The Internet is one way around this, because so far it is free and accessible to all and I presume it would be very difficult for the Saudis or any other government to impose the kind of regulations they want. It will be very interesting to see what kind of impact this will have and how the Saudis will try.'

More constructive than restricting information is its free exchange, and an equal dialogue between East and West, says Professor Akbar Ahmed. 'For the first time we are seeing serious attempts at dialogue and interchange of ideas and some mutual respect, which is important. On one side you had the Prince of Wales and his speech at Oxford, the Pope saying that Islam is a respected world civilisation, that contributed a great deal. In the Muslim world, you have people like King Hussein, Mahathir in Malaysia, people who are constantly making an effort to come to the West, to universities, to think-tanks, to dispel the idea that we are all mad fanatics.'

Muslims want to contribute an Islamic perspective to life in a modern industrial society, says Dr Dalil Boubakeur, rector of the Paris Mosque. The alternative, of continued prejudice and marginalisation, will only help spawn an angry Islamic under-class, that will turn increasingly to a radical, confrontational Islam and polarise further the divisions between the Wests Muslims and their host countries. Better by far then to let Muslims in the West introduce a new approach – or rather a much older one – founded in spiritual values, rather material ones,' says Dr Boubakeur.

'Muslims who are living in another country than their original one, have a new way to discuss life, religion, nationality, philosophy, which are not only about the problems of life in their own countries. Islamic life can be part of communal life in France, and Muslim values can help provide answers to problems of modern life, to make an *Ijtihad* [intellectual renewal]. For instance, on artificial insemination, that brings a lot of theological problems in Islam, on abortion, on genetic engineering, problems of malformed foetuses.'

There is a word in French, *misère*, which does not translate exactly into English. It means misery, depression, angst and alienation, the symptoms of life in depressed inner city ghettos across Europe and the United States. Islam can help solve *misère*, says Dr Boubakeur. 'Islam gives an explanation for ethical questions. We also have an attitude towards *misère*, on racism, and on the problems of the world, such as Bosnia. The Muslims there have their civilisation, their humanity, their spirituality, they are not without origin, people coming from the sky. Muslim people want to participate in the civilisation from which they were excluded for centuries, centuries. Now, it is difficult, I know. Muslims want to remember their past civilisation, which is not dead, absolutely not. We say that civilisation is not a fact only of one part of the world, of one country, the American way of life, or the European one, but civilisation is for all men in the world. We are all brothers, there is not a humanity of first-class and second-class people. That is the message of Islam.'

There is something more that Islam can bring to Europe, immeasurable, intangible, but nonetheless vital, say believers in all religions: God and spirituality. The missing part of the jigsaw of life in the late twentieth century. 'Islam offers a high spiritual life, one very open to God and unity of mankind and to philosophical insights into life, both spiritual and rational. Islam recognises the unity of God and a consideration that reason is not all, in our knowledge of life and the world and the cosmos. It leaves a part to mystery,' he says.

There is mystery, of God, religious belief and spirituality, and there is reality, of dealing with the world as it is, as Dr Zaki Badawi said, and not as some Muslims would like it to be. The challenge for the Islamic world is learning to deal with the West. To understand, that just like the Muslim nations, the Judeo-Christian half of the globe is a complex grouping of different states, nationalities and outlooks.

That necessary, subtle and intuitive interplay is already happening, as the two cultures are blending and fusing, often in unexpected places. Much of this book was written to the background of music by Natacha Atlas, and Nusrat Fateh Ali Khan. Atlas, who sings in Arabic, was born in Belgium of mixed English, Jewish and Arab ancestors. Her music blends Arab

song, hip-hop, dub and dance, a new sound for a generation
whose hearts are turned East, but who live in the West. Nusrat
Fateh Ali Khan – another favourite of World Music fans – sings
Sufi-influenced Pakistani devotional songs of such atmospheric
rhythmic power that his voice can make you feel as though your
soul is being turned inside out. I play both on a CD, the computer technology within it the latest manifestation of the
mathematical advances that began over 1,000 years ago in the
Islamic scientific academies of Baghdad. There is a continuum
of knowledge, science and culture that stretches across the
centuries, and across the globe. The West's new Muslim communities too, are part of that advance.

In mosques and Muslim academies across Europe and
America, Islamic scholars are defining a new Islamic theology
for the 1990s. In Bosnia, Islam has been reborn, harder and less
starry-eyed about western ideas of human rights. In Britain,
France and Germany, artists, musicians and writers have
blended pictures, music and words to create a Euro-Muslim culture that fuses the Islamic traditions of north Africa and Turkey
with that of the host countries. In Turkey the struggle continues
for the soul of the Islamic Welfare Party, between the young
women activists, influenced by western ideas of women's liberation and the sexist, conservative old guard. In Albania, Muslim
activists have revitalised Islamic life, tolerant and heterogeneous,
firmly in the Ottoman tradition. In the United States a Muslim
political lobby is competing for influence in Washington and
the White House.

I think they are all succeeding, slowly. I hope so, for as the
Quran says:

Oh Mankind! We created you from a single pair of a male
and female, and made you into nations and tribes, that
you may know each other, not that you may despise each
other.

Surah 49: verse 13

ISLAM: A SHORT GUIDE

'There is no God but Allah and Muhammad is the prophet of Allah.'
The *shahadah*, or core Islamic creed

Islam is the religion of Muslims. The word 'Islam' itself is Arabic and best translates into English as 'submission'. It comes from the Arabic word *salaam*, which shares the same semitic root as the Hebrew word *shalom*, both of which mean peace; peace not just in the absence of conflict, but a deep, inherent tranquillity. A less literal but more intuitive translation of the word 'Islam' would be something like 'submission to the peace that comes from following in the path of Allah (God)'. What this means in practice can perhaps best be understood by visiting a mosque when dozens, or hundreds of Muslims prostrate themselves as one, intoning their prayers, united in their faith and belief.

The semantic roots of the word 'Islam' are important, because for believing Muslims, Islam is more than just a matter of weekly attendance at a mosque. Rather it is a faith that provides a holistic unity, that balances matters of faith, *din*, with those of *dunya*, matters of the world. For Muslims the peace of submission ensues from following the path of Islam in every matter, from brushing one's teeth (Muhammad brushed his five times a day) to the implementation of the correct provision of civil rights for religious minorities under Islamic rule.

Muslims believe that Allah revealed his divine truths to Muhammad, who was born in Mecca about the year AD 570 in the Christian calendar. Unlike Christians who believe Jesus was the son of God, Muslims do not revere Muhammad as a divine figure. He was the *insan-i-kamil*, the perfect man, but a man nonetheless. Muhammad specifically warned Muslims against worshipping him, rather than Allah.

Muhammad became a prophet in the year 610 at the age of forty. He worked as a trader in Mecca, with the caravans that criss-crossed the deserts of Arabia and the Levant. He was a well respected local figure, known as *Al-Amin*, the one who is trusted. A contemplative man, he liked to retire to a cave on Mount Hira, where he would meditate and pray. It was there, during the night that Muslims now call 'the Night of Power and Excellence', that he received his first revelation, when the archangel Gabriel commanded him to 'recite'. The revelations, memorised by many Muslims during the time of Muhammad, continued for twenty-two years, and were written down as the Quran.

The Quran, divided into *surahs* (chapters) and verses, is the primary source for Muslim law and beliefs, supplemented by the *hadith* (sayings of Muhammad), which have been collected and systematised. Both the Quran and the *hadith* are firmly in the tradition of Jewish prophets such as Amos and Jeremiah, calling for social justice, protection of the poor, widows and orphans, and threatening the power and legitimacy of the unjust oligarchies who oppress their subjects. Muhammad knew the consequences of what he preached and he was at first overwhelmed with humility, but nevertheless continued with the role God had thrust upon him. He encountered stiff resistance from the Meccan élite to his message of egalitarianism, monotheism and social justice, but persisted before his faith triumphed in Arabia.

That was in the seventh century of the Christian era, although Muslims use a different calendar, based on a lunar cycle. Today there are over one billion Muslims in the world, mainly spread throughout the Middle East, Africa, the Indian sub-continent, south-east Asia, Europe, and the United States. Most people associate Islam with Arabs, as the land now known as Saudi Arabia was the birthplace of Islam, specifically the cities of Mecca and Medina. In fact Indonesia is the world's most populous Muslim country, and many Arabs, especially those now living in the United States, are Christian.

Although Muslims believe in the idea of the *ummah*, the international community of faith and brotherhood uniting every believer, they are differentiated by nationality, culture, politics, and theology. Over three-quarters of all Muslims in the world are Sunni, who take their name from the *Sunnah*, the customs and practices of Muhammad. Within Sunni Islam there are four main schools of law: *Maliki*, *Shafi*, *Hanafi*, and *Hanbali*, which reflect varying perspectives of Islamic interpretation and traditions from flexible and liberal to more conservative and literal.

The main split in the Muslim world is between Sunni and Shiah Islam, with between ten and twenty per cent of Muslims across the world professing allegiance to mainstream Shiah Islam, or one of its variants. Most are concentrated in the Middle East, particularly Iran and Iraq. The Sunni/Shiah split originated in a dispute over the succession to Muhammad after his death. Shiahs believe that Ali, the first young male Muslim and Muhammad's son-in-law, should have been the first *Caliph* (or successor to Muhammad after his death) rather than the fourth. Some Shiahs do not recognise the first three Caliphs, although Sunnis do recognise Ali as a Caliph. After Ali and his son Hassan were assassinated, Ali's other son Hussain led an army against the fighters of the Caliph Yazid at the battle of Karbala in 680.

A few dozen Shiah (partisans) faced hopeless odds against an army of thousands. They were slaughtered and Hussain's body was beheaded. Over 1,300 years later the Battle of Karbala is still of deep and profound significance for present-day Muslims, whether Sunni or Shiah. The motifs of martyrdom, revolution and uprising – as well as the disregard for death that can characterise Shiah Islam – could all be seen in the events of both the Iranian revolution and the Iran–Iraq war.

But whether Sunni or Shiah, all Muslims are united in their adherence to the five pillars of Islam, which are the core of their faith. These are:

1. The Creed (*shahadah*)
The statement that 'There is no God but Allah and Muhammad is the prophet of Allah' is known as the *shahadah*. This is recited during prayer, religious ceremonies and as an assertion of Islamic faith. The *shahadah* is the core tenet of Islam and by reciting it in front of two Muslim witnesses, a non-believer converts to Islam. The *shahadah* itself is split into two parts. The first half is known as the *tawhid*, the expression of God's unity. He is omnipresent, omniscient, without beginning, or end, forever indivisible. The Christine doctrine of the Holy Trinity is

totally alien to Muslims, who believe God can never be divided or manifest himself as a divine being in a human body.

The second half of the *shahadah* is called *risallah*, the acceptance of Muhammad and all the previous prophets as messengers of God. Islam recognises the prophets of Judaism and Christianity such as Abraham, Isaac and Jacob, as well as Jesus and Mary, as conduits for divine revelation. The virgin birth, the symbolic miracles and the Gospels are confirmed in the Quran. But the idea that God had a son is specifically denied.

To describe Islam, as some non-Muslims do, as 'Muhammadanism' is not only deeply offensive, but also a nonsense. Muslims revere Muhammad as God's messenger but they do not worship him, only Allah. Implicit in the *shahadah* is the core Muslim belief that Muhammad was the *last* messenger of God, perfecting the recognised truths of Judaism and Christianity in the final version of God's one true religion. As the Quran says (Surah 5: verse 3):

> This day I have perfected your religion for you, completed my favour upon you and have chosen for you Islam as your way of life.

Those who claim divine revelation for messengers after Muhammad are committing *apostasy*, denial of the faith – a crime which can be punishable by death for Muslims.

2. Prayer (*salat*)

A Muslim must pray five times a day, every day: before sunrise (*al-fajr*), noon (*az-zuhr*), mid-afternoon (*al-asr*), after sunset (*al-maghreb*) and before midnight (*al-isha*). Ideally a Muslim should pray in a mosque, but if for practical reasons of work or travel this is impossible, then a Muslim may pray in any quiet, clean place, facing Mecca, often on a rug kept especially for praying. There is no priesthood in Islam, and any believing Muslim, who knows the Quran and is of high moral character, may lead the prayers. Prayers are usually led by the *Imam*, the mosque's resident scholar.

The way the mosque has evolved across the world illustrates how Islam absorbs the culture of the local environment in which it grows. Prayers can be offered in any space that is in a state of ritual purity, free of impurities such as excrement. In Bradford Muslims pray in terraced houses, in central Africa mosques are built from mud and tree trunks. A mosque must include a *mihrab* (an arch facing Mecca) and a supply of clean, drinkable water for worshippers to perform their ablutions. The *minaret*, the tall tower from which the *muezzin* (caller) summons the faithful to prayer, is an Ottoman addition.

3. Poor tax (*zakat*)

Zakat is a tax on all Muslims living above the poverty line, who have amassed some capital, for the economic relief of poor Muslims. It is not charity, which is an additional duty. *Zakat* is paid on wealth according to the amount of property and goods that a Muslim owns, at 2.5 per cent. However, it is forbidden to establish any kind of bureaucracy to monitor or collect *zakat*, rather it should be paid out of an individual's conscience. *Zakat* is part of Islam's message of egalitarianism, that all men are equal in front of Allah. *Zakat* also illustrates how Islam is a religion of the community, that Muslims have an obligation to their less well-off co-religionists. Usury, the practice of giving or receiving interest, is forbidden for Muslims, and hoarding wealth is frowned on. Money should be used instead to benefit the community, either through *zakat*, charity, or honest commerce.

4. Fasting (*sawm*)

Every Muslim who has reached puberty must fast between dawn and dusk for the thirty days of Ramadan, the ninth month of the Islamic year. *Sawm* is how Muslims show their obedience to Allah and ability to do without food, drink, tobacco or sex. Muslims prepare for the day of abstinence by getting up an hour before dawn and having a large breakfast. The timing of Ramadan varies from year to year as Islam operates by the lunar calendar. Nursing mothers, the sick, and travellers are exempt from *sawm*, but they must make up for lost days by fasting later in the year. *Sawm* can be problematic for Muslims living in countries far to the north or the south, such as Britain or the United States, when the time between dawn and dusk can be over twelve or even sixteen hours. The end of Ramadan is marked by a feast to break the fast, *Eid-al-Fitr*, a time of great happiness and celebration.

5. Pilgrimage (*Haj*)

All Muslims must attempt the *Haj*, the pilgrimage to the Great Mosque at Mecca that houses the *Ka'bah*, Islam's holiest site, at least once during their lifetime. Muslims believe that the *Ka'bah* was built by the Judaic prophet Abraham (known to Muslims as Ibrahim). But by the time of Muhammad's lifetime the *Ka'bah* was a shrine to polytheism, filled with idols, until Muhammad destroyed them and began to preach the message of Islam. The core ritual of the *Haj* is *tawaf*, circling the *Ka'bah* seven times anticlockwise, when the *hajji* (pilgrims) attempt to touch or kiss the black stone which Muhammad put in the wall of the Ka'bah.

Until the advent of international jet travel going on the *Haj* was the most difficult journey a Muslim would have to make. Now its spiritual importance remains, although getting to Mecca from Bangladesh or Birmingham is a lot easier. A Muslim man travelling on the *Haj* must be healthy, sane, solvent and provide for his family while he is away. Muslim women may also make the *Haj*, although if they are unmarried they must be accompanied by a male chaperon whom they cannot marry, such as a father or a brother. Non-Muslims are strictly forbidden from joining the *Haj*.

Hajji start preparing for their journey at the end of Ramadan, by praying extensively and observing meticulous personal hygiene. *Hajji* wear a special garment of two unsewn pieces of white cloth, with sandals on their feet, while they observe a series of extensive rituals to complete the *Haj*.

There can be as many as two million people on the *Haj*, from all over the world, in any one year, and Muslims who have completed the *Haj* say the experience is one of the defining moments in their life.

Steven Barboza, author of *American Jihad: Islam after Malcolm X*, describes going on the *Haj* thus:

'For me it was wonderful. When I first saw the Great Mosque of Mecca I looked out the window of the bus, I saw the people on the plaza in front of it, all dressed in long robes, wearing white or pale blue, and it looked like everybody was dressed to go to their own wedding. I saw this marvellous structure with a greenish-grayish tint to it. When the people assembled to pray, when I saw the vast throng of people kneeling, and the complete silence and serenity of it, all with two million people, it was awe-inspiring. It inspired a feeling of peacefulness. It was a spiritual trip. It's about taking a journey into yourself; even though you're among two million people, you're alone. They call it a practice session for the Day of Judgment. You go through all these motions and emotions with two million people and yet you're alone. You do exactly what I said, you journey within yourself. And I found that to be wonderful. Afterwards I felt more inspired to live the religion by the letter. It brought some amount of solace to me. It made me see as an eyewitness that Islam is practised by people around the world.'

The *Haj* ends with the Feast of Sacrifice (*Eid al-Adha*), also known as the Great Feast, where the *hajji* sacrifice animals such as cattle, camels, sheep or goats, just as Ibrahim was permitted by God to sacrifice a ram instead of his son Ismail. The *hajji* can eat the meat, but most should be given away to the poor and the needy. A Muslim who has completed the *Haj* can preface his or her name with the word '*Hajji*'.

These, then, are the five pillars of Islam, but they are merely the foundation of a Muslim's faith. For readers interested in learning more about the details of Islam I recommend the following works: *Living Islam* by Professor Akbar S. Ahmed (Penguin); *What is Islam* by Chris Horrie and Peter Chippindale (Virgin) and *Islam: The Straight Path* by Professor John L. Esposito (Oxford University Press).

NOTES

Chapter 3 – Europe's Forgotten Islamic Heritage
1 Quoted in Bernard Lewis, *The Muslim Discovery of Europe*, p. 155.
2 Quoted in H.T. Norris, *Islam in the Balkans*, p. 29.
3 Bernard Lewis, ibid, p. 227.
4 Fouad Ajami, 'The Other 1492: Jews and Muslims in Columbus's Spain' in the *New Republic*, vol 206, no 14, p. 22.
5 Bernard Lewis (ed), *The World of Islam*, p. 181.
6 Bernard Lewis, *The Muslim Discovery of Europe*, p. 222.

Chapter 6 – France: The Dysfunctional Family
1 Bernard Lewis, *The Arabs in History*, p. 166.

Chapter 8 – Turkey: The Veiled Revolution
1 Andrew Wheatcroft, *The Ottomans*, p. 21.

Chapter 10 – The Future
1 Poem by Ibn Arabi, in Akbar S. Ahmed, *Living Islam*, p. 72.
2 Sir Abdullah Suhrawardy, 'The Sayings of the Prophet Muhammad'.

BIBLIOGRAPHY

Books

Aburish, Saïd K. *The Rise, Corruption and Coming Fall of the House of Saud*. London: Bloomsbury, 1995.

Ahmed, Akbar S. *Living Islam*. London: Penguin/BBC Books, 1995.

——. *Postmodernism and Islam*. London: Routledge, 1992.

Almond, Mark. *Europe's Backyard War*. London: Mandarin, 1994.

Andrić, Ivo. *The Bridge on the Drina*. Chicago: University of Chicago Press, 1977.

——. *The Days of the Consuls*. London: Forest Books, 1992.

Ayliffe, Rosie. *Turkey: The Rough Guide*. London: Rough Guides, 1994.

Barboza, Steven. *American Jihad*. New York: Doubleday, 1994.

Bousfield, Jonathan, and Richardson, Dan. *Bulgaria: The Rough Guide*. London: Rough Guides, 1994.

Brooks, Geraldine. *Nine Parts of Desire*. London: Hamish Hamilton, 1995.

Chippindale, Peter, and Horrie, Chris. *What is Islam?* London: Virgin Books, 1993.

Coughlin, Con. *Hostage*. London: Warner Books, 1993.

Council on American–Islamic Relations. *A Rush to Judgement*. Washington DC, 1995.

Dent, Bob. *Blue Guide Hungary*. London: A & C Black, 1991.

Dunsford, Martin; Holland, Jack; Bousfield, Jonathan, and Lee, Phil. *Yugoslavia: The Rough Guide*. London: Rough Guides, 1990.

Esposito, John L. *The Islamic Threat*. Oxford: OUP, 1995.

Glenny, Misha. *The Fall of Yugoslavia*. London: Penguin, 1993.

Haque, M. Atiqul. *Muslim Heroes of the World*. London: Ta-Ha Publishers Ltd, 1990.

Helsinki Watch. *War Crimes in Bosnia-Hercegovina*, Volumes 1 and 2. New York, 1993.

Johnson, Paul. *A History of the Jews.* London: Phoenix, 1995.

Lari, Sayid Mujtaba Rukni Musawi. *Western Civilisation Through Muslim Eyes.* Houston, USA: Free Islamic Literatures, Inc.

Lewis, Bernard. *The Arabs in History.* London: Hutchinson, 1970.

——. *Islam and the West.* Oxford: OUP, 1993.

——. *The Muslim Discovery of Europe.* London: Phoenix, 1994.

Lewis, Bernard (ed). *The World of Islam.* London: Thames & Hudson, 1994.

Lewis, Bernard, and Schnapper, Dominique (eds). *Muslims in Europe.* London: Pinter, 1994.

Maass, Peter. *Love Thy Neighbour.* New York: Knopf, 1996.

Malcolm, Noel. *Bosnia: A Short History.* London: Papermac, 1994.

Mohammad, Omar Bakri. *Essential Fiqh* [laws]. London: Islamic Book Company.

Nielsen, Jørgen S. *Muslims in Western Europe.* Edinburgh: Edinburgh University Press, 1995.

Norris, H.T. *Islam in the Balkans.* London: Hurst and Company, 1993.

Richardson, Dan, and Hebbert, Charles. *Hungary: The Rough Guide.* London: Rough Guides, 1995.

Ruthven, Malise. *Islam in the World.* London: Penguin, 1991.

Said, Edward. *Orientalism.* London: Penguin, 1995.

Silber, Laura, and Little, Alan. *The Death of Yugoslavia.* London: Penguin/BBC Books, 1995.

Simpson, John. *Behind Iranian Lines.* London: Fontana, 1988.

Simpson, John, and Shubart, Tira. *Lifting the Veil.* London: Coronet, 1995.

Thompson, Mark. *A Paper House.* London: Vintage, 1992.

Watt, W. Montgomery. *Muhammad.* Oxford: OUP, 1978.

Wheatcroft, Andrew. *The Ottomans.* London: Viking, 1993.

Internet
Islamic Computing Centre
www.islam.org/iqra/index.htm
Islamic Resources on the Net
www.utexas.edu/students/msa/links/other.html

Cyber Muslim Information Collection
www.uoknor.edu/cybermuslim

The Wisdom Fund
www.twf.org

The Truth About Islam
www.twf.org/truth.html

The Sayings of the Prophet
www.twf.org/sayings.html#jihad

Azhar Mosque of the Internet
http://thales.nmia

INDEX

Note: references in *italics* indicate illustrations.